ening hours:

THE DYNAMICS
OF RESILIENT
FAMILIES

Resiliency in Families Series
Hamilton I. McCubbin, Series Editor

The theme of Resiliency in Families places the creation, integration, application, and dissemination of knowledge about the power of families of all forms, structures, ethnic groups, and cultures to recover from adversity as the highest priority in our agenda. Research on the resiliency in families underscores the importance of understanding the natural resistance resources in families and the capabilities and patterns of functioning upon which families call to manage the ebb and flow of life and all its hardships. From this orientation, the well-being of families can be best understood by studying the natural capabilities of families to endure, survive, and even thrive in the face of crises. Although helpful, the theories and methodologies flowing from the study of dysfunctional families may limit and skew our search for the productive responses and capabilities of families. The resiliency in families may have the greatest potential of coming to light through theories and research that focus on why families succeed and endure in spite of adversities and crises. With this in mind, we offer this series of publications devoted to search for knowledge about families at their best.

Volumes in This Series

Stress, Coping, and Health in Families: Sense of Coherence and Resiliency. Edited by Hamilton I. McCubbin, Elizabeth A. Thompson, Anne I. Thompson, and Julie E. Fromer

Resiliency in Native American and Immigrant Families. Edited by Hamilton I. McCubbin, Elizabeth A. Thompson, Anne I. Thompson, and Julie E. Fromer

Resiliency in African-American Families. Edited by Hamilton I. McCubbin, Elizabeth A. Thompson, Anne I. Thompson, and Jo A. Futrell

The Dynamics of Resilient Families. Edited by Hamilton I. McCubbin, Elizabeth A. Thompson, Anne I. Thompson, and Jo A. Futrell

THE DYNAMICS OF RESILIENT FAMILIES

EDITORS

HAMILTON I. McCUBBIN

ELIZABETH A. THOMPSON

ANNE I. THOMPSON

JO A. FUTRELL

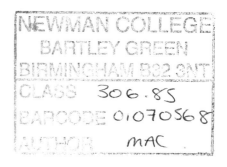

RESILIENCY IN FAMILIES SERIES

SAGE Publications
International Educational and Professional Publisher
Thousand Oaks London New Delhi

Editorial Board

Dedication

Dedicated to the memory of our dear friend and colleague Aaron Antonovsky, who supported our work in the field of resiliency and whose scholarship we will continue to promote.

For information:

SAGE Publications, Inc.
2455 Teller Road
Thousand Oaks, California 91320
E-mail: order@sagepub.com

SAGE Publications Ltd.
6 Bonhill Street
London EC2A 4PU
United Kingdom

SAGE Publications India Pvt. Ltd.
M-32 Market
Greater Kailash I
New Delhi 110 048 India

Printed in the United States of America

Library of Congress Cataloging-in-Publication Data

Main entry under title:
The dynamics of resilient families / edited by
  Hamilton I. McCubbin . . . [et al.].
    p. cm.—(Resiliency in families; v. 4)
  Includes bibliographical references.
  ISBN 0-7619-1390-4 (alk. paper)
  ISBN 0-7619-1391-2 (alk. paper)
  1. Family—Psychological Aspects Congresses. 2. Family—Mental health
    Congresses. 3. Family—Research Congresses. 4. Stress (Psychology)
    Congresses. 5. Resilience (Personality trait) Congresses. I. McCubbin,
    Hamilton I. II. Series: Resiliency in families series (Thousand Oaks,
    Calif.) ; v. v.
  HQ728 .D95 1999
  306.85—dd21   99-6191

This book is printed on acid-free paper.

99 00 01 02 03 04 10 9 8 7 6 5 4 3 2 1

Contents

Preface

The Dynamics of Resilient Families is the fourth volume in the Resiliency in Families Series and the first volume devoted specifically to qualitative research. This collection emerged from an innovative roundtable conference held on the University of Wisconsin-Madison campus. This conference brought together scholars from a variety of disciplines, each of whom studies the resilient and often growth-producing processes and outcomes of families facing conflicts and adversity.

This volume encompasses a wide variety of topics. The use of qualitative methods allows novel themes to emerge about central issues in family studies. Several of the chapters focus on the resilient adaptation and creation of meaning for families facing health-related crises. For example, Kerry Daly explores the reorganization of self, goals, and relationships for couples experiencing infertility issues; Elizabeth Thompson's study of mothers of adult children with AIDS points to the use of day-to-day coping strategies to face the uncertainty of the illness progression; Catherine Chesla's research explores the meaning of self-care skill development for couples living with diabetes; and Ann Garwick and colleagues' examination of cross-cultural differences in families' constructions of meaning around a child's chronic illness looks to the different explanations that families use to understand their children's illnesses. All of these chapters focus on families that are facing unexpected, and, in most cases, unwanted, family health crises.

The remaining chapters in the volume focus on families' adjustments to unexpected life events and changes. Helen Mederer's study examines the impact that changes in the commercial fishing industry have had on traditional fishing families. She points to family role flexibility, family cohesion, and social support as sources of resilience in the face of major family life changes. Barbara Golby and Inge Bretherton's study of postdivorce mothers focuses on the adjustment to post-divorce parenting and suggests that a mother's sense of effectiveness in parenting and her flexibility in dealing with conflict are two important themes in resilient adaptation. Katherine Allen's chapter examines the process by which older parents create meaning out of having a child who is gay and stresses the important theme of incorporating the changes in perspectives and behaviors that accompany coming to terms with a child's sexual orientation. Jane Gilgun's chapter examines the outcomes and adjustments of adults who experienced adversities in childhood and identifies the role of an individual's human agency in overcoming early life experiences. These chapters offer an in-depth and unique understanding of the meaning of crisis and unexpected life events. Each of the chapters illuminates the innovative and adaptive processes adopted by individuals and families to cope with family adversity. The use of qualitative methods allows the families to articulate their own personal perspectives on and meanings of these events.

A unique aspect of these qualitative chapters is that the researchers did not set out to study family resiliency. Rather, in studying families in crisis and family processes, the resilient and growth-producing meaning of these events to families emerged as central themes. Qualitative research can add to our understanding of why families are resilient and how they are able to embrace family crises as manageable challenges rather than insurmountable tragedies.

The chapters in this volume represent the diversity of approaches that are gathered under the umbrella of qualitative methods. These chapters demonstrate a variety of techniques for and approaches to collecting and analyzing qualitative data. In addition, the differences in the methods employed in these studies can further the dialogue on qualitative methodology for the study of families.

The use of qualitative methods in the study of families presents a unique opportunity for scholars to question and expand our understanding of family resiliency. The in-depth and emergent nature of qualitative research raises challenges to our previous understanding of family resiliency and also offers the unique opportunity to incorporate the participant's personal constructions of meaning in the development of family resiliency theories. By incorporating families' constructions of meaning around the issue of coping with adversity, and by looking to families for in-depth illustrations of how resilient family processes emerge, we can further the dialogue on how families positively adapt to crisis, as well as challenge and expand our previous theoretical understandings of family resiliency.

Hamilton I. McCubbin
Elizabeth A. Thompson
Anne I. Thompson
Jo A. Futrell
Editors

Acknowledgments

This volume highlights the use of qualitative research in the study of resiliency in families. By hearing the stories of individuals and families, we gain a more in-depth sense of the adjustment and adaptation process that families go through when faced with difficult situations. The process of creating a volume like this is a process that involves the individual voices and contributions of many people. As in the past, we have been fortunate to benefit from the support and expertise of many talented individuals. We thank Marion Brown of the University of Wisconsin Foundation for her continuing support of the Center for Excellence in Family Studies and the Institute for the Study of Resiliency in Families. We are also grateful for the contributions of our research team members, especially Kelly Elver and Sae-Young Han for the preparation of the documents and for their technical expertise. We continue to call upon the talents of our good friend and technical advisor, Wade Masshardt. We thank Christy Davenport, Gloria McCord, and Anne Connor for their ongoing support of our conferences and publications. We are also indebted to our colleague and friend, Terry Arendell, for encouraging us to explore the contribution of qualitative research to the issue of resiliency in families.

With the inauguration of our new book series with Sage Publications, we are especially thankful for the guidance and experience of their exceptional editorial staff, especially Margaret Zusky, Acquisitions Editor, for having the vision to encourage the development of the Resiliency in Families Book Series. We also thank Jennifer Morgan, Permissions Editor, Diane Foster, Managing Editor of Book Production, and Wendy Westgate, Production Editor, along with their extremely talented technical editorial staff.

Finally, we thank the contributors for their willingness to share their work through this publication and through the conference that inspired this volume. The advancement of our understanding of resiliency in families is greatly enhanced through qualitative inquiry, and we feel fortunate to highlight the diverse and thought-provoking work of these exemplary scholars.

Hamilton I. McCubbin
Elizabeth A. Thompson
Anne I. Thompson
Jo A. Futrell
Editors

1

Crisis of Genealogy:
Facing the Challenges of Infertility

Kerry J. Daly

It's important to say that I produced the child. It's kind of selfish but I feel it is important to me.
--A woman who has known about her infertility for 22 years

I think you would love an adopted child, but I don't think you would feel it is your own. I want to have my own to carry on my name and genes. I think there would be a sense of pride in having your own.
--A husband who has been trying for 5 years

I feel like I have to give back to them [i.e., dreamed for children] what my parents have given me.
--A husband who has known about a fertility problem for a year

Having your own. Pride. Selfish but important. Giving back. These are the existential rudiments of parenthood. In the face of the unexpected experience of infertility, they constitute a crisis of genealogy. Tree metaphors are most commonly used to explain genealogy. With their many branches, common stems, and traceable paths, "trees" are very useful tools for understanding ancestry, parentage, descent, and lineage. They are symbols of strength and life and represent the pride of family heritage. Genealogical trees have everything to do with generational continuity. We usually think of family blood as the sap of these trees where all of the genetic goods--from big noses to superior intelligence--are passed from one generation to the next. In short, genealogical trees play an important role in shaping our understanding of place and belonging. By providing a sense of rootedness, the genealogical tree provides a window on our organic place: what we have grown from and what we expect to produce in the regenerative cycle of life.

The language of infertility stands in sharp contrast to the tall, living regenerative tree of genealogy. "Barren," "fruitless," and "sterile" shift the focus from the lush foliage of the tree to the hot, rocky ground where nothing grows. Infertility represents a crisis of genealogy. Infertility precipitates a crisis of belonging, rootedness, and growth.

In this chapter, I explore what it means to experience infertility as a crisis of genealogy. Even at a time in our culture when family forms are more diverse and the importance of blood ties has diminished, it would appear that biological continuity continues to be salient for those who experience a fertility problem. For the couples who experience this unexpected life event, the crisis occurs on many levels: psychologically, in terms of self-worth; physically, in terms of deficiency and disease; socially, in terms of isolation, loneliness, and shame; and developmentally, where the generative potential of the future is compromised. In this regard, the chapter offers a substantive theory of the experience of infertility.

However, given that I have been asked to contribute this chapter to a book on resiliency, it is not simply a substantive theory on infertility. Rather, the opportunity to contribute to this book serves as an invitation to contribute to a more formal theory of resiliency. Prior to this invitation, resiliency did not enter into my writings about infertility and adoption. I did not ask questions about resilient behavior in my questionnaire. However, once I began to explore the theoretical dimensions of resiliency in relation to other life experiences, the parallels with infertility were many and exciting. Although creating formal theory in this way may represent a departure from the orthodoxy of grounded theory, it does, nevertheless, provide a creative and synergistic forum for the further development of the resiliency concept. Hence, in addition to outlining a substantive theory of infertility, this chapter is also concerned with adding to a formal theory of resiliency.

The Infertility Literature

Infertility can be seen as a "life crisis" (Bresnick, 1981; Bresnick & Taymor, 1979, p. 156) or a "stressful life event" (Zaslove, 1978, p. 2) that evokes a series of social-psychological responses. As a life crisis, infertility takes its toll on the relationship and on individual self-esteem, as well as the ability of individuals to function, to communicate, and to feel normal (Mai, Munday, & Rump, 1972). Even though families are becoming more diverse in their structure and practice and family size has been steadily declining, we continue to live in a pronatalist culture that clings to the idea that married couples should have children (Blake, 1974; Miall, 1994; Veevers, 1980). Parenthood, for married couples, continues to be seen as a "moral obligation" (Laurence, 1982) that has its roots in both religious beliefs and cultural norms (Pohlman, 1970, p. 7). Not only are couples expected to have children, but they are expected to have children "on time," usually about 2 to 3 years after marriage (Neugarten, Moore, & Lowe, 1968; Veevers, 1980). Infertility disturbs the normative schedule of life events. Because infertility results in a deviation from the social expectation that married couples become parents, it is subject to stigma (Miall, 1986) and results in "injury to self-esteem and self-image . . . with deleterious consequences for mental health because of the pressures of social disapproval" (Rosenfeld & Mitchell, 1979, p. 178). In a review of resilience and adversity, Cohler (1987) outlines the characteristics of life events that typically involve a resilient response. Those are events that persons feel they have little control over; that are undesirable, unexpected, and "off time"; that have major implications for maintaining the person's understanding of self and the meaning of life; and that are additive or interactive in effect. Infertility is easily construed as one of these life events that adversely affects mental and physical health.

The designation of infertile is typically applied to the couple because reproduction involves male and female contributors, which at a cultural level, is usually seen as occurring within a heterosexual relationship (Sandelowski, 1993). There is a strong emphasis in the infertility literature on the predictable changes that couples experience in relation to infertility. Link and Darling (1986, p. 57), for example, talk about the monthly adjustment to the "reality of another failure" that follows the menstrual cycle with a pattern of "hope, expectation and despair." Other models are based on stages of "infertility resolution." Menning (1977) and Shapiro (1982) have applied Kubler-Ross's stages of dying to the process of resolving infertility and delineated the stages of surprise, denial, isolation, anger, guilt, depression, grief, and finally resolution. Renne (1977) identifies the four stages of the process as shock, protest, despair, and resolution. Mazor (1979, p. 108) describes the process as involving denial and disbelief; helplessness and loss of control over life plans; feelings of being "damaged and defective," which give rise to anger and fear; a period of mourning; and finally, an acceptance based on a reassessment of "how to best realize their own creative, generative and nurturant potentials in the absence of biologic children." Hertz (1982,

p. 98) suggests that couples go through a period of astonishment, fear and anxiety, a sense of losing control over one's life plans, concern about bodily integrity, worries about sexuality, guilt and punishment, and finally, anger.

These models suggest a neat and linear progression from the shock of the initial awareness to some form of resolution. But as Kraft and colleagues (1980, p. 622) point out, a "complete" or "final" resolution of infertility is not absolute, for the issue continues to reverberate and can be revived even though it may essentially be worked through. Likewise, Menning (1977) suggests that it is a process that may not have a distinct end point. Zaslove (1978, p. 2) asserts that some couples may experience "chronic depression, frustration, guilt, anger, feelings of isolation, alienation and inadequacy." Rosenfeld and Mitchell (1979) also point out that alienation and isolation may be prevailing symptoms of infertility.

This nonresolution of the infertility crisis may be the result of a number of a factors: The loss associated with infertility may be ambiguous and unrecognizable, which makes it difficult to grieve; the loss may be "socially unspeakable"; and a social support system may be absent due to the "uncertain" nature of the loss (Menning, 1980, p. 317). In addition, as Bierkens (1975, p. 179) points out, "acceptance of childlessness is sometimes impaired by the persistent hope for a miracle."

The Resiliency Literature

Resilience is infrequently used to explain the way that adults cope with unexpected or challenging life events. Rather, the theoretical tradition of resilience is rooted in research that examines the way that children and adolescents survive in the face of adverse conditions. Beginning with Werner and Smith's (1989) classic longitudinal study of the children of Kauai, which began in 1954, the study of resilience has focused on the way that children successfully adapt and avoid succumbing to enduring risks, despite the presence of severe and ongoing adversity (see also Cicchetti, Rogosch, Lynch, & Holt, 1993). Other research has examined the experience of resilience in terms of short-term functioning in the face of acute or chronic major life stressors (e.g., divorce) or resilience as recovery when the immediate danger or stress recedes (e.g., abuse) (Masten, Best, & Garmezy, 1990). According to Werner and Smith (1989), resilient children are more likely to have greater internal locus of control; a more positive self-concept; a more nurturant, responsible, and achievement-oriented attitude toward life; and informal sources of support. Subsequent literature has identified a number of factors associated with successful recovery from adversity: the presence of at least one strong parent or adult caregiver (Egeland, Carlson, & Sroufe, 1993; Masten et al., 1990), self-efficacy and self-confidence, internal locus of control, and good problem-solving ability (Masten et al., 1990).

Although the literature that examines resilience among adults is not nearly as extensive, some of the same characteristics have been identified. In studies of how adults have coped successfully with highly stressful situations (ranging from coping with chronic illness to doing well in highly stressful professions), the conclusion is that the resilient individual has a "hardy personality." This personality is characterized by a strong internal locus of control, an ability to see the positive aspects of change, and an ability to find meaning and value in what one is doing (Joseph, 1994). Others have examined resilience as a kind of plasticity or reserve capacity in old age (Staudinger, Marsiske, & Baltes, 1993). In this research, the emphasis is not so much on risk and protective factors but rather on the identification of conditions that can lead to optimal growth and development in old age despite the presence of threat, challenge, or risk (Staudinger et al., 1993).

Whereas much of the early emphasis in the resiliency literature is on characteristics of the individual that are necessary to adapt in the face of severe stress, more recent works have begun to acknowledge the confluence of a variety of factors both within the individual and within the immediate context. Like adaptation in general, resilience is always contextual (Masten et al., 1990). Specifically, Haggerty and Sherrod (1994) suggest that resilience has to do with physiological and psychological characteristics, the degree of prior success in dealing with life's difficulties, developmental periods of vulnerability, the timing and sequence of experiences, and a host of factors that may lie outside of the individual's control including the response of peers, family, and community supports. As this would suggest, stressors and successful adaptation involve complex environmental and transitional processes (Haggerty & Sherrod, 1994; Masten et al., 1990). From this perspective, resilience involves the ability to use both internal and external resources successfully to resolve stage salient developmental issues (Egeland et al., 1993). Corresponding to this, there is an emerging consensus that resilience is not a unidimensional construct but rather is an experience that occurs in many domains of adjustment with some persons being resilient in some domains and not others (Kaufman, Cook, Arny, Jones, & Pittinsky, 1994; Luthar, Doernberger, & Zigler, 1993). There is also an acknowledgment in the literature that there is a "self-righting tendency" at play when there is a crisis in these complex systems (Cicchetti et al., 1993). This applies to both individuals and families. Masten and associates (1990, p. 438) conclude that individual development is "highly buffered and self-righting." Similarly, in a study of the adverse changes associated with the transition to old age, there is a kind of natural resiliency of the self (Brandstadter, Wentura, & Greve, 1993). Adverse events that were objectively and subjectively beyond the individual's span of control did not seriously undermine the individual's sense of control over personal development and did not involve a generally increased risk of depression (Brandstadter et al., 1993). There has also been an interest in understanding the interactive mechanisms by which compensatory, self-righting tendencies are initiated when problems or crises arise in family systems (Cicchetti et al., 1993).

Embedded in the findings of the resilience literature are a number of theoretical assumptions about which factors play a critical role in explaining resilient behavior. Whereas much of the early resilience literature within psychology took a psychopathology position, some of the later work carried out by developmentalists focused on competence (Cicchetti et al., 1993; Luthar et al., 1993). The attempt to understand resilience has also moved from trying to identify attributes that characterize the resilient individual to understanding family responses, systemic dynamics, and contextual processes. There has also been a shift from seeing resilience as a static and predictable response to an identifiable stressor, to conceptualizing it as a dynamic developmental process that involves changing conditions and adaptations (Cicchetti & Garmezy, 1993; Cicchetti et al., 1993).

The work of McCubbin, McCubbin, and Thompson (1993) has played an important role in shifting the focus of resiliency from internal and external factors associated with the individual to an examination of resiliency as it is experienced in families. When faced with a crisis situation that demands changes in established patterns of functioning, families find their direction in the "family schema," which incorporates shared beliefs, standards, priorities, and expectations. The family schema serves as a basis for the family's appraisal of the crisis situation and, in turn, shapes the coping behavior and strategies families employ in the management of the associated stressors and hardships. Other researchers have identified a number of family system characteristics that are associated with resilience: parental competence, shared parental values, good family communication, and a high degree of parental receptiveness about their child (Hauser, Vieyra, Jacobson, & Wertlieb, 1989).

Although these developments in the literature have broadened the lens and made the study of resilience more complex, they continue to overlook, or pay little attention to, some other theoretical viewpoints that might advance our understanding of resilience. For example, issues of power and control, which in some ways define the parameters of adaptability, do not have a strong presence in the literature. Similarly, although there has been an effort to identify sex differences in resilient behaviors, there has been very little attention given to the sociopolitical ramifications of gender as either a constraining or privileging force in the adaptation to stressor events. Finally, in recent years there has been a move toward understanding complex human behaviors from a social constructionist perspective, with an emphasis on capturing the complex stories and definitions of experience from the viewpoint of the social actors. Here the emphasis is not so much on outcomes and factors but on the myriad of meanings that are part of the experience. It is in this regard that Masten and colleagues (1990) have called for a shift in research from the "what" questions of description to the "how" questions of underlying processes that influence adaptation. Specifically, there has been a call to shift from the study of risk variables to the study of the process of negotiating and managing risk situations (Rutter, 1990, cited in Egeland et al., 1993).

Qualitative research, which is well suited to understanding these processes and strategies, has been underused in the study of resilience. Beardslee's (1989) work is one of the few exceptions. Using an open-ended, life history data-gathering method, he examined the role of self-understanding in resilience. Of critical importance for resilience were strong relationships and realistic appraisals of the capacity for, and consequences of, action. Self-understanding and strong relationships are ongoing and developmental, and as a result, resilience was conceptualized as a process whereby individuals came to a better understanding of their responses over time, and were then in a position to better manage the stresses.

In my examination of the relationship between infertility and resilience, I am particularly interested in the process by which couples manage the stress of infertility individually; as a family; and within their social environment consisting of family, friends, and acquaintances. In carrying out this study, I used a grounded theory approach, which meant that there was no effort to test a particular theory but rather to allow the theory to emerge from data. As a result, there was an effort to allow a variety of theoretical emphases to come into play based on participants' definitions of the situation. This inductive posture, therefore, allowed for the emergence of developmental themes, individual attributes, family processes, power dynamics, and broader sociocultural influences.

Research Design

To capture couples' perceptions of this process, a combination of written questionnaires and semistructured interviews was used. The questionnaire provided information on demographics, marital satisfaction, and attitudes, and the interview asked open-ended questions to capture couples' subjective perceptions of their infertility experience.

This research followed the principles of grounded theory (Glaser & Strauss, 1967). There were two phases. The first phase involved participant observation at five infertility support group meetings and unstructured, taped interviews with five infertile couples. The objective of this phase was to become sensitized to the salient issues and to generate substantive themes and categories that could be more systematically analyzed in the second phase. In the second phase, a structured, but open-ended, interview schedule was established on the basis of the categories identified in phase one. Examples of these categories were commitment to parenthood, salience of motherhood versus fatherhood, infertility as a problematic, loss of control, the response of significant others, and critical incidents in the consideration of adoption as an alternative.

Both spouses were present in all interviews, because the husband and the wife each has a separate, subjective reality that makes data collected from only one spouse unreliable when generalizing to the couple (Saffilios-Rothschild, 1969). It is also consistent with the idea that infertility and parenthood involve a degree of shared meaning and shared identity because both are typically experienced as a couple. Although they may have different subjective viewpoints on the experience of infertility or parenthood, there is, nevertheless, an underlying intersubjective reality. On a very practical level, interviewing spouses together was advantageous insofar as spouses jogged one another's memories and were able to corroborate statements made by each other, which served to improve the reliability of their comments. In addition, men have typically been difficult to recruit for studies on private family topics such as this, and wives were often a welcome ally in encouraging husbands to participate. Drawbacks of interviewing couples involved the potential for conflictual and embarrassing issues not to emerge. In this regard, there may have been a more collusive tendency in the couple to protect their backstage behavior than might be the case when interviewing spouses alone. There is also the possibility that gender alliances are formed between a single interviewer and the spouse of the same sex (Daly & Dienhart, in press). In addition, conjoint interviews may result in some unanticipated disclosures by one spouse that violate the privacy or consent of the other spouse (LaRossa, Bennett, & Gelles, 1994).

Couples were sampled from several different sources. Of the 76 couples who agreed to be interviewed, 39 (51%) were from a fertility clinic in a large teaching hospital in southern Ontario, and 37 (49%) were from two Children's Aid Societies, also in southern Ontario. In the fertility clinic, eligible couples (no children; a fertility problem) were asked to participate by the physician, and if they agreed, they were then approached directly by the researcher. With adoption agencies, letters were sent out by the agencies that requested participation from couples who were on the adoption waiting list. Couples responded by returning a consent form to the researcher. Two couples were excluded from the final analysis because they did not meet the eligibility requirements, leaving a final sample of 74 couples.

The median age of the sample was 30 years for husbands and 29 years for wives. Couples had been married for a mean average of 6 years. Ninety percent of the couples were in their first marriage. The sample was highly educated with one third of men and one fifth of women holding university degrees. Corresponding to the high levels of education, the sample also consisted of a relatively high concentration of respondents in professional or managerial positions. Approximately one third of husbands and one quarter of wives held positions at a professional or management level.

The majority (84%) of the sample were born in Canada. When asked about their ethnic background, approximately one quarter of the sample indicated that their ethnic background was Canadian. The largest proportion of both husbands (36%) and wives (47%) were of British, Scottish, or Irish background, and this was consistent with the general population. Approximately two fifths of the sample were Protestant and one third were Catholic.

The fertility problem was believed to be with the wife in almost three fifths of the cases. In only 18% of the cases was the fertility problem exclusively male related, and in 15% of the cases there was a combined problem between husband and wife. In 9% of the cases, there was no diagnosis. This is referred to as idiopathic infertility or "normal infertility" (Wallach, 1980) and is estimated to occur in 5% to 10% of all cases.

The mean length of time for having suspected a fertility problem was 5 years. The range was from just under 1 year to 22 years. For those who did not know at marriage of their fertility problem, the mean length of time for becoming aware of a fertility problem was 3.5 years after marriage, suggesting that these are the critical years for making childbearing decisions. By 5 years of marriage, 85% had identified themselves as having a fertility problem.

Once a fertility problem was suspected, the mean length of time before medical attention was sought was 10 months. About one third of the sample went to a doctor immediately. By 1 year after suspecting a problem, three quarters of the sample had sought medical assistance. Only 5% of the sample waited for more than 2 years to get medical help.

A Substantive Theory of Infertility

Characteristics of Infertility as a Stressor Event

Infertility is an unexpected life event. What is supposed to happen is that you grow up, get married, and have children. This is the expected, taken-for-granted course of life events. Playing house, taking care of dolls, reading fairy tales, or caring for younger siblings play a key role in establishing parenthood as the expected future horizon. One woman, who wanted to stay home and take care of children explained:

> I have this feeling of inadequacy because I can't have any children. As a little girl, you're playing with dolls and all this and you're prepared right from when you are a little one. You're prepared to be a mother--role playing and the whole bit. And then all of a sudden I can't. Like it's a whole switch in your mind. You're prepared for this whole thing and then Bingo!--you can't and you have to start thinking differently.

Similarly, for one husband these expectations for parenthood were so internalized that the desire to become a parent was something fundamentally human: "I've never thought of not having children. If you are married, its the natural thing to do. It's like a natural instinct or an uncontrollable urge to have children."

On the basis of these taken-for-granted beliefs about parenthood, couples usually assumed that they would simply become parents when they chose to do so. Their starting point was the presumption of fertility, which was seen as something that they could simply "turn on" at the appropriate moment after a period of having "turned it off" with the aid of contraceptives. As one man put it, "You use birth control all the time and you just think its going to happen when you want it to." Another man expressed a similar frustration when he said: "You grow up trying not to get girls pregnant, and then when you want to, you can't!"

For many couples, infertility is the kind of life event that happens to other people. As a result, shock and surprise was the usual response. One man succinctly described the news of infertility: "I was surprised. I always thought that these things happen to other people!" Another man explained his feelings of surprise and anger after hearing that he was sterile:

> I had the feeling of "what did I do to deserve this?" I don't drink, I didn't run around with women. We build our lives together and it's an ideal situation to bring up kids. What the hell is this [i.e., infertility]? Other people run around impregnating women. Why the hell does this happen to me? I felt it was an injustice to me--but I'm not bitter. It's like someone called the wrong number. Why me?

Infertility is an ambiguous problem. As a medical problem, infertility can have many causes, no cause, or many possible contributing factors--all of which contribute to an ongoing sense of uncertainty in the infertility experience. Infertility is also a problem that is experienced within many domains, all of which are interrelated and complex. If infertility is the physiological problem, then involuntary childlessness is the social-psychological counterpart. Infertility is usually a poorly defined physiological problem that is accompanied by social-psychological questions about identity and self-worth. As a result, there is a great deal of social awkwardness that couples encounter in trying to manage both infertility and involuntary childlessness.

One of the key reasons why infertility is experienced as an ambiguous problem is that it is a private and hidden condition. Within social situations, couples lamented the inability of others to appreciate the nature of their problem. This difficulty was partially attributed to the nonobvious nature of infertility: "It's really something that people don't see or understand. Like you aren't missing an arm or anything like that. But you still have that physical handicap. You can't do what you want to do."

Although there was tremendous variation in the kind of fertility problems that were diagnosed, there was, with all diagnoses, except those couples who were definitely sterile ($n = 6$), a sense of uncertainty about whether they would become biological parents.

In the face of the ambiguity and the unexpected challenges associated with infertility, couples were most likely to approach the field of medicine with a sense of optimism and hope. As they did with all other physical ailments, these couples turned to the medical profession to fix the problem and bring an end to their uncertainty. Only a small number of couples ($n = 9$) knew of a fertility impairment prior to the time when they decided to start a family. When the other couples first suspected that something might be wrong, the most common reaction was that it wasn't really a problem, that the doctor would be able to straighten it out, and that it was just a matter of time before they would get pregnant.

Over the course of their tests and treatments, most couples did not receive diagnoses of absolute sterility, but rather, had certain problems identified that might impede the normal process of reproduction. This is consistent with other studies of infertility that indicate the medical diagnosis of a fertility problem is typically an open-ended process characterized by medical definitions of the situation that are constantly in flux (Greil, Leitko, & Porter, 1988). In this study, most couples received a diagnosis of a fertility problem that did not absolutely exclude the possibility of getting pregnant, but only lessened their chance. This led to a reluctance to embrace the term infertile, which is associated with an obvious and certain finality. Rather, couples typically lived in a frustrated, ambiguous present with a guarded but optimistic future. By way of illustration, several couples expressed resentment that the interviewer would refer to them as having a fertility problem. In one case in particular, a woman had known about scarring, adhesions, and partially blocked fallopian tubes for about 10 years but was extremely reluctant to identify herself as someone with a fertility problem or to define her situation as problematic. Before the interview began, she had this to say:

> I tried to call you all day to tell you not to come. You see, I went to the doctor again this week and he said there really wasn't a problem --the tubes are still open and there is no good reason why I shouldn't get pregnant. Since you want to talk to people who have a fertility problem--right?--I didn't think you would want to talk to us.

With each and every menstrual cycle, there was a renewed sense of hope that "it would work this time." Without the definitive diagnosis that said they could not get pregnant, couples had to deal with an seemingly endless string of "maybes." One woman described this feeling:

> It's the not knowing that if you had tried it again it might have worked. The possibility is always there for me because there is no really serious block. It's always hanging over you. And if you don't try, you feel like it might have worked. You are always waiting to see if it happens.

Whereas the majority of couples experienced some level of ambiguity about their medical diagnosis, the uncertainty was most acute for those who experienced idiopathic infertility. These couples had been through a lengthy period of tests and treatments but were still without a diagnosis. For many of these couples, coming to an acceptance of infertility as a problem was particularly difficult. Even though couples felt a definite helplessness and lack of control over changing their situation when there was no diagnosis, they were still reluctant to identify themselves as someone who had a fertility problem. One man explained this helplessness: "Without them finding anything definite, we don't really feel like we have a problem. If they could say it was definite, then we could make plans to do something definite about it."

For most couples, however, the simple passage of time and the event of nonpregnancy were more crucial than the medical diagnosis for defining the situation as problematic. Most couples indicated that they came to believe there was a problem simply by the fact that they were not using birth control and not getting pregnant. The medical process of tests and treatments shaped the way the problem was defined by creating, on the one hand, the optimistic expectation that something could be done, and on the other, by delivering the disappointing news that a particular test or treatment was unsuccessful. There was a general pattern that many couples referred to as the "roller coaster" whereby they got their hopes up following a treatment, only to have them dashed with the onset of yet another menstrual period.

The event of nonpregnancy, described by one woman as "month after month of 'nothing' happening," was the key for taking on the identity of someone who is infertile. For another couple, the absence of change that would come with parenthood and the loss of control over achieving it created the problem:

> When you have a child, your life changes. Now, for us, it doesn't change. When you plan to have kids you see that that is the way it should be. Our life has been incredibly easy for us. We got the jobs we wanted. We got the house we wanted. This [i.e., parenthood] we couldn't have.

The diagnosis of a physiological problem served to concretize what they had come to expect after a period of trying unsuccessfully to get pregnant. For these couples, the diagnosis offered some explanation for their failed efforts and allowed them to more definitely define their situation as problematic. In this regard, a diagnosis of sterility was more clearly identifiable as a "critical incident" (Strauss, 1959). As one man explained:

> I never really thought about not being able to have kids. Maybe subconsciously but I didn't want to believe it. Then I more or less

forced her to go to the doctor. She didn't want to find out there was a problem. It never sunk in there was a problem until they told me we definitely couldn't.

When the long-sought-after diagnosis finally arrived, there was sometimes a sense of relief at no longer having to live with the ambiguity of not knowing whether there was a problem. At last the previously dispersed feelings could be focused on a specific problem. For one man, this offered a tremendous sense of release:

When she told me [i.e., about the diagnosis], she just fell apart and I walked away--I was so angry at her, at the doctor--I was angry at everyone and anyone--but then there was relief--a load came off because of all the pressure that had been building up.

For some couples, the long process of tests and treatments created ambivalence about the importance of children in their lives. Whereas most couples decided to have children as part of the normal course of events in their marriage, the discovery of a fertility problem resulted in an intensive analysis of why they wanted children. Hence, not only was the physiological problem of infertility fraught with uncertainty, but the meaning of parenthood was open to misgivings.

H: There is indecision now. Do we really want one now for what it will bring or because we can't have one?

W: For 7 years of trying you ask the question so many times--you get so unsure--"Do we really want one?" and "Why?" It is now so confusing--you ask the question so many times that I'm not sure that we really even want children any more.

Loss of control. Most couples felt that having a fertility problem had changed their sense of control over their lives. At the most fundamental level, infertility meant a loss of control over one's own body. As one woman described the experience:

For me there has been a loss of control. It is no longer my choice as to whether or not I can get pregnant. People I know come off the pill and they get pregnant--that makes me mad. I just don't have control over my body.

Women were more likely than men to say that having a fertility problem had an effect on the extent to which they felt like they had control over their lives. Whereas women had more invested in the motherhood role, men tended to more easily retreat into work-related activities. This is consistent with research on community attitudes toward infertility that suggests that among both women and men, motherhood continues to be seen as a stronger biological and social imperative (Miall, 1994).

Losing control over becoming a biological parent was frequently attributed to the power that physicians were perceived to have. In this regard, doctors were perceived to have control over whether they became parents. As one woman described the physician's role, "The doctor is the main player, he is everything!" Another man described the feelings of dependency that this engendered: "We feel a lot more helpless now than when we first started. There is a lot of giving up to and depending on the doctors. Although we still feel like we can choose options, we are dependent on them."

Anger was also a common response when the couples could not control the timing of parenthood. This anger was often focused on the doctors in charge of their treatment. Couples criticized doctors for the way they managed their medical treatment. As one woman pointed out:

> The frustrating thing about it is the slowness in the process--the delays and the miscommunication between the medical staff and us. The demands that they have shortchange the attention that we get. One doctor was really incompetent. He told me it was all in my head.

Over time, however, there comes the eventual and dreaded realization that maybe not even doctors have control over whether they will become parents. The loss of control over their bodies, and over the medical process that was supposed to fix it, precipitated a loss of control over their life plans.

Compromised future: Infertility as a developmental problem. Infertility disrupts the normal developmental trajectory. At an individual level, it means being unable to move forward into the generative challenges associated with parenthood. As a couple, the family development trajectory is also jeopardized. Their shared future horizon loses shape as a result of their frustrated attempt to realize the dream child that they so longed for.

The loss of control over the next developmental step was most often expressed in terms of their life being "on hold." Waiting for parenthood preempted other life activities. This was described as a "moratorium in life," "a limbo," or "waiting for a bus--a holding pattern." Especially for women, the loss of control over the timing of pregnancy was perceived to interfere with other life commitments. Because the future was constructed around the desired transition to parenthood, there was a reluctance to make other kinds of plans in case these plans would in some way interfere with parenting if and when it happened:

> You are always waiting to see if it happens. It's very hard to make plans to go back to work, going back to school. If you do and get pregnant, you leave. Yes, it does control you. I just can't commit myself to anything right now.

Normative age expectations played an important role in defining infertility as a developmental crisis. Parenthood was usually expected to occur within marriage after an initial "settling down" period of several years. One woman described her difficulty in hiding her childlessness because of the time norms that influence the transition to parenthood:

> It's [i.e., childlessness] a hard thing to hide. You are no sooner married than people start asking. For 2 or 3 years you can put them off. But after awhile, what are you going to say? Now I find it easier just to tell them straight out. Why beat around the bush?

Another man described his feelings of being set apart from his peers as a result of falling behind in the transition to parenthood:

> People ask whether I have kids and how long have I been married. Then they look at me funny when I say I don't after having been married for 13 years. After that, I feel like I'm not like everyone else and I feel less of myself.

Friends of the same age who were beginning to have children created peer pressure by focusing attention on children and the parenting experience. The awareness that they were falling behind their peers seemed to heighten their awareness of infertility as a developmental problem. For one man, a reunion with friends highlighted the sense of falling behind and intensified the importance of parenthood: "We went to a college homecoming and many of our friends had children and that was difficult--people expect that you will have children."

Indications are that infertility had more dire developmental consequences for women than men. Consistent with the continuing ideology and practice of mother as the primary parent, women tended to experience infertility more acutely as a developmental crisis. Whereas men continued to have their work as a primary commitment, women more often focused on the importance of becoming a mother as their central developmental task. As one man expressed it, parenthood was not as primary as it was for his wife:

> I am more frustrated for her than I am for myself. If we don't ever have children, my life isn't going to stop. There are many other interesting things in life that I can do. But if she doesn't have a child, she will be more frustrated because she has her whole life wrapped up in it.

Consistent with the findings of other research, women and men seemed to concur about the greater implications of infertility for women (Miall, 1994). Another woman elaborates on the consequences of infertility for her sense of development:

> I feel that somewhere along the line I have failed and I know that other people say that that isn't right. You can't help it. People just expect women to have babies. That's what we were put here for! (laughing). It's people who make you feel like a failure. It will never go away because people will never let you forget.

A challenge to the marriage. Although the physiological problem of infertility is typically identified in either the husband or the wife, being blocked from parenthood is a shared problem. For most couples, involuntary childlessness is experienced as a shared problem, a problem that can be either a destructive force in the relationship or a strengthening one. As one woman described it: "We feel it [infertility] is a couple problem . . . these things either split people or bring them closer together . . . it has brought us closer together."

Through the repeated disappointments of it "not happening this month" to the stale and perfunctory sex that accompanies having intercourse at the right time of the fertility cycle, infertility created a number of shared strains in the relationship. Many talked about the impact on their sexual relationship:

> It has taken its toll on our sexual relationship. There is always this feeling like we had to do it on a certain day or at a certain time and that was really hard on us. You had the feeling of being rejected. We had to have intercourse. It took the fun and pleasure out of it. It gives a sense of emptiness.

Nevertheless, most couples in this sample talked about the cohesive impact of the infertility experience. For one husband, "infertility is a problem that is there to be solved . . . not something where we blame each other or argue about it." One woman explained her experience of it:

> What has been very positive is how he has been supportive. It has brought us together. I have never felt this much commitment to another person. He has seen me vulnerable, frightened, and scared--

and he has responded. It has been a testing thing, because we had a plan and we've had all these obstacles to get over. I've seen relationships tested. There was a fear in my mind that Ken would leave me. It's my infertility--do I have the right to deny him kids? You think as a couple, but we are individuals and he could go his own way and have kids.

For a minority of couples, the absence of children precipitated a re-evaluation not only of whether to have children and their value to them but of the purpose and the viability of the marriage itself. For example, two couples were, at the time of the interview, seriously considering separation as a result of infertility. Two other women indicated that a previous marriage had split up on account of infertility. A man with a sperm problem explained:

> We have had a lot of discussions about whether or not the marriage is viable. I feel that if it is important for her to have children and we can't then maybe the marriage should dissolve. Being married for 11 years and finding out that something you assumed was automatic threatens your marriage. To have to divorce because of it is traumatic to think about.

A family crisis. Infertility raises to the surface the cultural ideology of the nuclear family as the dominant family form. The medical condition of infertility robs couples of their "membership" in "mainstream" family:

> W: You don't feel like you are part of the mainstream. Even watching TV the emphasis is on having kids. It is even difficult to make friends because they expect you to have children.
>
> H: It makes you very sensitive that the whole world is geared towards the nuclear family.
>
> W: It's like a membership. You aren't part of the group when you have a fertility problem. Our friends who have children seem to apologize for them.

Within their own extended families, infertility carried the heavy weight of disrupting generational continuity. It was in the midst of well-intentioned parents and brothers and sisters that the crisis of genealogy became most evident. The potential grandparents were a particularly salient force in conveying the expectation that their children have children. For one woman, this expectation was very clearly announced when her mother asked, "Do you think that I will have a grandchild before I die?" For others, the expectation was less overt but clearly present:

> I think my parents are expecting that we will have our own biologi-
> cal children. They haven't really said anything out loud but deep
> down, I think they would like to see us have our own biological
> children because then it's the continuation of their family--I guess I
> feel guilty that we can't give them biological grandchildren and that
> I would be letting them down--although I'm sure if I ever said that
> they would be mad at me for saying it.

The presence of subtle expectations from grandparents resulted in a
sense of responsibility for carrying on the family line. Hence, to not
have children meant not only being let down themselves but letting
down the generations before them. One of the consequences of this
was to feel less valued in their own families. As one woman explained:

> Our families think we are selfish because we are frivolous with our
> money. They don't come and visit us as much as my sister who has
> two kids. It seems that they don't like us as much because we don't
> have kids.

Social isolation. Infertility is socially isolating. As one woman so succinctly expressed, "I feel sometimes like we're the only ones in the
world who have this!" For some couples, the research interview was
one of the first opportunities to talk about what had been experienced
as a private and embarrassing problem. At the end of an interview,
one couple had this to say:

> H: It's good doing this kind of thing [i.e., the interview]. You hear
> about so many people going through it but no one talks about it--I
> guess it's too embarrassing.
>
> W: This is good to do because you go to the clinic and it takes so long
> to get in. You know that there are a lot of other couples going but
> you just don't know what is happening with them. So I think it will
> help to hear about other couples [i.e., from the research].

Couples repeatedly emphasized the difficulties they encountered in
trying to help others in coming to a shared definition of their infertility. For most, there was a clear division between those who could
understand their situation and those who could not. Couples expressed
the view that people who did not share the problem were unable to
understand their situation. As one woman put it:

> People who don't have the problem just can't understand. Like it's
> just natural to have kids and people put so much energy into not
> getting pregnant. To take fertility pills, people think you are crazy!

Others who had children or who were single were generally considered unable to understand their predicament. One couple highlighted

some of the misinterpretations and unsolicited advice they received
when they decided to tell others about their infertility:

> H: The guys I have told, most of them respond with sympathy like
> "It's too bad." Some guys mean it, but for others it's like you stubbed
> your toe. When I first mentioned it at work I felt shunned--they say,
> "What the hell is that?" "Are you shooting blanks?"

> W: Some girls say when I tell them that I have endometriosis, "Well,
> is it cancerous?" Others say, "Well, I had a friend who had that and
> she got pregnant" or they read this article and she got pregnant
> doing this. They make it sound so simple but I know it's not that
> easy. I get so angry because they give you false hope. I wish people
> wouldn't give me advice. I don't think that people can understand
> unless they have gone through it.

One woman talked about how motherhood was often the preferred
topic of discussion in various social settings and how this focus contributed to a sense of isolation: "I feel like a real outsider because
anytime we go to parties, the ladies get together and talk about the
children. I feel left out."

Many factors appear to contribute to the couple's experience of infertility as a socially isolating condition. It is a hidden, ambiguous problem that is poorly understood and, as a result, is open to insensitive
responses. The problem itself is not always clearly defined medically,
making it difficult to communicate to others. Because infertility deals
with sensitive, private matters of sexuality and reproduction, it is not
easy to talk about with others. Matters of sexuality and childbearing
are often considered inappropriate to discuss publicly. Finally, infertility is not openly disclosed or discussed because of the feelings of
shame and failure that it typically engenders.

Strategies of Resilience

Facing the challenges of infertility involved a number of complicated
processes. Couples were required to draw on both their internal resources of hope and perseverance and the external help of their physicians, friends, and family. Distinct from the focus on individual
characteristics in the psychopathology literature, this study focuses
on the strategies that couples used to successfully cope with and
overcome the challenges. Because involuntary childlessness is a couple's
problem, it is also an inherently social problem. The strategies of
resilience outlined below are concerned with the way couples defined
and coped with problematic situations within the context of their
shared vision of the future; the professionals with whom they came in

contact; and their circle of friends, work associates, and family members.

Hope, Denial, or Perseverance? Holding to the Goal in the Face of Uncertainty

Being resilient in the face of infertility meant coping with uncertainty. Infertility was usually not experienced as a neatly defined problem, because of underlying uncertainties associated with the medical diagnosis. Although a small number of couples had received a definite diagnosis that they were completely sterile, most lived with a diagnosis that indicated some level of a fertility problem but that did not rule out the possibility of conception. In some ways, the seeds of hope were nourished by the soil of uncertainty.

Couples used a variety of strategies to maintain their commitment to become parents. Staying optimistic was one of the key strategies used by these couples in persevering with their uncertainty. One man explained the challenge:

> We're like many other couples insofar as you have to play it day by day. You have to be positive. Your mental outlook has a lot to do with it. You've got to stay up. You can't let it get you down.

One woman, who had gone through 4 years of testing without a diagnosis, explained how hope seemed to override the rational conclusion that there was indeed a problem:

> We don't have a problem. It's just taking longer. So it depends what you call a problem. Even now we aren't sure that there's a problem. I don't allow myself to think that there is a problem so I believe that I will get pregnant.

Although one can readily point to denial for this couple as a "dysfunctional" response to their problem, there is a sense in which their unwillingness to embrace the problem keeps them steadfastly locked on the goal of becoming parents. Indeed, for most couples in this study, the importance of parenthood seemed to intensify through the course of their infertility experience. One of the ways that they were resilient was to not only maintain a commitment to their goal in the face of significant obstacles but in fact to intensify that commitment. The majority of couples indicated that parenthood had become more important to them since discovering a fertility problem because it was no longer something they could take for granted. One man expressed it this way: "People keep telling you to stop worrying about infertility.

But it's like telling a kid to stop thinking about his presents on Christmas morning."

As couples deepened their investment by going through a seemingly endless regimen of tests and treatments without a solution, their expectations for an appropriate reward at the end seemed to intensify. For some, there was a kind of bargaining or an appeal to the basic principles of justice that accompanied this commitment. As one woman said:

> I sort of felt that, well, I'm going through all this and the reward at the end is that I'm going to get pregnant. In a way, I had that in my head. If I'm a really good girl, then I'll get pregnant.

The stronger commitment to having children was also related to the loss of control. As one woman put it: "Because the decision of whether or not we have children has been removed from us, then I think that there is a stronger urge to have kids."

One of the positive ramifications of encountering a fertility problem was that the meaning and importance of parenthood in their lives was much clearer. Because parenthood had been so frequently brought forward from its taken-for-granted place, the reasons and expectations for parenthood were better understood. Their resilience was expressed not only as a deepened commitment to the goal of becoming parents but also as a clearer vision of what that would mean for them.

Hope and the promise of success in the future played an important role in sustaining these couples from day to day. Their resilience was rooted in a conviction that they would ultimately triumph in their efforts to become parents if they stayed committed to the goal and did everything possible to get there. The focus was on maintaining a sense of hope in the face of adversity. The reasons for their optimistic attitude were that "we must continue to hope and have a positive attitude"; "there is no good reason that we are not getting pregnant"; or that "it will work the next time and we will get pregnant." For one couple, maintaining an optimistic attitude was the easiest way of coping with infertility:

> If you think that it's not going to happen, you get depressed. The other extreme is being defiant and giving up. Staying optimistic makes it easier. If you tread water, it's easier to stay above than going down and up again.

Temporal Reorientation

Even for some of the most optimistic couples, however, the years of repeated disappointments meant investing more in the present than in the future. While still maintaining hope that they might someday become parents, one couple who had been trying to get pregnant for 6 years found it more realistic to invest energy in the present than in the future:

> H: We live more for ourselves rather than for something that may never be there. I don't know what the future is going to hold. We have moved into a two-bedroom house now from a large house where we were planning to have kids.

> W: We don't plan ahead like we used to. We used to bank money for kids. Now we bank a little and go on holidays. We spend it on each other. If we die, who are we going to give our money to?

For this couple, resilience involved a temporal reorientation from the future to the present. Because the experience of infertility is rooted in an unrealized future and the frustration of being blocked from an anticipated goal, their resilience involved shifting their gaze from the hopes of the future to the realities of the present.

Perseverance and a Belief in Success:
The Role of Medicine in Sustaining Hope

Infertility is first and foremost treated as a medical problem. As a result, physicians played a powerful role in shaping the course of events. This is consistent with other research where couples primarily define their infertility not as a social-psychological problem but as a medical condition requiring medical diagnosis and treatment (Miall, 1994). Not only were physicians responsible for the tests and treatments associated with the physiological problem, but they appeared to have a great deal of control over the outlook for the future. Most couples looked to their physician with some variation on the traditional theme of "What are my chances, doc?" and as a result, looked to their physician as a way of defining how much hope they should have. One man elaborated on the doctor's influence: "I am optimistic that we can have a biological child because the doctors seem to have the same optimism and hope and they seem to believe that there is a solution."

Even when there is no immediate solution to their problem, some couples vigorously held on to the promise of medicine to discover a solution in the future. For one man, whose wife had partially blocked fallopian tubes, there was still a strong sense of optimism: "Our doctor said that we have a good chance. You talk to the doctors and there are new breakthroughs all the time." Even in the face of repeated failures, the doctor continues to have the power to provide the possibility of success. One woman who had been trying for five years described her feelings: "Each time I go for a test, I think it is going to make it better, and then nothing happens. I say, 'Why am I doing this?' But I will keep going until the doctor says that there is no chance."

The promise of reproductive technologies also fueled the optimism about the future. For one woman, the reluctance to give up is reflected in a persistent drive to continue the medical process until she is told she can no longer do so: "If I don't get pregnant, I will go through IVF [in vitro fertilization] until they say that I can't anymore. And that could be another 10 years because I'm eligible until I'm 38."

Other couples felt they had to do everything possible before they could call an end to biological parenthood. In some cases, this end was elusive in that technology was perceived as continuing to generate new possible solutions to the problem. A woman who had been through 8 years of testing and treatment continued to hope to have a biological child:

> I grasped at straws--surgery after surgery, to see if they could fix it. I'll still do it if the doctor says that there is a new procedure. I'll try it. Like last year I went in again. I'll go again, being the guinea pig that I am.

The continuing promise of new and sophisticated reproductive technologies resulted, for some couples, in a "magnificent obsession" where sophisticated and extensive treatments present a seemingly endless promise of hope (Sandelowski, 1993). Because in vitro fertilization is one of the most sensationalized means to treat infertility, the "test tube baby" has become the "iconic representation of the adversity and hope embodied in the contemporary experience of infertility" (Sandelowski, 1993, p. 42). Whether it is defined as obsession or persistence, medical treatments played an important role in sustaining these couples through the course of physiological uncertainty and adversity.

Disclosure, Accounting for Infertility, Eliciting Support

In light of the isolating, "shameful" characteristics of infertility, one of the key mechanisms for regaining a sense of control over the problem was to move from a closed- to an open-awareness context. In a closed-awareness context, one interactant does not know either the other's identity or the other's view of his or her identity. In an open-awareness context, each interactant is aware of the other's true identity and his or her own identity in the eyes of the other. Infertile couples tended to create a more open-awareness context over time, which allowed their reference group to identify them as having a fertility problem (Glaser & Strauss, 1981, p. 54).

By way of explaining this increased openness, one man pointed out that people begin to suspect that there is a problem, which then requires explanation:

> With most of my friends it was not until about 2 or 3 years after we found out that we had a problem that I could tell them. Initially I just said, "Well, we're sure having fun trying!" but people are not stupid and you soon have to face up to it--so I told them that we have a problem.

Others explained that it got easier to talk about it as time went on because they got over the feelings of "shame" and "inadequacy" that were present at the beginning and over time, "it made me feel better to talk about it." One woman talked about the importance of telling others as a way of coping with the intensity of the infertility experience: "I would suggest that people confide in a friend. Although I wanted to tell my husband everything, it helped to tell someone else. It was a relief to tell people and not to bottle it up."

For some, the greater ease in accounting for their childlessness emerged as a result of developing a vocabulary for talking about it. The responses that they learned to use in situations ranged from simple statements like "We have a problem" or "We can't" to more elaborate statements designed to make others think about the situation. For one woman, this meant becoming an "educator" to help others understand the situation: "I just tell them straight out--'We can't have kids'--boom! that's it. I don't need the social pressure. I take it on myself to educate people." From relationships with other couples who shared the problem of infertility, and could therefore share in the definition of the situation, there emerged a sense of comfort from feeling less isolated:

> Because I know others, I don't feel so isolated. It's nice to see that others are going through it as well. I feel more comfortable knowing I'm not the only one going through it. Seeing others and their experiences and seeing that their feelings are the same is comforting.

Consistent with the finding that motherhood was a more salient role than fatherhood, women tended to talk with other people about matters related to having children more frequently than did men. This is a reflection of different cultural expectations for women and men. Women are seen to experience more intensively a set of biological and social pressures to reproduce (Miall, 1994). Men were much less likely than women to talk about having children and were much more selective in discussing infertility. As one man pointed out: "I've only told one person at work and he also had a problem [fertility]. But we just didn't go in to it. With other male friends its just not something you bring up." As another man indicated, most people assume that infertility is a "woman's problem" when you mention it, and they just aren't interested in going into it with you:

> When I tell the guys about it, they just aren't that interested. They don't usually follow it with questions. Some say, "Oh, is it 'women's problems'?" and then don't talk about it. She gets a lot more questions about it.

In this respect, men were not called on to account for the infertility in the same way as women, and therefore, they were more likely to avoid discussions of it. By contrast, women were more likely to be in situations where childlessness was more apparent and problematic. As one woman expressed, "With women the issue comes up a lot more. 'When is it going to be your turn?' " As a result, women were required to be more adaptive in the way that they talked about their infertility.

Adoption as a Way of Staying the Course

Adoption was one alternative for some couples who wished to maintain their commitment to parenthood. However, pursuing adoption involved a fundamental reevaluation of what it means to be a parent. For these couples, seeking to adopt meant sorting out having a child of "your own" versus becoming a parent. One woman talked about what it means to think about becoming an adoptive parent when you can't have a child of your own:

> I think that you have to be completely convinced that you couldn't have your own baby. Then, is it your own baby or a baby that you want? You have to come to a point where if your own baby is not

possible, or so dim that you then ask the question--Do we just want a baby? Or was it to have our own baby?

Being able to make the distinction between having your own baby and having a baby created an important new awareness in the crisis of genealogy, for it represented a shift from primary identification with biological, genetic parenthood to an identification with social parenthood. The pursuit of adoption as another means of becoming a parent meant both coming to terms with infertility and anticipating the challenges of adoption:

> The signs that tell you that you are ready are that you can accept that you have a problem, accept taking help, and accept the child of someone else's making. It's an acceptance of what it would be like if the child were to search and how I would feel. I had to think about whether I was ready to accept all the things that an adopted child could throw at you.

Adoption introduced a new set of uncertainties into the process of trying to become parents. Foremost among these was the uncertainty of the child's genetic heritage. One man said: "You worry about the kind of person who gives up a baby." Another expressed fear that the adopted "kid would be stupid or have birth defects." In response to these concerns and uncertainties, couples made the effort to find out as much as they possibly could about adoption by talking to agencies and friends or acquaintances that had adopted. One of the resilience strategies was to watch a little closer those families who had adopted to try to get the reassurance that they had "turned out all right."

Those couples who chose adoption as a way of regaining control over their parenthood choices faced the paradox of once again having to give up control. The decision to move forward with adoption was a kind of resilience strategy insofar as it was a resource that allowed them an alternate means to achieve their goal of becoming parents. It involved redefining the meaning of parenthood, but allowed them to stay committed to their goal of becoming parents. After the years of "nothing happening," adoption allowed them to feel like they were moving forward and could regain a sense of control. As one woman put it, "It was a big relief when I signed up for CAS [the public adoption agency]. I knew I would eventually have a child. I knew I could plan for something."

However, in the same way that their efforts to become biological parents resulted in a dependency relationship with their physician, their effort to become adoptive parents required that they enter a dependency relationship with social workers in the adoption process.

In the couples' efforts to regain control over their decision to become parents, they first must give control to the adoption personnel. The adoption agents had the power to reject a couple for adoptive parenthood on the basis of their evaluation of them as suitable parents. Whereas adoption for many of these couples was a kind of resilience strategy in the face of their involuntary childlessness, it actually gave rise to the need for new resiliency strategies to deal with the challenges of adoption. One woman who had been on the adoption waiting list for 4 years described how their dependence on the adoption agency lay at the root of these feelings of loss of control and anger:

> It has opened my eyes to the frustration of going through the process. You are at their beck and call when they decide that the match is made. You have no control. You have to submit yourself to the process.

Furthermore, in light of the diminishing supply of adoptable babies (Bachrach, London, & Maza, 1991; Sobol & Daly, 1994), infertile couples were subject to increasingly selective practices by the formal agents of the adoption process. This increased selectivity served to heighten the power that was held by adoption workers and corresponding to this, increased the dependency of couples on these workers in their drive to become adoptive parents. Whereas adoption was entered into as a kind of resilience strategy to the crisis of parenthood, in the end, it required that couples draw on some of the same coping behaviors that allowed them to deal with the uncertainty and loss of control associated with infertility.

Shifting commitment from biological parenthood to adoptive parenthood was typically a long process that lasted for several years. Rather than a radical alteration of identity that occurs with the adoption placement itself, the redefinition of parenthood to accommodate adoption was a gradual and incremental experience. The resilience required to come to terms with infertility and prepare for adoption was something that changed over time. Rather than a single turning point, there were a series of changes that were visible in hindsight that marked the growing identification with adoptive parenthood. One man explained:

> There isn't a point when you are totally ready to take on things like this. But it's feeling ready to have a family, and that comes from being more aware of children. Suddenly you see children more directly and are more aware of them. Before you didn't notice kids as much. It's hindsight that shows you the change.

Two different patterns emerged regarding the way that couples moved toward adoption as an alternative route for becoming parents: sequential and concurrent. For some couples, the processes of relinquishing biological parenthood, on the one hand, and taking on adoptive parenthood, on the other, occurred in a sequential manner. For these couples, there had to be some sense of certainty that they would not become biological parents before moving on to a consideration of adoptive parenthood. For these couples, coming to a distinct end point with infertility was the critical turning point for becoming adoptive parents. This meant for some couples that adoption would only be an option "after all avenues of having our own would be exhausted" or "when we are certain that we can't have our own" or "once you've played all your cards with infertility" or "when the biological door is closed."

For others, however, commitments with biological parenthood and adoptive parenthood were experienced concurrently. For these couples, there was a continual vacillation between biological parenthood and adoptive parenthood; they continued to hope for a biological child at the same time as they increasingly invested themselves in becoming adoptive parents. In the face of a limited time span within which to have children, some couples were open to the prospect of being both biological parents and adoptive parents. In this respect, getting pregnant was still important but adoption was the back-up means to parenthood as a result of "not wanting to pass up having children at all." For others, the possibility of having "one of each" is entertained as the way of achieving their desired family size:

> I've always been open to adoption. We've talked about both--what if we were to adopt and then get pregnant. I think that we could adopt and still keep trying to have our own. I wouldn't mind having one of each.

Some couples "hedged their bets" in recognition of the long wait for adoption. As one man described it:

> People tell you it takes so long, it takes so long [to adopt]. So we had a few tests. Quite a few people were pushing us to get on the waiting list saying that you can always cancel out. So once we had a few tests and they still couldn't find anything wrong--that's when we went ahead with it [adoption].

As part of staying the course to reach their ultimate goal of becoming parents, couples talked about the importance of gathering information about both infertility and adoption. Information gathering in itself became an important resiliency strategy. One woman provides

some insight into the importance of information for coping with infertility and coming to a state of readiness to take on adoption:

> To be ready for adoption, you really have to research it. You go and
> get as much information as possible. With infertility, that's what I
> did. That was maybe a sign that I was accepting it. So with adoption,
> I will go and find out. It is a way of accepting it.

Discussion of adoption with others outside the marriage also played
an important role in getting themselves and others ready for adoptive
parenthood. Through the process of disclosing their consideration of
adoption to friends, family members, and people who had experience
with adoption, couples were able to take the role of these others in
getting a perspective on themselves as they would fit into this new
role identity. By monitoring others' reactions to them as prospective
adoptive parents, couples could then realign their actions so as to best
fit with the expectations for the transition to the new role.

These interactions with others served to place couples within the
boundaries of this potential new role identity. In so doing, not only
did couples begin to see themselves in this new role, but others would
increasingly identify them as prospective adoptive parents. In keeping with this, one woman described how she would tell others about
adoption as a way of preparing both herself and them for the new
role:

> Sometimes I tell people about adoption to see what their reaction is.
> I want to see how they respond. I knew that there were some nega-
> tive ideas. It's part of the preparation. If they have something crummy
> to say [i.e., about adoption], I want to hear it now before I have a
> child.

Creating a more open-awareness context played an important role in
managing the socially isolating aspects of both infertility and adoption. When they allowed others in on their private world, they were
more confident in their sense of who they were and were more likely
to feel secure in their relationships.

Toward a Formal Theory of Resiliency: Contributions From Infertility

Infertile couples encounter dramatic and unexpected life events that
call out for a resilient response. Whereas the previous section outlines
a substantive theory of resiliency in the face of infertility, the next
section outlines a formal theory of resiliency. In other words, using
the key categories and properties of infertility as a particular sub-

stantive area, I offer a formal theory that broadens the scope of these findings to the more general process of resilience. A grounded formal theory is an effort to highlight the generic social processes involved in the experience of resiliency to broaden the scope and relevance of key underlying principles. A formal theory of resilience, based on the substantive findings of this research, includes four key elements: (a) an unfailing commitment to the shared goal; (b) fluctuations between fatalism and control; (c) reorganization of self, goals, and relationships over time; and (d) increased openness and resourcefulness.

Commitment to the Shared Goal

Central to the resilient behavior demonstrated by these couples was the unfailing commitment to the goal of becoming parents. Infertility presented major obstacles to this goal, but through it all, they stayed fixed on their shared dream. The shared goal sustained these couples through the day-to-day tribulations of failed treatments, insensitive remarks, mechanical sex, and the frustration of endless delays. From an outsider's perspective, at times it seemed fully irrational to hold on to such a goal when the odds of success seemed impossible. Nevertheless, they did hold on to the goal, and it did sustain them in their ongoing efforts.

These findings indicate that a continuing commitment to the goal plays a central role in any process of resilience. To maintain hope and continue moving through the obstacles along the way, it is critical to have a future orientation that justifies the efforts, sacrifices, and hardships encountered.

The Dynamics of Fatalism and Control

One of the central features of the infertility experience was the feeling that their lives were out of control. The couples talked about being unable to control their fertility and their bodies when they expected to be able to do so, they spoke about the loss of control over their individual and family development plans, and later in the process spoke about their lack of control over the adoption process. In response to this loss of control, couples used a variety of strategies to regain control. In spite of these efforts, the overall pattern was one that seemed to reverberate between a sense of fatalism that their success was in the hands of doctors, God, or luck and a sense that they could do something by trying harder, being more assertive with doctors, getting the timing of sex right, or going through the procedures to move toward adoption.

There is a temptation to think about resilient individuals as those who can seize control of a situation to do something to change it. However, most people who find themselves in adverse situations must cope with a set of conditions that is frequently beyond their ability to change. Hence, for infertile couples, there was an experience of moving between their powerlessness to make a pregnancy happen and their ability to feel in control of the next tests and treatments. This reverberation in control is a mark of many resilient strategies. Whether it be the abused child who moves between tactics devised to avoid "getting into trouble" and situations that are overwhelming or the chronically ill patient who moves between trying to stay fit and giving up activity to the disease, resilience involves fluctuations in the degree of control. The resilient individual is not one who naively seeks to control the situation but instead takes control when possible and realistically acknowledges and accepts powerlessness at other times.

Reorganization of Self, Goals, and Relationships Over Time

The crisis of infertility typically occurred over the course of many years. As a result, couples encountered a number of changing conditions and stressors in their efforts to become parents. Throughout this analysis, for example, participants' comments are prefaced with the phrase "over time . . ." Their ability to be resilient rested in the way that they were able to deal with these changes over time. Although some of the traditional infertility literature has conceptualized these changes as a linear-stage model similar to grief models, it appears that the process of coming to terms with infertility is much messier. Linear models stress a pattern that begins with initial shock and ends with acceptance or closure, but few of these couples even made reference to anything resembling "closure." Acceptance for these couples meant admitting defeat, which they were reluctant to do. Rather, what appeared to work for them were redefinitions of the situation that allowed them to move forward with a goal that was manageable. For example, couples began to question the meaning of parenthood by trying to articulate whether it was a "child of their own" that they wanted or whether it was simply to become a parent (which could be achieved through adoption or donor insemination). Infertility also precipitated reevaluations of the importance of work and career plans, how they spent their money, or what it meant to be a good spouse in the relationship.

Strategies of resilience are typically not neat and tidy linear trajectories. It would appear that "final resolution" is not a particularly salient or honored goal in the process. Rather, infertility was something that these couples learned to live with. Infertility did not go away as they had hoped and it was not resolved, but instead required them to modify their expectations and definitions to meet its emerging demands. Hence, rather than a linear resolution model, resilience may be more appropriately viewed as a many-tiered scaffold whereby emerging problems are conceptualized and dealt with as they arise. The building of the scaffold is the ongoing business of coping with the challenges in the domains of identity, couple relationship, and shared meanings and goals.

Increased Openness and Resourcefulness

Infertility is typically a private experience that touches on the sensitive areas of sexuality, reproduction, and dreams of the future. Failing to become parents "on time" violates normative expectations and often results in insensitive remarks and comments that allude to the couple's selfishness or sexual incompetence. The result was that infertility was usually experienced at the beginning as a socially isolating experience. Many couples made reference to the difficulty they had in conveying the significance of the problem to others who seemed not to be able to grasp the gravity of their pain and frustration. Over time, however, couples learned how to tell others about their infertility and appeared to gain confidence in the way that they approached these disclosures. Informing others and bringing them in on the "private" world of infertility helped them to moderate the otherwise stigmatizing effects of their childlessness.

Related to this, couples grew more resourceful in gathering the support of various professionals. For example, couples tended to become more demanding of physicians as time went on. They requested that their family doctor refer them to a fertility specialist, and if that continued to be unsatisfactory they asked to be referred to one of the specialized fertility clinics at one of the teaching hospitals. Many requested reproductive technologies as a way of moving toward their goal of parenthood. For those couples that pursued adoption, they investigated public, private, and international alternatives as a way of maximizing their chances of becoming parents.

The trend toward more openness and resourcefulness was an important resilient strategy. Facing infertility, like any other adverse condition, involved a process of learning how to tell others and how to elicit their support. In the course of doing this, individuals were able to have a better sense of who they were by bringing into alignment their own sense of self and the expectations and reactions of others. In this regard, increasing openness played an important role in understanding the way that their identity changed in the face of adversity. Although the disclosure of self during times of difficulty increases vulnerability and at times heightens the risk of being misunderstood, it plays a vital role in reshaping who one is in the eyes of others. In this regard, increased openness is an important resilience strategy because it supports the integrity of the individual's changing sense of identity.

Conclusion

The results of this analysis suggests that resilience is not something that can be measured in terms of success, but rather it is a process of navigating an ongoing set of challenges that get in the way of an important goal. Staying fixed on the goal seems to be as important as the strategies that are employed or created to deal with the many problems and obstacles that arise. Gathering support, redefining identity, and being resourceful by drawing on the help of others are important elements in maneuvering through the choppy course of resilience.

At the end of this analysis, however, I am left with the disconcerting feeling that I have little to say about who is resilient and who is not. All of the 74 couples I talked to were navigating the course. Were some more buoyant or successful than others? Were some more resilient than others? The answer is a fully equivocal "No!" Although my impressions as a researcher were that some were coping better than others, to say that they were more resilient would be contingent on setting a standard of successful adaptability. In my view, this is simply not possible to do.

There are many difficulties that one encounters when trying to establish these standards. First, do we measure successful outcomes in relation to each of the problems that are encountered along the way or do we use arrival at the goal as the measure of success? For infertility, is it a matter of successfully negotiating a difficult social situation such as an infertile woman getting through a baby shower, or is it getting a baby at the end of the process? Do we assess resilience by their perseverance to reach the goal or by their adaptability to life's immediate and day-to-day challenges?

Second, there has also been a tradition within the resilience literature to assess how "intact" the individual or family is at the end of the storm. Have they survived the storm? Are they stronger? Or are they worse for the wear? I would argue that we need to shift these kinds of assessments from "better" or "worse" and rather seek to understand the way that these crises transform lives. A crisis like infertility invokes a dramatic resocialization of self that involves fundamental changes in the couple relationship and redefinitions in many of their primary social relationships (Daly, 1992). Resilience research needs to examine these transformations of self and relationships to understand the process of change that is at times positive and forward moving, at times negative and apparently destructive, and at other times holding steady without dramatic alteration.

Finally, resilience is not an individual attribute, nor do I believe that it can be reduced to some kind of score that is in any way meaningful. Rather, resilience is a capability that ebbs and flows in the course of negotiating complex physiological, psychological, and social challenges. Any judgments that we might choose to make about resilience need to be attentive to how individuals assess their own ability to navigate through the minute steps of a difficult process, that for some, goes on without end.

References

Bachrach, C. A., London, K. A., Maza, P. L. (1991). On the path to adoption: Adoption seeking in the United States, 1988. *Journal of Marriage and the Family*, 53, 705-718.

Beardslee, W. R. (1989). The role of self-understanding in resilient individuals: The development of a perspective. *American Journal of Orthopsy chiatry*, 59, 266-278.

Bierkens, B. P. (1975). Childlessness from a psychological point of view. *Bulletin of the Menninger Clinic*, 39, 177-182.

Blake, J. (1974). Coercive pronatalism and American population policy. In R. L. Coser (Ed.), *The family: Its structure and functions* (pp. 276-317). New York: St. Martin's.

Brandstadter, J., Wentura, D., & Greve, W. (1993). Adaptive resources of the aging self: Outlines of an emergent perspective. *International Journal of Behavioral Development*, 16, 323-349.

Bresnick, E. R. (1981). A holistic approach to the treatment of the crisis of infertility. *Journal of Marriage and Family Therapy*, 7, 181-188.

Bresnick, E. R., & Taymor, M. L. (1979). The role of counselling in infertility. *Fertility and Sterility*, 32, 154-156.

Cicchetti, D., & Garmezy, N. (1993). Prospects and promises in the study of resilience. *Development and Psychopathology*, 5, 497-502.

Cicchetti, D., Rogosch, F. A., Lynch, M., & Holt, K. D. (1993). Resilience in maltreated children: Process leading to adaptive outcome. *Development and Psychopathology*, 5, 629-647.

Cohler, B. J. (1987). Adversity, resilience and the study of lives. In E. J. Anthony & B. J. Cohler (Eds.), *The invulnerable child* (pp. 363-424). New York: Guilford.

Daly, K., & Dienhart, A. (in press). Navigating the family domain: Qualitative field dilemmas. In S. Grills (Ed.), *Fieldwork settings: Accomplishing ethnographic research*. Newbury Park, CA: Sage.

Daly, K. J. (1992). Interactive resocialization: The case of adoptive parenthood. *Qualitative Sociology*, 15, 395-417.

Egeland, B., Carlson, E., & Sroufe, L. A. (1993). Resilience as process. *Development and Psychopathology*, 5, 517-528.

Glaser, B., & Strauss, A. (1967). *The discovery of grounded theory: Strategies for qualitative research*. New York: Aldine.

Glaser, B., & Strauss, A. (1981). Awareness contexts and social interaction. In G. P. Stone & H. A. Farberman (Eds.), *Social psychology through symbolic interactionism* (pp. 336-347). New York: Wiley.

Greil, A., Leitko, T., & Porter, K. (1988). Infertility: His and hers. *Gender & Society*, 2, 172-179.

Haggerty, R. J., & Sherrod, L. R. (1994). Preface. In R. J. Haggerty, L. R. Sherrod, N. Garmezy, & M. Rutter (Eds.), *Stress, risk and resilience in children and adolescents: Processes mechanisms and interventions* (pp. xiii-xxi). Cambridge, UK: Cambridge University Press.

Hauser, S. T., Vieyra, M. A. B., Jacobson, A. M., & Wertlieb, D. (1989). Family aspects of vulnerability and resilience in adolescence: A theoretical perspective. In T. F. Dugan & R. Coles (Eds.), *The child in our times: Studies in the development of resiliency* (pp. 109-133). New York: Brunner/ Mazel.

Hertz, D. G. (1982). Infertility and the physician-patient relationship: A biopsychosocial challenge. *General Hospital Psychiatry*, 4, 95-101.

Joseph, J. M. (1994). *The resilient child: Preparing today's youth for tomorrow's world*. New York: Plenum.

Kaufman, J., Cook, A., Arny, L., Jones, B., & Pittinsky, T. (1994). Problems defining resiliency: Illustrations from the study of maltreated children. *Development and Psychopathology*, 6, 215-229.

Kraft, A. D., Palombo, J., Mitchell, D., Dean, C., Meyers, S., & Schmidt, A. W. (1980). The psychological dimensions of infertility. *American Journal of Orthopsychiatry*, 50, 618-628.

LaRossa, R., Bennett, L. A., & Gelles, R. (1994). Ethical dilemmas in qualitative family research. In G. Handel (Ed.), *The psychosocial interior of the family* (pp. 109-128). New York: Aldine.

Laurence, J. (1982). The moral pressure to have children. *New Society*, 5, 216-218.

Link, P. W., & Darling, C. A. (1986). Couples undergoing treatment for infertility: Dimensions of life satisfaction. *Journal of Sex and Marital Therapy*, 12, 46-59.

Luthar, S. S., Doernberger, C. H., & Zigler, E. (1993). Resilience is not a unidimensional construct: Insights from a prospective study of inner-city adolescents. *Development and Psychopathology*, 5, 703-717.

Mai, F. M., Munday, R. N., & Rump, E. E. (1972). Psychiatric comparisons between infertile and fertile couples. *Psychosomatic Medicine*, 34, 431-440.

Masten, A. S., Best, K. M., & Garmezy, N. (1990). Resilience and development: Contributions from the study of children who overcome diversity. *Development and Psychopathology*, 2, 425-444.

Mazor, M. (1979, May). Barren couples. *Psychology Today*, pp. 101-112.

McCubbin, H. I., McCubbin, M. A., & Thompson, A. I. (1993). Resiliency in families: The role of family schema and appraisal in family adaptation to crises. In T. H. Brubaker (Ed.), *Family relations: Challenges for the future* (pp. 153-177). Newbury Park, CA: Sage.

Menning, B. E. (1977). *Infertility: A guide for the childless couple*. Englewood Cliffs, NJ: Prentice Hall.

Menning, B. E. (1980). The emotional needs of infertile couples. *Fertility and Sterility*, 34, 313-319.

Miall, C. (1986). The stigma of involuntary childlessness. *Social Problems*, 33, 268-282.

Miall, C. (1994). Community constructs of involuntary childlessness: Sympathy, stigma and social support. *Canadian Review of Sociology and Anthropology*, 31, 392-421.

Neugarten, B. L., Moore, J. W., & Lowe, J. C. (1968). Age norms, age constraints and adult socialization. In B. L. Neugarten (Ed.), *Middle age and aging* (pp. 22-28). Chicago: University of Chicago Press.

Pohlman, E. (1970). Childlessness: Intentional and unintentional. *Journal of Nervous and Mental Disease*, 151, 2-12.

Renne, K. S. (1977). There's always adoption: The infertility problem. *Child Welfare*, 56, 465-470.

Rosenfeld, D. L., & Mitchell, E. (1979). Treating the emotional aspects of infertility. *American Journal of Obstetrics and Gynecology*, 135, 177-180.

Saffilios-Rothschild, C. (1969). Family sociology or wife's family sociology? *Journal of Marriage and the Family*, 31, 290-301.

Sandelowski, M. (1993). *With child in mind: Studies of the personal encounter with infertility*. Philadelphia: University of Pennsylvania Press.

Shapiro, C. H. (1982). The impact of infertility on the marital relationship. *Social Casework*, 63, 387-393.

Sobol, M., & Daly, K. J. (1994). Canadian adoption statistics: 1981-1990. *Journal of Marriage and the Family*, 56, 493-499.

Staudinger, U. M., Marsiske, M., & Baltes, P. B. (1993). Resilience and levels of reserve capacity in later adulthood: Perspectives from life span theory. *Development and Psychopathology*, 5, 541-566.

Strauss, A. (1959). *Mirrors and masks: The search for identity*. New York: Free Press.

Veevers, J. E. (1980). *Childless by choice*. Toronto: Butterworths.

Wallach, E. E. (1980). The frustrations of being "normal" yet "infertile." *Fertility and Sterility*, 34, 405-406.

Werner, E. E., & Smith, R. S. (1989). *Vulnerable but invincible: A longitudinal study of resilient children and youth*. New York: Adams, Bannister and Cox.

Zaslove, H. K. (1978). Infertility as a life event. *Journal of Human Stress*, 4, 2.

2

Mapping Resilience as Process Among Adults With Childhood Adversities

Jane F. Gilgun

Resilience, or successful outcomes under conditions of adversity, is a concept in need of delineation. Researchers have observed that resilience is a process involving complex relationships among risks, resources, and contexts (Boss, 1987; Egeland, Carlson, & Sroufe, 1993; Gest, Neeman, Hubbard, Masten, & Tellegen, 1993; McCubbin, McCubbin, Thompson, & Thompson, 1995; McCubbin, Thompson, Thompson, & Fromer, 1995; Masten, Best, & Garmezy, 1990; Rutter, 1987). While recognizing that individuals actively process and construct ongoing experiences, researchers have left unexplored the roles of human interpretation in resilience processes. How persons negotiate risks and have good outcomes are puzzles that intrigue scholars and the general public as well.

In the present chapter, I focus on the interpretations of adults who have experienced adversities in childhood and adolescence. I was specifically interested in how persons dealt with risks and used or did not use assets that were available to them. My conceptual framework was a combination of social work's ecological perspective and research and theory on risk and resilience within developmental psychopathology, a branch of child psychology (Gilgun, 1996a). My methods were interpretive phenomenological (Benner, 1994a) life history interviews that were tape-recorded and transcribed. In the course of analyzing the data for this study, I began to see that human agency--the will to do or to be something--has a major role in resilience processes. As far as I know, this concept has not been explored in resilience research.

The discovery of the possible centrality of human agency in resilience processes is a type of discovery that is the hallmark of grounded theory (Gilgun, 1995; Gilgun, Daly, & Handel, 1992; Glaser & Strauss, 1967; Strauss & Corbin, 1990).

Family Stress and Developmental Psychopathology

Research on resilience has occurred in two separate but somewhat related domains: family stress and developmental psychopathology. Both focus on positive outcomes under conditions of adversity and each is concerned with family relationships. Child psychologists have taken the lead in the field of developmental psychopathology, whereas family stress researchers generally have been family scientists interested in how adults cope with contemporaneous stress.

In the family stress literature, the processes of interest are individuals' appraisals of contemporary events, how they marshal resources, and how they cope (Boss, 1987; McCubbin, Thompson, et al., 1995). Thus, family stress research has focused primarily on the unfolding of events after the stressors have occurred and has long recognized that how individuals interpret life events is pivotal in how they respond (McCubbin & Patterson, 1983; McCubbin & McCubbin, 1996), a stance rooted in a symbolic interactionist heritage (Blumer, 1969/1986).

Boss (1987) advocated for the use of qualitative methods to grasp personal meanings and interpretations in family stress research. As Boss observed, research on meaning requires qualitative methods. She pointed out that qualitative research conducted in the 1930s provided many of the fundamental concepts of contemporary family stress research. Most contemporary stress research, however, has been conducted through large-scale surveys and standardized instruments. Open-ended interviews where informants set the pace and create their own conceptual frameworks do not appear in family stress research methodologies.

In developmental psychopathology, the focus is on child adaptation, with parent-child relationships as a major variable and the major resource for successful outcomes (Cicchetti & Garmezy, 1993; Cummings & Davies, 1996). Interest in children's subjective experiences and appraisals are not the norm in this research. Thus, accounts of individuals' interpretations rarely appear in research accounts, although researchers acknowledge that individuals are actively involved in resilience process (e.g., Egeland et al., 1993; Gest et al., 1993). As Egeland and colleagues (1993) noted about resilience as process,

> The individual actively participates in this process, bringing to new experiences attitudes, expectations, and feelings derived from a history of interactions that, in turn, influence the manner in which environmental cues and stimuli are interpreted and organized. (p. 518)

Like most other fields, developmental psychopathology uses surveys, questionnaires, standardized instruments, and complex statistical analyses (e.g., Gest et al., 1993) as the means of understanding processes. These researchers sometimes use structured interviews (e.g., Egeland et al., 1993; Werner & Smith, 1992). These methods, however, are not conducive to generating how individuals actively participate in resilience processes; the methods themselves undermine any goal of capturing human interpretations.

Developmental psychopathology has both a retrospective and a prospective focus and examines risks and assets that are the historical antecedents of good and poor outcomes (Cicchetti & Garmezy, 1993). Often the research is longitudinal, such as the project of Werner and associates that is now in its fourth decade (Werner, 1993; Werner & Smith, 1992) and the 20-year project of Sroufe, Egeland, and associates (Egeland et al., 1993). Within developmental psychopathology there also is a tradition of retrospective research on adults, such as the long-term follow-up studies by Rutter and others (Quinton, Rutter, & Liddle, 1984; Rutter & Quinton, 1984), conducted on women who were institutionalized as children, and the work of Egeland, Jacobvitz, and Sroufe (1988), on the outcomes of adults maltreated in childhood.

As retrospective research that examines how adults negotiate historically occurring risks and assets while grappling with contemporaneous adversities, the present research is closer to the traditions of developmental psychopathology than to family stress research. In my emphasis on interpretation, however, I am linked to family stress research. Thus, in the following discussion, the concepts primarily are from research and theory on developmental psychopathology, with some integration of concepts from family stress research and theory.

Resilience as Outcome

The general definition of resilience within developmental psychopathology involves the interactions of risks and assets that result in good outcomes (Gilgun, 1996b; Masten et al., 1990). Assets and risks reside within individuals, families, neighborhoods, and social policies and programs, as viewed from an ecological perspective. Individuals can be termed resilient only when they have been subjected to risk conditions. Egeland and colleagues (1993) view resilience as unfolding within a supportive context, a context that can deteriorate or ameliorate over time. The deterioration may undermine what until then has been a successful adaptation to risk conditions, or amelioration can shift the balance between risks and resources so that individual functioning improves. Thus, individual functioning can fluctuate over time (Cohler, 1987; Egeland et al., 1993; Murphy, 1987). In addition, resilience may vary across developmental domains at the same points in time. Some persons, for example, may do well in school or work, but have difficulties with interpersonal relationships, or the obverse.

Resilience can be viewed as both a set of behaviors and internalized capacities. Behaviorally, resilience means recovering from, coping with, or overcoming adversity (Masten et al., 1990). As internalized processes, resilience, in the words of Cohler (1987), refers "to the capacity to maintain feelings of personal integration and sense of competence when confronted by particular adversity" (p. 389). Cohler observed that persons who demonstrate resilience cope through flexible, problem-solving, and help-seeking behaviors rather than through brittle and rigid responses to adversities and other stresses.

Resilience, however, is an abstract term. In the conduct of research, the outcome of interest usually is within a particular developmental domain. Resilience as an outcome, an adaptation, or a form of coping can be conceptualized in abstract, general terms or in terms related to specific developmental domains. An example of an abstract statement about resilience is the following: Individuals may lead pro-social lives although they have risk conditions that predict the development of violent behaviors (Gilgun, 1996a, 1996b). A specific statement about resilience is the following: Bart had issues with his sexual identity and homophobia after he was sexually abused but through therapy he gained some peace about his sexual orientation (Gilgun & Reiser, 1990).

There are other issues with definitions of resilience. Resilience itself is defined as a good outcome. What, however, constitutes a good outcome? Is it the absence of poor functioning when persons have risks? Who decides whether a person is functioning well or not? Even persons who generally are not functioning well often have areas of high functioning. On the other hand, fairly well-functioning persons may have areas of maladaptation. General ideas of what constitutes a good outcome, such as loving well, working well, and expecting well, provide guidelines for defining the outcomes of interest in particular studies. Expecting well generally means that individuals are optimistic about the future, their opportunities, and their interpersonal relationships. Because of the multitude of possible resilient outcomes, Cicchetti and Garmezy (1993) urge researchers to include "specifics on the operationalization of resilience . . . in all research reports" (p. 499).

Another problematic aspect of understandings of resilience is the connotation of the term outcome. Outcome connotes an end point to a process. Clear and clean definitions become problematic when outcomes and adaptations are viewed as punctuation points in ongoing interactional processes that occur simultaneously in multiple domains with multiple persons over time. Resilience as punctuation points, however, leads to the principle that resilience points themselves become integrated into processes that become part of ongoing adaptation and coping.

Resilience as Interactions Between Risks and Resources

Risks are a component of resilience. Probabilistic, statistical concepts, risks predict that a portion of an at-risk group will experience adverse outcomes, but cannot predict which individuals within high-risk groups will have the associated outcome. For example, it is well known that being abused in childhood is a risk for the intergenerational transmission of child abuse, but most persons who have this risk are not known to be abusive to children (Egeland et al., 1988; Kaufman & Zigler, 1987), including men who were sexually abused as children and adolescents (Gilgun, 1990, 1991). Being a member of an at-risk group can predict only a vulnerability to the outcome (Gilgun, 1996a, 1996b; Masten, 1994; Masten et al., 1990). Vulnerability, then, is a concept that can be applied to individuals, when they are members of at-risk groups (Masten, 1994; Masten & Garmezy, 1985).

In addition, individuals may experience risk pile-up, similar to McCubbin and colleagues' (1980) concept of "stress pile-up" (p. 861), where they have other risks besides the specific risk condition for a specific outcome. They still may not have the associated outcome, but they may have other adverse outcomes. For example, in my studies of men sexually abused in childhood, most of them did not become perpetrators of child sexual abuse but many had issues with sexual identity and sexual compulsiveness (Gilgun, 1990, 1991, 1996b; Gilgun & Reiser, 1990) and frequently had issues with chemical dependency. Their experience of sexual abuse was not their only developmental risk; commonly, they experienced other forms of childhood maltreatment and parental discord and chemical dependency. Their risks were cumulative.

Yet persons who experience risk pile-up may experience resilience in several domains. In their decades-long study of persons with cumulative risks, Werner and Smith (1992) found that those with resources within themselves, their families, and other social groups developed into competent, caring adults. Their counterparts with fewer resources and similar risks had variety of problems in childhood, adolescence, and adulthood. These studies suggest risk pile-up increases the chances that persons will have adverse outcomes, but these risks do not guarantee poor outcomes. Some persons with vulnerabilities may have an assortment of resources or social assets that see them through serious adversities.

Social assets are important concepts in resilience research. They are "the positive counterparts of risk" (Masten, 1994, p. 6). Like risks, they are a statistical concept. Not all persons with assets such as high IQ, physical attractiveness, social skills, parents who care about them, safe neighborhoods, and good socioeconomic backgrounds turn out well, nor do all persons from impoverished, violence prone neighborhoods and poor families have maladaptive outcomes (Canada, 1995; Jarrett, 1994, 1995; Richters & Martinez, 1933). Individuals may have many assets that could potentially help them to deal successfully with risks, but if they do not use them, they do not function as assets at all. On the other hand, persons with a few assets may use them in the constructive management of adversities. Human agency and interpretation, then, are pivotal in resilience processes.

When individuals use assets to deal constructively with risks, the assets are termed protective factors. They, therefore, are elements in resilience processes that counter the influence of risk. Examples of factors associated with resilience include affection from at least one parent; harmonious parental relationships; persons inside and outside the family who encourage and facilitate the child's ability to cope and who foster positive values; exposure to persons who model prosocial behaviors; and personal qualities, such as abilities to verbalize emotions and thoughts, to empathize with others, and to elicit positive responses from others (Cicchetti, 1987, 1996; Garmezy, 1987; Masten, 1994; Masten et al., 1990; Richters & Martinez, 1993; Rutter, 1987; Werner & Smith, 1992). These personal attributes are hypothesized to develop from secure attachments to parents and parental figures during infancy, early childhood, and/or across the life span (Bowlby, 1973; Cicchetti, 1987, 1996; Cummings & Davies, 1996; Egeland et al., 1993; Egeland et al., 1988; Masten & Garmezy, 1985). In adulthood, supportive spouses and therapy are associated with successful parenting of adults maltreated or experiencing institutionalization in childhood (Egeland et al., 1988; Kaufman & Zigler, 1987: Rutter, 1987).

Just as there are risk pile-ups, or cumulative risks, so are there cumulative protective process. A child who experienced secure attachments is more likely to respond positively to others outside of the family and thus elicit positive responses that result in the development of relationships of trust. In turn, these relationships lead to further positive experiences and the development of coping styles that bode well for future development (Cummings & Davies, 1996; Sroufe, Egeland, & Kreutzer, 1990; Werner, 1993). Persons who have experienced cumulative protective processes are likely to cope well when confronted with risk situations.

The Present Research

In the present research, I am interested in outcomes in multiple developmental domains. As discussed earlier, my work is within the tradition of developmental psychopathology. I depart from the usual practices in developmental psychopathology in that I am using qualitative methods to understand processes of resilience. My work, therefore, connects with Boss's (1987) advocacy for the use of qualitative methods to grasp personal meanings in family stress research. In taking interpretive phenomenological perspectives, I am bringing something new to both traditions. The retrospective nature of my data also departs from mainstream developmental psychopathology, which values longitudinal studies over all others, although, as mentioned, some researchers have done retrospective studies. Finally, I view the term developmental psychopathology as unfortunate, in that it has strong connotations of disease-focused, nonecological, and internally oriented perspectives, in spite of its emphasis on positive adaptation (Gilgun, 1996a).

Interpretive phenomenology is particularly germane to this type of research. Like symbolic interactionism with which it shares a philosophical heritage (Gilgun, in press; Van Manen, 1990), it posits, among other things, that persons are situated in the world and are constituted by and help constitute their worlds (Chesla, 1995). Thus, although they may be unique in many ways, they also are part of a world shared by others (Benner, 1994b). An examination of their lived experiences is likely to be germane to and shed light on the experiences of others.

Given these assumptions, it follows that generalizability in interpretive phenomenological research is based on logic different from that of random sampling. Findings are not numbers and probabilities but researchers' interpretations of informants' interpretations and meanings. Researchers do not presume that findings exhaust all possible patterns and meanings that may characterize phenomena (Benner,

1994a; Bogdan & Knopp Biklen, 1992; Gilgun, 1994, 1995; Morse, 1992; Patton, 1990). On the other hand, researchers assume that findings foster understanding of other similar situations. Generalizability in phenomenological research is analytic, where findings from a study are examined for their fit with other similar situations (Gilgun, 1994). In general, in qualitative research, if findings do not fit subsequent cases, the findings are modified to fit the case.

Method

The present chapter is based on a long-term research project that is seeking to understand the development of violent behaviors and how perpetrators experience their own violent acts (Gilgun, 1990, 1991, 1992, 1996a, 1996b; Gilgun & Reiser, 1990). Thus, the outcomes of interest for the larger study are the presence or absence of violent behaviors when persons have risks for such behaviors. Details of the method of this larger study are in Gilgun (1996b).

For the present chapter, my purpose was to map resilience as process. Outcomes are important insofar as they helped me to designate who in my study was resilient and who was not. I used the guideline of loving well, working well, and expecting well and of being law abiding at the time of the interview as my general definition of resilience. I reanalyzed seven life histories, five men and two women, to prepare for writing this chapter, although I report on only three of them. All but one of the informants--a man--lived within the law, although one of the women maintained a career as a call girl that was secret from her husband and children. All seven are white and have educations ranging from high school graduate to Ph.D. I recruited these seven informants from therapists working with adults with childhood adversities, from self-help groups, and from a medium-security prison. Informants are volunteers. Five of the seven were married or in committed relationships. The remaining two informants had never been married but had maintained committed relationships over long periods of time. Ages ranged from 27 to 50 with a modal age of 36.

I chose these seven cases from among the larger sample of 66 adults, 13 women and 53 men, about two thirds of whom had committed serious violent acts, such as murder, attempted murder, armed robbery, rape, and child molestation. Like the larger sample, informants for the present study experienced many types of childhood adversities. The childhood risks that informants experienced included many types of childhood abuse and neglect: child sexual abuse; witnessing violence within families and neighborhoods; child physical and emotional abuse; and physical, medical, and emotional neglect. Harassment by other children was common in this sample. Other risks were parental chemical dependency, parental separation and divorce, abandonments and deaths of parents and other significant people, and racial discrimination.

The Interviews

The average number of interviews was 8, with a range from 2 to 25 per informant. The average number of interview hours was 12, for a total interview time of about 70 hours. In addition, many hours of interviews with other informants whose histories I did not analyze for the present chapter shaped my understandings and interpretations of the case studies I did use. I was the sole interviewer. By many standards, these are unusually lengthy interviews. I found, however, that the amount of time was well spent for several reasons. One is the sensitive nature of childhood adversities. A certain amount of trust must develop between interviewers and informants before they feel comfortable talking about these topics. Two, understanding resilience or its lack is challenging. Informants often are not clear in their own minds about the meanings of events and how events are related to others. This is expected, because individuals themselves often are nonreflective and do not make connections among components and processes of their lives (Leonard, 1994). Also, I might not always have drawn out my informants at points where later I realize I want to know more. Three, the detail that I sought took a long time to obtain, given the number of years for which informants were accounting. My overall goal of trustworthy constructions of informants' perspectives was the basis of these lengthy interviews.

In these phenomenologically oriented interviews, informants described their experiences in their families of origin and their current families and how they fared in other social groupings such as peer groups, schools, churches, and youth-serving organizations. Their relationships with peers and adults over time and their sexual development histories, including their interpretations of major events in these histories, were examined. Exposure to violence, as targets, as witnesses, and as consumers of violent print and film media, was of particular interest in this research. Informants' interpretations of their experiences were important in these life history interviews because this research assumed that (a) personal interpretations are a basis of human actions, and (b) understanding how individuals who experienced childhood adversity interpret their lives and their actions provides a basis for the development of prevention programs and programs for victims and family members.

Informants signed an informed consent. I encouraged informants not to answer any questions they did not want to answer and to stop talking if they began to feel anxiety. They were free to withdraw from the research at any time without prejudice. The institutional review board of my university approved the research protocol.

Data Collection, Analysis, and Interpretation

I tape-recorded the interviews, had them transcribed verbatim, and then coded them to identify risks, assets, and outcomes, and the processes that link them. For this chapter, I did the analysis without the help of research assistants. I sought to delineate chains of events and interpretations of these events using the concepts of risks, assets, protective factors, outcomes, and resilience. For the ongoing analysis of the interviews, several research assistants and I did the analysis.

In the interviews, I encourage informants to tell their own stories from their points of view, in their own words and in their own ways. The "truth" of informants' stories is not an issue for this research; I am interested in how they construct and interpret events. For me, it is a given that their interpretations of past events may change as their life circumstances change. In the interviews, I do a minimum of guidance and the guidance I do is based on an ecological framework that helps me to investigate resilience processes in a variety of settings, such as families, schools, and communities.

I understand that I have an influence on informants' accounts. My verbal and nonverbal language cue informants, and they undoubtedly shape their stories in response to these cues. The questions I asked and the responses I had usually were not detached and objective. I often felt deeply connected to my informants, often in a comfortable way, but sometimes I felt serious disjuncture and stress. The sources of the disjunctures, of course, were part of my interpretations and responses, but on reflection my disjunctures were usually either rooted in the triggering of my own personal risk processes or by being so shocked I disconnected temporarily from my informants.

Representing Lived Experience

Interpretive phenomenology is primarily an ontological perspective that shifts researchers' attention from traditional Cartesian concerns with epistemology, or how we verify what we know and how we know what we know (Leonard, 1994). Interpretive phenomenology is focused on what it means to be a person present in worlds that constitute you and that you constitute. Developmental psychology also recognizes these reciprocal relationships between individuals and their environments, where environments shape individual development and perception but where individuals also shape their environments. Researchers' goals are to represent individuals' lived experiences in authentic ways, while recognizing that researchers too are interpretive beings constituting and being constituted by their worlds. Thus, there are no absolute criteria for judging the truth value or validity of phenomenological, interpretive research (Benner, 1994b). The value of an interpretive case studies lies in its authenticity and its ability to shed light on what it means to be in the world. For instance, if phenomenological researchers state that their study is focused on cancer patients' lived experiences, then the results of such research can be judged on whether the findings provide perspectives on what having cancer means to persons with cancer.

Results

The informants whom I termed resilient in the present study had multiple risks for poor outcomes, such as childhood maltreatment, parental death, and parental chemical dependency. In their set of risk factors, they were similar to many of the informants who were serving prison terms for violent behaviors. The persons with resilient outcomes had factors in their lives that helped them adapt to, cope with, and/or overcome some of the effects of these risks, and they often displayed problem-solving, help-seeking behaviors. In terms of processes, in the accounts of the persons whom I am terming resilient, I saw the following general pattern: experiences of multiple risks over time; using resources within the self and the environment to cope; developing a pro-social sense of agency; coping with, adapting to, and overcoming the risks at the time of their occurrence and well into the future; and adult relationships that were affirming and helpful in terms of dealing with everyday stress.

The case studies below illustrate these points.

Phil: A Pro-Social Sense of Agency

In the following excerpt, Phil, age 34, whom I term resilient, was married, had children, and worked at a highly responsible job. He was attractive and articulate. His wife was a strong source of support as he dealt with the challenges of running a large company. About 3 years prior to participating in the present research, he had joined Alcoholics Anonymous (AA) and was sober from then on. He had also had therapy for 2 years for sexual addictions; that is, he saw his masturbatory practices and his relationships with women as problematic and wanted change. He had distant relationships with his extended family. Until he went into therapy, he saw himself as turning out like his father:

> I acted out with all kinds of women; he had all kinds of girlfriends. I
> drank; he drank. I drank hard liquor; he drank hard liquor. I had his
> rage; I just took on his rage.

Among many childhood and adolescent risks, Phil had experienced
parental sexual abuse:

> My father and mother both abused me. I forgot about that. I jumped
> into bed with them one time. I don't know why--because of a storm,
> and I was between my father and my mother, and my father had put
> his penis between my legs, and I was fondling my mother's breasts.

His father abused him many times after that, but his mother did not.
Both his parents were chemically dependent, his father had multiple
affairs, he witnessed his father's sexual abuse of his older sister, and
he also was abused sexually by two different men outside of the family when he was between the ages of about 10 and 14. One man was
his physical education teacher and the other was a pharmacist for
whom he worked part-time after school. He experienced his parents
as perpetrators of psychological maltreatment, including name-call-
ing. For example, his parents often told him he was stupid. These
combinations of risk experiences led him to feel as if there was something wrong with him, but they also seemed to spur him on to master
important tasks. In the following excerpt, he talked about his life
when he was in the eighth grade. It begins with his account of lobby-
ing his mother to go to the school of his choice. The excerpt illustrates
how risk processes are linked, and in some cases, how what Phil
called "survival" leads to moderation of risks:

> I was standing at the counter eating lunch one day, and I was bug-
> ging her [mother] about it, and she says, "Phil, you're too stupid to
> get in Morgan [the private school of his choice]." She said, "You'd
> never pass the entrance exams. You're going to have to go to Sylvester
> [the public school]." And I think that a wave of shame came over me
> at that point, that I started feeling real self-conscious about every-
> thing, and there's also all the abuse at that time had taken effect,
> and this phys ed teacher in grade school had abused me like fifth,
> sixth, and seventh grade, and by this time I was on Valium, because
> I had severe headaches, and I couldn't, I couldn't go to school I had
> such severe headaches. Because that guy would come to me at a
> class and abuse me in his office, and then one time he--I escaped. I
> ran out of his office, and he chased me for many blocks, and I hid in
> a trash barrel, a five-gallon drum, and I hid in that and threw trash
> over me, and I got away from him. But anyway, by this time, I was
> on Valium because I couldn't go back to school. I had such bad
> headaches. So I was dealing with that, but no one ever knew that.

> But I walked in the house after coming out of the trash barrel full of carbon and ketchup, all this crap on top of me, and my mother was so blasted she didn't realize it. It was just a matter of surviving. So anyway, I ended up going to Sylvester, and I was real withdrawn by that time.

This outpouring documents the interconnections between a series of risks and also shows the desperate attempt that Phil made to successfully avoid a perpetrator, an act that can be viewed as positive coping, although his mother appeared oblivious to his physical and emotional state when he returned home. His headaches and use of Valium may be linked to his prior maltreatment. All three factors probably undermined his school performance. The abuse by a teacher may be connected to reluctance to go school. Thus, because he did poorly in school, he was unable to go to the school of his choice. His mother called him stupid. This is risk pile-up. There's a circularity here. Perhaps had he not experienced maltreatment at home, he might have gotten into his first-choice school. That his mother called him stupid is an example of a double-bind: She blamed the child although she had helped put him in a position he did not want to be in.

Agency and father's maltreatment. His father also contributed to Phil's sense that he was stupid. The following story not only illustrates this, but it also places his relationship with his father in a larger context. Finally, and perhaps most significantly for the purposes of understanding resilience processes, Phil showed a strong positive sense of agency in how he responded to his father's cruelty:

> Well, we were working on a car one time, which is kind of--it sticks out in my mind, because I was lying underneath my car and working on it, and my shoulder touched his shoulder, and it burned, and I just hated it. I never touched him otherwise. We never shook hands, never did anything. And it just burned. So anyway, he said, "Give me an open-ended wrench." And I got a wrench. And it wasn't an open-ended wrench, and he says, "You stupid son of a bitch." He says, "You fucking kids are so stupid." He rolled out, and he went and got his own tool. So what I did is that I went and I got a Sears magazine, and I studied the tools, what was what, so I could--so he would never have to do that to me again.

Learning the names of all the tools was a positive coping strategy, as was his decision to run from a perpetrator and hide in the trash can.

Phil not only developed a pro-social sense of agency and a sense of competence, but he also established affirming relationships with others. He had a lifelong best friend named Dave in whom he confided most of his feelings and experiences, and, when he was 16 and had his first girlfriend, he told her his life story, leaving out only the sexual abuse. As an adult, he talked frankly to his wife about his problems at work, and she appeared to have been an important factor in his vocational success.

An alternate father. As an adolescent, Phil found an alternate father in Bob, Dave's father, who affirmed his sense of self-efficacy. He said of Bob: "I think he liked me because I was industrious. Dave and I would go to Dave's house and Bob would help us, and we'd get into conversations." Bob taught Phil how to repair electronic equipment, and by the time he was 16, Phil was running a small business and making good money repairing small appliances, radios, and televisions. As Phil was learning how to repair this equipment, he sometimes made mistakes, but Bob was kind to him. Phil in turn would help Bob when Bob needed an extra pair of hands: He said, "Bob was a model for me. I would watch him and help him. If I got into trouble, Bob would help me." In other conversations about Bob, it appeared that Phil consciously sought to be like him.

Into adulthood, he continually attended school, acquiring skills that eventually led him to head a manufacturing concern. He attributed his hard work in school as attempting to prove to his father that he was not stupid. He said:

> I suffered from severe low self-esteem for many years. I went to trade school, and I couldn't get into the class. I wanted to be an electrician, because my father used to be a tradesman, and I couldn't study in school. I was a wreck. I was just the bottom of all the grades. I got into the Technical Institute, and the guy said, "You're nuts." I took the entrance exam, and I didn't know any math. He says, "You can't be an electrician. You don't know any math," and it was just a knife in my heart. I thought I could finally prove myself to my dad, and I couldn't do it. So I took this other course, industrial hydraulics, pneumatics. And I got in there, straight As. I just got a job, went back to night school and did the electricity course, took the refrigeration and air conditioning course, took electronics courses, and I'd get all this stuff. I kept trying to prove myself to my dad and prove that I was smart. And then I was sick of trade school, and I went to college. Anyway, things started clicking in my life, and I still suffered from this self--this issue that I'm stupid.

Determined to succeed in school and to show his father that he was not stupid, Phil displayed a strong sense of agency. He did well in school and that led to vocational success. Although Phil had a single explanation for his school achievements, I believe there were other factors as well: He probably liked to learn, he may have set high standards for himself in terms of the kinds of jobs he wanted, and he probably formed some satisfying relationships with some of his teachers, as he had formed such a relationship with Bob.

A competent wife. Phil's wife, Sal, helped him deal with work stress by "listening." She also was a capable household manager, which he recognized, although he put himself down--typical of persons who feel defective:

> I was like a big baby. I couldn't take care of myself. She [Sal] took care of me completely, totally. She was like my mother, and if I was angry about work, she'd listen. If I was--she would wash the clothes, clean the house, handle the bills, I wouldn't have to worry about the money. That was her problem, not mine. I would go to work, take my paycheck, give it to my wife.

He was in school while married, and Sal's ability to care for the household effectively undoubtedly gave Phil the time to devote to his studies.

Sal may have been instrumental in his decision to join AA and to enter therapy. She fought with him, refusing to give in to Phil's self-defeating decisions. When one of their infants died, Phil at first refused to go to a grief group, which was what Sal wanted. He said, "I fought. I did fight. I didn't want to go to that thing." He went, however, because Sal "fought with me" and "convinced me to go." She said to him, "You owe this to me. You do owe this much to me."

Sal's "fighting" with him and his becoming "convinced" was based on his desire to keep his marriage and to avoid abandonment. He said:

> I thought that if I was going to save my marriage, because I think, come to think of it, Sal had threatened to leave a couple times, if I didn't start taking care of it, holding up to my deals, she would leave. That triggered my abandonment, and that made me react, and my abandonment came from my mother [who] would get into a fight with my father and grab her suitcases and walk out the door. She'd tell us kids that we were bad and that she was never coming back, and we were on our own, and that's when I was abused in one of her little times that she left.

Phil, then, responded to his wife's request that he go to the grief group, which in turn led to his joining AA and then getting therapy for his sexual issues. Whether his response was based on a desire to maintain a relationship he wanted or a desire to avoid abandonment, or some combination, is not entirely clear. Here, as when he talked about his vocational success, he is giving a single explanation for situations that could be much more complex.

Overall, then, Phil can be thought of as displaying resilience. He overcame serious adversities, and he displayed many of the coping and problem-solving behaviors that have been noted in previous research and theory, as discussed above. His fortuitous marriage to a capable woman who was willing to struggle with him over pivotal issues, and his responses to her, shows the interactional nature of resilience processes. Sal was an asset, but if he had not responded to her, she would not have become part of his resilience processes. Earlier in his life, he also showed a capacity to make effective use of the resources in his environment. Bob, his best friend's father, was an important resource for him; in turn, Phil responded well to Bob, learned a great deal from him, and then was able to build a business while still a teenager, a business that increased his confidence in his abilities and that could have been a factor in his adult vocational success.

Interlacing of risk and resilience. Phil's history also demonstrates that risks continued to be interlaced with resilience processes. He succeeded in school, but his need to prove something to his father was a possible risk condition that appeared to be undiminished even though he proved that he could succeed in school. Another example of possible undiminished risks in resilience processes is his response to his wife after she threatened to leave him. Is being motivated by fear of abandonment, even partially, a sign that risks are still present and not overcome?

A personal quality that may have been a factor in his ability to respond to environmental resources was his emotional expressiveness. Throughout the telling of his story, he is clear about how he was feeling at any point in his life. As an adult, as the excerpts from his interview demonstrated, he was able to maintain what appeared to be an emotionally expressive marriage. Emerging in my overall research program is the idea that emotional expressiveness is an essential component of resilience processes (see, e.g., Gilgun, 1996b).

Another emerging concept in my research is agency, for which I have no satisfactory conceptual definition. As is clear from Phil's story and from others that I have not reported here, a person's will, or sense of determination, appears to be pivotal in how risks and assets are used. I return to this concept later in this chapter.

Phil's chemical dependency issues and sexual behaviors were problematic even at the time I was interviewing him. Thus, although he overcame a great deal, he had ongoing issues with which he was coping. His resilient outcome, therefore, was not untainted with risk processes. Resilience, adapting to, coping with, and overcoming risk, therefore, is a relative and ongoing condition. Phil's life history is paradigmatic of other histories that show resilience processes. I discuss the next two cases more briefly. My purpose in these cases is to deepen understanding of the resilience processes under discussion.

Agency: A Component of Andy's Resilience Processes

Andy, 27 years old at the time of the interviews, had a well-paying job that he liked and a committed 5-year relationship, and he was looking forward to the future with pleasure, anticipating, among other things, adopting a child and becoming involved as an actor in a small theater company. At that point in his life, Andy fit the general definition of a good adult outcome: working well, loving well, and expecting well. He also can be termed resilient because he learned to manage substantial risk conditions. Whether he will maintain his resilience is not clear because it is possible that risks he encounters later in life could overwhelm his resources.

Over his lifetime, Andy experienced many risks and assets, some of which became protective factors. His risk processes led to a sense of being a bad person and to long-term feelings of depression. When he was a senior in high school, he confided in a trusted high school English teacher about his depression and his belief that he was gay. She helped him find counseling and a coming out group that led to his self-acceptance as a gay man. Although the counseling helped him to come to terms with his gay identity, he continued to have serious issues with depression. In his early 20s, after being unable to succeed in a New York design school far from his Midwest home, he returned home feeling like a failure and overdosed on pills. His sister found him in the living room, and he recovered in the hospital. He sought counseling a second time.

Risks. The components of Andy's risk processes included parental divorce when he was 8 years old; harassment by other children for his slight build and fair complexion; sexual abuse by his adolescent uncle when he was 8 to 12 years old; unhappiness over his gradual awareness that he was gay; negative reactions of others to his interests in design, sewing, and knitting; and one instance of sexual abuse by his father when he was 16. He gradually developed feelings that he was somehow bad and over time became depressed, which was such a usual state for him that he didn't know he was depressed. Andy was at high risk for risk pile-up and negative outcomes. Each negative event in his life contributed to his sense that he was a bad person.

Assets. Andy's assets included being a member of an ethnic and racial group that was the norm in his community; a pro-social family; a mother, sister, and extended family whom he experienced as somewhat attentive; friendships that sometimes were emotionally expressive and affirming; long-term success in his school work; enjoying and being good at designing, sewing, and knitting; a determination to pursue his interests despite discouraging responses from others; talents in photography, writing, and editing; a form of intelligence that included wanting to understand himself and others; searching for guidance and a rationale for being who he was; and a determination to be who he was, what I call a sense of agency. Both his teachers and his classmates recognized his talents. He was editor of his high school yearbook and throughout his school career his art teachers consistently affirmed his abilities.

This long list of assets suggests that Andy grew up in supportive environments, where other persons provided him with affirmation of his talents and where he found pro-social successes. He had a sense of what it means to be connected to work he loved, and he resisted the attempts of others to turn him from his interests in women-identified activities and vocations. His negotiation of his assets and his risks led him to have a strong sense of agency that he was going to live his life his own way. Challenged by many for his interest in activities and vocations most identified with women, by the end of high school he had decided to do what he wanted with his life regardless of how some others perceived him.

Resilience processes. Although Andy experienced a long-term undiagnosed bout of depression, including a suicide attempt, he did not kill himself. What kept Andy alive? What gave meaning to his life that helped him to realize that he needed help? What keeps any of us alive? As I searched the transcripts for answers, I found that he expressed a strong will to be what he wanted to be; that is, his sense of agency may have been part of protective processes that kept him alive. He said:

> I took an English class called "A Different Path," and this was my favorite English teacher. She's a woman who, I don't know that much about her, except what we did in school, but she--this class was we were studying people who chose other than the norm. It was more like you learned self-truth and things important to you rather than how to fit into the society as a mold of someone else, everybody else, and that really helped me reinforce the idea that I was doing what was right. I studied Thoreau and people, Emily Dickinson, people

that weren't considered normal, but maybe were true to themselves or happy because of something inside that was telling them, you're okay. You can do what you want, and that was a big influence on me.

Andy's words present a definition of agency: exercising the will to do what you want. He read these words in the class of the English teacher in whom he confided about his gayness and depression.

At another point in the interview, Andy returned to this theme of ultimate meaning and agency. He talked about how his parents didn't want him to go to fashion school in New York, but to go to college and be an architect. He had a strong sense of self; not only did he not do what his parents wanted him to do, he also did not abandon his interest in sewing and design. The following excerpt not only shows his sense of will, but it also shows that he was able to listen to others and take their advice, perhaps an important element in resilience processes. He said:

> My parents always wanted me to go to college, but they wanted me to be like an architect or something, not involved with art or sewing or anything like that. So basically in junior high school I took the classes you had to take to do that. I took a lot of drafting, mathematics, and things like that. But when I was going to high school, I went to my counselor, and she said, "Well, what do you want to do?" And I said, "I want to be a fashion designer," and she was like, this boy is crazy. I said, "I want to take as many art classes and so on as I can." I did that. My high school counselor was a woman, and she didn't think this was a good idea at all, so she said, "Well, I think it's fine that you do that, but I think that you should also have marketable skills, so I think you should take typing and shorthand besides the art and sewing that you like." So I did that, too. I didn't do that well, but I got through 2 years, but I took the classes that I wanted to take, sewing and art.

At another point in the interview, Andy reflected on his decision to do what he wanted to do:

> Just thinking about it right now, this minute, I think there were so many things in my life that I did because it was what I had to do and because it was expected, and that this was the one thing [fashion school] that I really wanted to do. So maybe that was a pact that I made with myself. That I wasn't going to compromise that as I had compromised so many other things in my life.

Agency, failure, and a suicide attempt. His failure in fashion school, where he was so determined to succeed, apparently overwhelmed his resources. This excerpt shows his willingness to take the counsel of others. In addition, his agency once more was engaged: to avoid being committed and to seek the help he knew he needed. He said:

> I tried to commit suicide. I was living at home. I had--this was a long time--when I was still young, probably about 19, I moved to New York, because I was all set to--I was going after my degree in design. I was going to do all this stuff. I moved to New York, and I couldn't cope with it. I had a friend who found an apartment, and we were both going to go to school, somebody who I attended school with here, and it just didn't turn out the way I thought, and I lost my money, ran out of money, and didn't get a job. I ended up coming back home and living with my mother, which was a terrible thing, because I had lived--actually I must have been older than that, 20 or 22--because I'd lived away from home already for 2 or 3 years. And to come home to live with my parents, . . . I was in a bad relationship. I tried to commit suicide and was told I would have to see a therapist or they would commit me. It was real odd. I don't remember, because like I said, I took a lot of pills, and I almost fell asleep once in the car, so I don't remember much about it until much later after the hospital. I went to the County Hospital, and I just remember, like I went into the therapist, and we talked for about an hour, and, you know, he says, "Well, we can commit you because of what you did." I said, "Well, I don't want to be committed." I told him that I was taking care of it, because I had scheduled an appointment with Ron [a therapist whom he subsequently saw for 3 years]. I had talked to someone about taking care of this. I had made an appointment to see Ron. I said, "I know I need help. I have an appointment to see somebody. If I start to do that, is that okay?" He said that was okay.

Scared into health. Like Phil, who was afraid of being abandoned by his wife and who therefore went to a grief group with her, an act that led to therapy and major positive personal changes, Andy was scared into health.

> It was scary. And like the man, the therapist I saw then, he told me, "If you ever try to do this again," he said, "then you're committed. Legally we commit you whether you want to be or not." And like that always scared me. I've had problems with depression since, but it scared me. Because I think, you can't do that, because if you don't, you risk being back in the hospital.

Some of the criminals I interviewed for the larger project did not appear to believe there were consequences for their behavior, or if there were, the actions were worth it or they wouldn't be caught.

An example of a risk process. Andy's strong sense of agency is central to his resilience processes. I would like to share one brief story about being teased in childhood that shows the hurt he experienced over being who he was. Not coincidentally, the teasing began after his parents' divorce when he may have been feeling vulnerable and after his mother, he, and his sister moved to a new neighborhood. There is a certain sweetness to the story that attenuates some of the pain:

> A: Yeah, because in school I had a lot of problems with other kids. Like growing up in school, I guess I was different, because I didn't have the same interests that boys my age did. I didn't really feel I was different. I just felt like . . . I kind of knew what I liked and did that, but I got teased a lot because of that. So I got called a lot of names and alienated. I wasn't in with a lot of people. I wasn't good friends with a lot of people.
>
> J: What names were you called?
>
> A: I was sissy, you know, sissy and pansy and stuff like that. . . . Which I didn't know--yeah, that was real weird--because I didn't know what a pussy was. I knew that that was a cat. And sissy and faggot, things like that.
>
> J: When you were 9, 10 years old?
>
> A: Yeah. I can remember the split [when his parents were divorced], because like kindergarten to second grade I was at one school, and then I went to a new school. We moved, and I remember moving. And more, it started to happen after that.
>
> J: After you moved. It didn't happen in kindergarten through second grade at all.
>
> A: No, no.

With these kinds of risks and the others he experienced, his assets helped him maintain a sense of integration. His suicide attempt is an instance where his resilience processes broke down, but he returned to his previous level of functioning. He was not able to succeed in fashion school in New York and this was almost more than he could bear, given his will to succeed in fashion. His sense of agency was reengaged in the hospital: He wanted to get help, and he wanted to avoid being committed.

Richard: An Antisocial Sense of Agency

A sense of agency is not always pro-social. Both Phil and Richard pushed themselves forward for the sake of pro-social goals. Many of the persons whom I interviewed and who were in prison for various acts of violence also displayed strong sense of agency, but they sought to succeed in often extreme antisocial ways, such as being the most vicious, intimidating person they could be or in being the best drug addict.

Richard, age 40, in prison for armed robbery and who had a 27-year history of chemical abuse and dependency and physical assault, provides an example. His outcomes thus far are not optimal, although he is taking major leadership roles in the prison system. His wife and young son visited him frequently in prison, and they have participated as a family in several prison family life education programs. He is devoted to his family and working hard at learning a trade in prison, but he is not sure he can resist chemicals and the associated lifestyle once he is released.

Risks. Like Phil and Andy, Richard had a long string of risks, such as paternal alcoholism, poverty, a young mother overwhelmed with family responsibilities, sexual abuse, physical abuse, emotional abuse and neglect, being teased and beaten by other children in the neighborhood, and having a learning disability that kept him from succeeding in school. He had some assets, such as being athletic, intelligent, and good-looking and having the ability to tell a good story. His mother worked at being effective, but she experienced stress due to insufficient resources. Richard's nuclear family had strong ties to his mother's extended family, but Richard did not like them, and one of his mother's uncles molested him. Often, when his father came home drunk, he was physically abusive to his wife, who then took the children and stayed for several days with her family. The family also moved frequently because they could not pay the rent. These were protective processes in the sense that they sheltered the mother and children from physical harm and kept a roof over the family, but these actions had negative effects on Richard.

The frequent moves took Richard away from organized activities in his neighborhood, such as Scouts and Little League, and he therefore was not able to succeed in areas where he did well, such as in meetings and games. He continually had to move to new schools, and each time he did, he was teased and often beaten by other children. Because of his learning disability, he was in special classes. Some of the other children called him "retard," "dummy," and "stupid." When he got older and was stronger, he started beating up other kids. He got a big kick out of harassing younger boys.

His sense of agency centered around wanting to feel powerful instead of being put down and in excelling at everything he did. When he was unable to succeed in school and was not able to participate in Scouts and sports, he turned to antisocial activities, which were readily available to him. He loved and wanted to be like his father, an alcoholic who rarely worked and frequented hobo camps. Richard often went with him to the camps. In kindergarten, his teacher asked the children what they wanted to be when they grew up. Richard said, "A bum." The teacher said, "No, you don't." Richard became a bum and thought it was a romantic, wonderful life, even when he woke up so sick from chemicals he wanted to die.

Richard desperately wanted to feel good about himself, and he sought the admiration of others, often through antisocial acts. He said about beating other children:

> I didn't want to really hurt them bad, but I just wanted them to be afraid, you know. That's what felt good is them being afraid, like I was afraid. That was a good feeling I got, is that they were afraid. And embarrass them in front of other, the other kids around. This one kid, Peter Mack [not his real name], he used to beat me up. And at, at sixth grade, what I did is I took his shoes and I threw them over this fence, and I had it planned out, when he was going to go get his shoes I was going to go over there and beat him up. And all the kids on the playground playing kickball were there. He went over there. BAM, BAM, BAM, BAM. Blasted him about three, four times. He was on the ground. He started crying. I kind of kicked him. And, you know, he was just crying. He was just embarrassed. And that felt good for me. To have the other kids see that. And then I started liking it, I think. I, I think I liked that because then I kind of turned into a bully. Then I started picking on kids when I went to junior high school. I was tough, you know.

He succeeded in being tough, and he was proud of it. His words suggest that he was making up for the humiliations he had felt whenever he was beaten up by others. He wanted to feel powerful, and he committed antisocial acts to do so.

He also enjoyed harassing and teasing younger, weaker children, again because that gave him feelings of power. He sought an audience when he picked on others:

> I used to really like the school peanut butter bars. So I'd have a few kids that I'd go and I'd just take them from them because I knew they weren't going to hit me back or something. And there was this one poor kid, I remember. Boy, I was just thinking about this the other day, about that kid. I felt real bad. I used to always catch him in the hall somewhere, but I would hide. And when the, you know, he was kind of a little dorky-looking kid with glasses and stuff, carrying his books. And I'd come up behind him and I'd surprise him. You know, at least two, twice a week. And I would kick him as hard as I could in the ass. WHAM. You know and books would go flying. And I, I remember I kicked him hard. And I used to kick with everything I got. And he wasn't ready for it. A lot, most of the time it was a surprise because I would be hiding, and I would just do that and laugh and think it was funny, but there was a part of me inside, I remember, I felt bad for him. Sometimes I felt bad because I knew

I really hurt him. Then I felt good because I thought it was funny that other, other kids were around.

Just as there are no such things as resilience processes without interlacing risks, perhaps many risk processes have some streams of assets, such as the regret and guilt that Richard expressed. He had a strong sense of agency in terms of getting the approval of other children and of avenging his own earlier humiliations.

He tried alcohol and glue sniffing when he was 13, and this gave meaning to his life. He felt wonderful, on top of the world. When he needed money to buy drugs and alcohol, he had many mentors in the neighborhood to show him how to get money. Friends introduced him to beating and robbing gay men, to armed robbery of drug stores, and burglary. He prided himself at being good at all of these activities.

Part of beating and robbing gay men involved engaging them in sex first. Eventually, he established relationships with some of the men who showered him with money, clothes, and opportunities to travel. He took a great deal of pride in being good at gay sex and of being attractive to other men. Part of the pride had to do with his sense of power of being liked, for being attractive:

> I liked it. I liked the feeling of, ah, but I always knew it was basically a sexual thing. I really knew that in my, in my mind I knew that it was. But it was still a, a sense of, you know, I was liked for something. I felt that I was real good at it. I don't know if you'd call it a soothing sense. I don't know. I think it was more of a powerful, you know, a feeling of power.

He wanted to be good at something, to have a sense of power, to be admired, to be liked. These were strong motivations in him, and he sought to fulfill them even at the expense of others. As an adult, confined to prison, he expressed regret at some of the hurt he had caused.

Discussion

As I have shown, human beings are the agents of resilience processes. Resilience appears to be a lot of work, struggle, and pain. Many persons have multiple cumulative risks. Some cope successfully in prosocial ways, choosing positive goals for themselves, such as Phil learning about tools from the Sears catalog after a humiliating experience with his father. Others chose positive goals for themselves, as Richard did in choosing to want to feel good and powerful, but his way of feeling better often involved hurting others. Both Phil and

Richard had a strong sense of agency coupled with goals that most of us would endorse. One chose pro-social methods, whereas the other did not. Andy maintained a strong determination to succeed in fashion in the face of years of derision from others, and, when this goal was frustrated, his resources were overwhelmed and he attempted suicide. Knowing he needed help and fearful of being committed to a mental hospital, he voluntarily sought counseling and kept at it for 3 years.

The findings of these case studies in combination with the four others I analyzed especially for this chapter and the other 58 interviews I have done on issues related to resilience provide a powerful database that I can link to previous research and theory. The concepts of agency, agency with pro-social and antisocial outcomes, and resilience processes as interlaced with risks augment our understanding of resilience.

I have taken an interpretive phenomenological approach that demonstrates the utility of this much underused method. This method has helped me demonstrate such concepts as risk pile-up, the importance of a supportive spouse, and active engagement with pro-social persons and activities. These ideas are well accepted but poorly understood. Finally, I have given a sense of what it is like to experience risk and resilience: to hide in a filthy trash can, to feel like a knife is in your heart when your father calls you "stupid," to be confused and isolated when other children call you "pussy." For too long, research has been concerned with quantities--how much, how many--but not sensitive to the central issue of the quality of human life. Interpretive phenomenological methods can contribute to understanding not only quality of life, but can also, as I have demonstrated, deepen understanding of known concepts and help discover and delineate new concepts.

Note

1. This chapter was originally presented as a paper at the Conference on Resiliency in Families: Qualitative Approaches, sponsored by the Center for Excellence in Family Studies, University of Wisconsin--Madison, June 16-18, 1996. This research was supported by Grant 55-024 from the Minnesota Agricultural Experiment Station.

References

Benner, P. (Ed.). (1994a). *Interpretive phenomenology: Embodiment, caring, and ethics in health and illness.* Thousand Oaks, CA: Sage.

Benner, P. (Ed.). (1994b). The tradition and skill of interpretive phenomenology in studying health, illness, and caring practices. In P. Benner (Ed.), *Interpretive phenomenology: Embodiment, caring, and ethics in health and illness* (pp. 99-127). Thousand Oaks, CA: Sage.

Bogdan, R., & Knopp Biklen, S. (1992). *Qualitative research for education* (2nd ed.). Boston: Allyn & Bacon.

Boss, P. G. (1987). Family stress. In M. B. Sussman & S. K. Steinmetz (Eds.), *Handbook of marriage and the family* (pp. 695-723). New York: Plenum.

Bowlby, J. (1973). *Attachment and loss: Vol. 2. Separation.* New York: Basic Books.

Blumer, H. (1969/1986). The methodological position of symbolic interactionism. In H. Blumer, *Symbolic interactionism: Perspective and method* (pp. 1-60). Berkeley: University of California Press.

Canada, G. (1995). *Fist, stick, knife, gun: A personal history of violence in America.* Boston: Beacon.

Chesla, C. A. (1995). Hermeneutic phenomenology: An approach to understanding families. *Journal of Family Nursing, 1,* 68-78.

Cicchetti, D. (1987). Developmental psychopathology in infancy: Illustrations from the study of maltreated youngsters. *Journal of Consulting and Clinical Psychology, 55,* 837-845.

Cicchetti, D. (1996). Regulatory processes in development and psychopathology, *Development and Psychopathology, 8,* 1-2.

Cicchetti, D., & Garmezy, N. (1993). Editorial: Prospects and promises in the study of resilience. *Development and Psychopathology, 5,* 497-502.

Cohler, B. (1987). Adversity, resilience, and the study of lives. In E. J. Anthony & B. Cohler (Eds.), *The invulnerable child* (pp. 363-424). New York: Guilford.

Cummings, E. M., & Davies, P. (1996). Emotional security as a regulatory process in normal development and the development of psychopathology. *Development and Psychopathology, 8,* 123-139.

Egeland, B., Carlson, E., & Sroufe, L. A. (1993). Resilience as process. *Development and Psychopathology, 5,* 517-528.

Egeland, B., Jacobvitz, D., & Sroufe, L. A. (1988). Breaking the cycle of abuse. *Child Development, 59,* 1080-1088.

Garmezy, N. (1987). Stress, competence, and development: Continuities in the study of schizophrenic adults, children vulnerable to psychopathology, and the search for stress-resistant children. *American Journal of Orthopsychiatry, 57,* 159-174.

Gest, S. D., Neeman, J., Hubbard, J. J., Masten, A. S., & Tellegen, A. (1993). Parenting quality, adversity, and conduct problems in adolescence: Testing process-oriented models of resilience. *Development and Psychopathology, 5,* 663-682.

Gilgun, J. F. (1990). Factors mediating the effects of child maltreatment. In M. Hunter (Ed.), *The sexually abused male* (pp. 177-190). Lexington, MA: Lexington Books.

Gilgun, J. F. (1991). Resilience and the intergenerational transmission of child abuse. In M. Q. Patton (Ed.), *Family sexual abuse: Frontline research and evaluation* (pp. 93-105). Beverly Hills, CA: Sage.

Gilgun, J. F. (1992). Hypothesis generation in social work research. *Journal of Social Service Research, 15,* 113-135.

Gilgun, J. F. (1994). A case for case studies in social work research. *Social Work, 39,* 371-380.

Gilgun, J. F. (1995). We shared something special: The moral discourse of incest perpetrators. *Journal of Marriage and the Family, 57,* 265-281.

Gilgun, J. F. (1996a). Development and adversity in ecological perspective: Part I. Conceptual framework. *Families in Society, 77,* 395-402.

Gilgun, J. F. (1996b). Development and adversity in ecological perspective: Part II. Three patterns. *Families in Society, 77,* 459-576.

Gilgun, J. F. (in press). Methodological pluralism and qualitative family research. In S. Steinmetz, M. Sussman, & G. Peterson (Eds.), *Handbook of marriage and the family* (3rd ed.). New York: Plenum.

Gilgun, J. F., Daly, K., & Handel, G. (1992). *Qualitative methods in family research.* Newbury Park, CA: Sage.

Gilgun, J. F., & Reiser, E. (1990). Sexual identity development among men sexually abused in childhood. *Families in Society, 71,* 515-523.

Glaser, B., & Strauss, A. (1967). *The discovery of grounded theory.* New York: Aldine.

Jarrett, R. L. (1994). Living poor: Family life among single parent, African-American women. *Social Problems, 41,* 30-49.

Jarrett, R. L. (1995). Growing up poor: The family experiences of socially mobile youth in low-income African-American neighborhoods. *Journal of Adolescent Research, 10,* 111-135.

Kaufman, J., & Zigler, E. (1987). Do abused children become abusive parents? *American Journal of Orthopsychiatry, 57,* 186-192.

Leonard, V. W. (1994). A Heideggerian phenomenological perspective on the concept of person. In P. Benner (Ed.), *Interpretive phenomenology: Embodiment, caring, and ethics in health and illness* (pp. 43-63). Thousand Oaks, CA: Sage.

⮜Masten, A. S. (1994). Resilience in individual development: Successful adaptation despite risk and adversity. In M. C. Wang & E. W. Gordon (Eds.), *Educational resilience in inner-city America: Challenges and prospects* (pp. 3-23). Hillsdale, NJ: Lawrence Erlbaum.

Masten, A. S., Best, K. M., & Garmezy, N. (1990). Resilience and development: Contributions from the study of children who overcome adversity. *Development and Psychopathology, 2,* 425-444.

⮜ Masten, A. S., & Garmezy, N. (1985). Risk, vulnerability, and protective factors in developmental psychopathology. In B. B. Lahey & A. E. Kazdin (Eds.), *Advances in clinical child psychology* (Vol. 8, pp. 1-52). New York: Plenum.

McCubbin, H. I., Joy, H., Cauble, A., Comeau, J., Patterson, J., & Needle, R. (1995). Family stress, coping and social support: A decade review. *Journal of Marriage and the Family, 42,* 855-871.

McCubbin, H. I., McCubbin, M. A., Thompson, A. I., & Thompson, E. A. (1995). Resiliency in ethnic families: A conceptual model for predicting family adjustment and adaptation. In H. I. McCubbin, E. A. Thompson, A. I. Thompson, & J. E. Fromer (Eds.), *Resiliency in ethnic minority families: Native and immigrant American families* (Vol. 1, pp. 3-48). Madison: University of Wisconsin System.

McCubbin, H. I., & Patterson, J. M. (1983). Family stress and adaptation to crisis: Double ABCX model of family behavior. In H. I. McCubbin, M. Sussman, & J. Patterson (Eds.), *Advances in family stress theory and research.* New York: Haworth.

McCubbin, H. I., Thompson, E. A., Thompson, A. I., & Fromer, J. E. (1995). *Resiliency in ethnic minority families: Native and immigrant American families (Vol. 1).* Madison: University of Wisconsin System.

McCubbin, M. A., & McCubbin, H. I. (1996). Resiliency in families: A conceptual model of family adjustment and adaptation in response to stress and crises. In H. I. McCubbin, A. I. Thompson, & M. A. McCubbin (Eds.), *Family assessment: Resiliency, coping and adaptation--Inventories for research and practice* (pp. 1-64). Madison: University of Wisconsin System.

Morse, J. M. (Ed.). (1992). *Qualitative health research.* Newbury Park, CA: Sage.

Murphy, L. B. (1987). Further reflections on resilience. In E. J. Anthony & B. J. Cohler (Eds.), *The invulnerable child* (pp. 84-105). New York: Guilford.

Patton, M. Q. (1990). *Qualitative evaluation and research methods* (2nd ed.). Newbury Park, CA: Sage.

Quinton, D., Rutter, M., & Liddle, C. (1984). Institutional rearing, parental difficulties and marital support. *Psychological Medicine, 14,* 107-124.

⬢ Richters, J. E., & Martinez, P. E. (1993). Violent communities, family choices, and children's chances: An algorithm for improving the odds. *Development and Psychopathology, 5,* 609-627.

Rutter, M. (1987). Psychosocial resilience and protective mechanisms. *American Journal of Orthopsychiatry, 57,* 316-331.

Rutter, M., & Quinton, D. (1984). Long-term follow-up of women institution-alized in childhood: Factors promoting good functioning in adult life. *British Journal of Developmental Psychology, 18,* 225-234.

Sroufe, L. A., Egeland, B., & Kreutzer, T. (1990). The fate of early experience following developmental change: Longitudinal approaches to individual adaptation in childhood. *Child Development, 61,* 1363-1373.

Strauss, A., & Corbin, J. (1990). *Basics of qualitative research: Grounded theory procedures and techniques.* Newbury Park, CA: Sage.

Van Manen, M. (1990). *Researching lived experience.* Albany: State University of New York Press.

Werner, E. E. (1993). Risk, resilience, and recovery: Perspectives from the Kauai Longitudinal Study. *Development and Psychopathology, 4,* 503-515.

Werner, E. E., & Smith, R. S. (1992). *Overcoming the odds: High risk children from birth to adulthood.* Ithaca, NY: Cornell University Press.

3

Reflexivity in Qualitative Analysis

Toward an Understanding of Resiliency Among Older Parents With Adult Gay Children[1]

Katherine R. Allen

I have three aims in this chapter. First, I will describe preliminary findings from an empirical investigation of older parents of adult gay and lesbian children, currently under way. Second, I will describe relevant aspects of my circumstances as a lesbian and a daughter as they pertain to the research I am conducting. Third, I will address the interweave of these two sources of knowledge through my use of reflexive understanding about family diversity over the life course. I believe that my ability to see and understand resilience in the families I study is deepened because I am a participant in the experience that I investigate (Krieger, 1991) and because I use the method of reflexivity as a way to enhance the trustworthiness of my data and analysis (Lather, 1991).

I want to understand how diversity and marginalization affect individuals and their families. How do older adults define and experience the structures and processes that affect their family relationships given the increasing diversity in which their younger kin live? The adult gay and lesbian children of presumably heterosexual older parents often are stigmatized and treated as second-class citizens. Learning that one has a gay child is not something for which most parents are prepared, emotionally or politically. The families of lesbians, gay men, and bisexual and transgendered people are politically vulnerable; it is still safe to target gay people as abnormal, defective, immoral, and less than human. Gay, lesbian, bisexual, and transgendered people in the United States face not only legal and social discrimination but also threats to their physical safety, despite an increasing awareness and acceptance of the normative range of sexual orientation (see Allen & Demo, 1995; Editors of the *Harvard Law Review*, 1990; McWhirter, Sanders, & Reinisch, 1990; Savin-Williams & Cohen, 1996). How heterosexual parents come to understand the experience and meaning of having a child who is gay and how they incorporate the changes in perspective and behavior that inevitably occur is the focus of my current inquiry.

In describing this study, I weave in my own story. I use my life circumstances as a woman and a scholar as a bridge to the broader methodological issue that I address in my research program—the relevance of reflexivity in the production of new knowledge and scientific understanding. Fonow and Cook (1991) define reflexivity as the tendency "to reflect upon, examine critically, and explore analytically the nature of the research process" (p. 3). As a feminist, I seek to give voice to experiences that have been hidden or missing from what counts as knowledge (Du Bois, 1983). In these investigations, I employ my understanding of self as a primary method of discovery (Krieger, 1991). My research agenda explicitly considers the particular of my own experiences in the world as an important factor in the production of knowledge (e.g., Allen, 1994, 1995; Allen & Baber, 1992). I use the particular as a pathway to understand more generalized knowledge.

A Study of Older Parents of Adult Gay Children

In 1995, I began to interview older parents of adult lesbian and gay children. I am using a modified ethnographic approach to intensive data collection (Henderson, 1994), consisting of in-depth interviews and participant observation in which I keep detailed field notes. I have completed 12 interviews to date, and I continue to conduct additional interviews. I also attend monthly meetings of a local chapter of Parents, Families and Friends of Lesbians and Gays (PFLAG), a national organization whose mission to is provide support for families and education to the wider public about gay issues. PFLAG's mission involves explicit advocacy for the families of those connected to gay people: One of their mottos is "keeping families together." I am a member of the national organization and a co-founder of the local chapter to which I belong. I have attended several meetings of a much larger PFLAG group in Dallas, Texas and have interviewed staff in the national office in Washington, DC. I have given presentations about gay families at local PFLAG meetings and regional and national PFLAG conferences.

I conducted 3-hour tape-recorded interviews with parents I found through a snowball sampling method, asking various chapter members who were parents of gay people to suggest other parents who might be willing to talk to me. I eventually came to see that it was also important to locate parents who did not belong to PFLAG; I again used personal contacts by asking gay adults I knew if I could interview their parents. I added several more parents in this way and interviewed one gay son and one lesbian daughter about their relationships with their parents. I have completed follow-up interviews, by telephone and at PFLAG meetings, with parents previously interviewed in person. Follow-up is important because of the temporal dynamics associated with these families and the continual reconstructing of what it means to come to terms with having a gay child. One example includes a mother's report of the declining health of her gay son, who is living with AIDS. Another example involves a mother's description of a lesbian daughter's recent pregnancy attempt. A third example involves a father's story of his formerly lesbian daughter, who is in the process of becoming a transgendered male.

Gender is an important consideration in this project. There are fathers of lesbian daughters, mothers of lesbian daughters, fathers of gay sons, and mothers of gay sons. Additional complexity of family circumstances include step-parenting relationships. In one family, the father and mother had a gay son, and the father also had a lesbian daughter by a previous marriage.

The sample, to date, includes in-depth interviews with one father of a lesbian daughter, one father of a formerly lesbian daughter who is now becoming a transgendered male, three mothers of gay sons, a father with a lesbian daughter and a gay son, a mother with a gay son and a lesbian stepdaughter, a mother of a lesbian daughter, a gay son, and a lesbian daughter. Field notes also include many personal narratives and theoretical memos reflecting my experiences and observations as a lesbian within the context of having two older parents and a gay brother. I have recently conducted separate in-depth interviews with my own mother and father.

After spending a year in PFLAG and observing my parents going through their own acceptance process of having two gay children, I came to understand that parents who join PFLAG are on a similar journey, with many diverse pathways, toward keeping their families intact. As one mother mentioned, the resilient process of coming to accept a child as gay is a matter of "tears, talk, and time." Parents whose children experience unanticipated life course events must mourn the loss of one's dream of a perfect child (Ryff, Schmutte, & Lee, 1996). PFLAG offers a supportive place for parents to educate themselves and each other. There is a burgeoning literature available in the popular press, and the parents I meet in PFLAG avidly buy, read, and loan books about parents with gay adult children. Important resources include Bernstein's (1995) *Straight Parents / Gay Children: Keeping Families Together*; Rafkin's (1996) *Different Daughters: A Book by Mothers of Lesbians*; and Griffin, Wirth, and Wirth's (1986) *Beyond Acceptance: Parents of Lesbians and Gays Talk About Their Experiences*. PFLAG parents had sought a support group and were reading literature designed for them. Even parents who live more than 60 miles away from the community in which the local chapter meets were motivated to attend monthly meetings for the opportunity to share reading materials and their stories with one another.

The interviews comprise a pilot study I conducted as a prelude to research in which I am involved with other colleagues (Allen, Demo, Walker, & Acock, 1996). Our preliminary analysis of in-depth interviews with eight parents revealed nine issues: (a) a parent's prior relationship with another person who had a notable difference or stigma; (b) the duration of the parent's awareness of the gay child's sexual orientation; (c) the presence of a confidant for the parents to share their feelings; (d) the quality of the parent-child relationship; (e) gay discontinuity (e.g., when a child who had proclaimed a gay identity behaved in a way that may indicate a heterosexual or other orientation); (f) the presence of other children in the family; (g) the threat of the AIDS epidemic; (h) the desire for grandchildren; and (i) whether the gay child was in a stable, intimate relationship.

In this chapter, I use resiliency as a metaphor to understand older parents' efforts to keep their families together in the face of a nonnormative life course transition experienced by one or more offspring (McCubbin, Thompson, & McCubbin, 1996). The analysis, overall, reflects the educational activities and emotional growth these parents seek in order to help themselves overcome the perceived hardship of having a gay child. By educating themselves about a subject matter that is, at first, foreign and upsetting to them, many are able to surpass even normative acceptance and embrace their child's difference as a way of expanding their knowledge of the full range of human experience. This report is a tentative sketch, and additional interviews are planned in order to expand and challenge the themes that are evident so far. The themes I will review involve the arduous process of coming to accept one's child, a process that is never complete, and the transformative experiences that allow parents to become advocates and even activists on behalf of their children.

No parent anticipates his or her child becoming gay, nor do many parents immediately welcome the news with joyous acceptance. The heterosexual narrative is as strong in this culture as the narrative that mothers protect children from all harm (Baber & Allen, 1992). Feminists refer to these narratives as being rooted in compulsory heterosexuality and compulsory motherhood (Rich, 1976, 1980). In the absence of competing narratives that prepare people for the unexpected, parents do not have anticipatory socialization for their loss of a child's normative identity (see Pillemer & Suitor, 1991; Ryff, Lee, Essex, & Schmutte, 1994). Nor do many, at first, have a trusted confidant to whom they feel comfortable disclosing this new information about their child. Paulette Goodman (1991), the past national president of PFLAG observed, "When a gay person comes out to his or her family, most parents crawl right in to the closet which their child has just left. For a time they feel that they will never be able to share this news with anyone else" (p. 3). All of the parents with whom I talked expressed a sense of surprise and initial disappointment that their children turned out to be gay. They differed, however, in terms of how long it took them to change their mind about gay being a "lesser life." Their process of coming to terms with having a gay child can be captured by the metaphor of a journey toward increasing acceptance. The parents who are able to go farther on this journey and even celebrate their child's differences experience the unanticipated benefit of embarking on new avenues of self-discovery. Indeed, they become champions for the civil rights and social acceptance of their children. Some parents, of course, have made more progress on this journey than others.

The parents I interviewed range in educational background from having a master's degree to not completing high school. All of them share the desire to learn more about lesbian and gay life in general, with the awareness that this is a stigmatized identity. Some responded immediately by going to the local bookstore and buying, as one mother noted, "everything I could get my hands on." Others relied on a spouse or gay child to supply them with information. Still others read in secret, tearing the covers off books to conceal the nature of their reading material.

I interviewed six parents I met through PFLAG. They differed from other parents who were not PFLAG members in that they had a wider range of people to whom they disclosed their child's sexual orientation. By getting involved in an organization, parents' acceptance intensifies. Benefits of belonging to a support and educational organization included hearing others' stories; having time to adjust to the new knowledge about one's child; and meeting gay parents, who reminded them that it was possible for their own gay children to make them grandparents one day. Their crash course in educating themselves transformed these parents rather quickly from not knowing much about gay life to having a "click" experience, where, all of a sudden, the discrimination against their gay child hit home, and they wanted to do something about it. As Bernstein (1995) wrote:

> As parents, it turns out, we can learn a lot from our gay kids about such significant matters as personal integrity and respect for individual differences. Legions of us have come to terms with our children's homosexuality and discovered that our lives were not diminished but actually enriched by the process. In this way, PFLAG functions as a sort of alchemist of the soul, converting bereaved parents into active celebrants of diversity. It leads us gently through the barbed thickets of misguided conventional wisdom and back to where we belong—our children's sides. In its support groups, we can let our anguish hang out, secure in the empathy of those who have experienced the same sense of devastation and loss. We can sense in others the healing qualities of time and understanding. And we soon become closer than ever to our children. (pp. 3–4)

Parents who possess the individual strength and group support to face down the shame and sense of failure inherited from the broader society find something more positive than the initial sense of loss that accompanies nonnormative transitions in their children's lives. Most parents become activists for their own child and some for the broader cause of gay rights (Allen & Wilcox, 1996). They are forced into deconstructing the myth that everyone is treated equally in our society. By acknowledging the inequities their child experiences, they challenge the illusion of safety and security that accompanies this myth, particularly parents of the majority race and class, who have taken their privilege for granted. Some eventually find a way toward creating new identities for themselves. All parents told stories of a new sense of personal empowerment as a result of their own coming out as the parent of a gay child.

Because this journey toward activism among parents who join PFLAG is so evident, it is important to locate more parents who are not accepting of their child. A limitation of snowball sampling, however, is that given the generalized stigma of having a gay child, it is hard to locate unaccepting parents, and it is challenging to establish the rapport necessary to discuss an issue that is difficult and painful for them. It is easier to find resilient parents, particularly those whose lives have become invigorated by having a gay child. Consequently, I am now interviewing parents who have not come to PFLAG. To hone

my understanding of the experiences of older parents who find acceptance difficult, I have turned to my own parents for insight. The
benefit is that my parents and I have come to new understandings of
each other in the process of my asking for their help in trying to grasp
parental difficulties about a child's life.

Nearly all of the parents interviewed to date tell a story about a
friend who is also the parent of a gay child, but who is "in denial"
about or rejects his or her child's gayness. Parents compare themselves to others in similar circumstances, and they are preoccupied by
how their children turn out (Ryff et al., 1996). PFLAG parents have
crossed a line in which they see themselves as different from their
former selves, no longer like that unaccepting friend to whom they
now compare themselves. To illustrate, in an interview with a 60-
year-old mother, I asked, "Have things changed for you since your son
came out? And since you've come out about having a gay son?"

> Oh, most definitely, and all for the better. It's certainly made me a
> better, stronger person, and a wiser person, and a richer person
> because I've met so many other lovable people. . . . I can say I
> wouldn't go back to the life that I had before.

Parents also report the disclosure of a child's sexual orientation to be
an experience that forces family members, many of whom have been
estranged, to talk with each other about "something real." Dealing
with this issue had many unexpected consequences. For example,
one mother of a lesbian daughter, after not resolving her feelings
about her daughter's divorce and decision to enter a lesbian relationship, eventually came to understand that her sadness about her
daughter's lack of a "storybook perfect" life reflected some of her own
childhood trauma. This mother, at age 60, began to deal with long-
buried knowledge that her own birth was out of wedlock. She described a gut-wrenching sense of unresolved loss, pain, and humiliation
about being "illegitimate" in the 1930s and 1940s, a time she perceived was far less tolerant from her own daughter's experience of
difference in the 1990s:

> My mother was divorced and had an affair with my father. He had a
> wife. . . and for all my life, he never divorced her, so he was in and
> out of my life. I never knew, and of course at some level I know I
> knew. . . all my life I was that glue that held, that kept him coming
> back. All my life I was used by my mother. . . . We never even talked
> about it in our family, until mother died, in fact, until I went into
> therapy. . . never, ever said it.

Regarding the influence of family-of-origin experiences on a parent's
ability to handle a nonnormative transition in a child's life, every

parent cited some circumstance that provided a bridge to enable him or her to understand his or her own child's difference. One mother grew up with a younger brother who had Down's syndrome. Another mother was raised by her father from the time she was an infant after her own mother died. One father had a gay brother; when this man was 12, he learned of his brother's sexual orientation. Their close relationship facilitated his acceptance of having two gay children. Another father's father was disabled from a farming accident, when he lost the use of his limbs. Still another mother's parents divorced when she was a child, an uncommon experience for her peers and one that she attributed to her own early marriage and pregnancy.

The parents I interviewed were able to put their child's gayness into perspective by comparing their gay child to their other children or to the children of siblings and friends. Having a child turn out to be an alcoholic or drug addict was far more negative to them than having a gay child. As a father of eight adult children described, having a daughter who is lesbian "makes no difference" to him, particularly in comparison to having two other children who have "drinking problems that I can't accept." There was also a hint of favoritism for one's gay child over others in the family. Particularly for mothers of gay sons, there was a unique bond that was not evident in the descriptions that those mothers had of their other children, nor between mothers and lesbian daughters. Many of these parents, as well, felt a sense of triumph in the accomplishments of their gay children, particularly when comparing them to children of friends who did not turn out as well but had greater privilege in the wider society. As the mother of a gay son explains, she eventually ended a friendship with a neighbor she had previously admired and respected. This friend was the first person the mother told about having a gay son. Later, she asked the friend to sign a petition to lift the gay ban on the military:

> Without a question or doubt, without a question in my mind, I just ran down to my friend and said, "Will you sign this?" And she just looked at me, and she said, "I can't. . . . " It hurt. She couldn't accept gays in the military. She thinks that my son is a fine son, but to me, that shows that she thought of him as less a man. . . . And she had three boys and none of them had served [in the military].

The intersection of gender and sexual orientation in the parent-child relationship and how this intersection is linked to parents' feelings of favoritism and comparison to other adult children are exciting sources of new information that I am continuing to gather in the interviews.

My Story: On Being a Lesbian and a Daughter

Every parent, like every gay person, has a "coming out" story that reveals a sense of changed identity and, for many, triumph over stigma and adversity. I want to share some of my own coming out story as a lesbian, particularly in regard to my relationship with my older parents, as a way to demonstrate reflexivity in qualitative analysis. Being a lesbian is relevant to my research because it has an impact on my access to gaining a sample, it shapes the kinds of questions I ask, and it is reflected in the nature of the responses.

At the same time, as other feminist scholars, such as Stacey (1988), Lather (1991), and Krieger (1991), have found, reflexive understanding is not a panacea for the dilemmas of subjectivity in qualitative research. The tension between research that makes a difference in an unjust world (Lather, 1991) and topics that threaten a researcher's ability to scrutinize her own issues is not easy to negotiate. It would be naive to conclude that reflexivity is a problem-free solution to the dilemmas posed by explicit subjectivity. Although I am impatient with research that asks the same old questions, or hides behind false neutrality, or does not go directly to the people under investigation, there are some dangers in doing the politicized inquiry I value. We need well-developed skills to avoid merely reproducing our own experiences and values in the collection and analysis of data.

With that caution in mind, I would like to share how my personal story affects the topics and processes I am drawn to study. Nearly 8 years ago, I began to understand that I was in love with another woman. At the time, I was still married to a man with whom I had lived since I was 21. After my son, Matt, was born, I knew that the way in which my husband and I had worked out the roles and private commitments to each other as adult partners was not working. I knew that it was only a matter of time before I chose another way to live my life. Around the time that things were intensifying with T.J., the woman with whom I now share my life, my brother, John, who has known he was gay for many years, decided it was time for him to share a residence with his partner of many years. This was a silent announcement to our family that he was gay, although he had never used the words with our parents. He tried to tell them, but their response was, "If you're going to tell me what I think you're going to tell me, don't." At the same time, my two best friends, who had been involved in long-term marriages, separated from their respective husbands and began to live together. These experiences opened some space for me to move toward my desire for a life with T.J. At 35, I found a new job, started a new life, and everyone—myself, my son, my husband, and T.J.—moved to Virginia.

Eventually, I came out to colleagues, in the classroom, and in my publications. It took me several years to tell my mother, and when I did, she put her hands over her ears so she would not have to hear me say the words, "Mom, I'm a lesbian." Her father died the next day, and although I know that one event did not cause the other, they remain connected in my mind, allowing me to ponder the mystery of how family events are reconstructed in memory. As my grandfather's generation lost its grip on the lives of others, my capacity to live my own life emerged. Heightening the significance of my disclosure and setting the stage for continued drama between us, I told my mother on the birthday we share, March 9.

My former husband and I negotiated a careful divorce, and we remain good friends. I am humbled by our enduring connection, despite some painful memories of how things did not work out for us. Seeing the pictures of his mother, father, and siblings from his recent wedding to his second wife brings a sense of sadness and regret. Yet I am still his confidant for many personal and professional issues. He appreciates the mothering that T.J. and I provide our son, and when he and his new family come to visit in Virginia, they stay in our home. Adding to our family's diversity, Ken is now in a biracial marriage, and he and his wife have a son of their own.

T.J. had a child, our second son, who is now 2 years old. T.J. and I are Zack's parents, but his biological father, "Papa Keith," is my brother's life partner.

My sons have complex and extensive relationships with an array of people who are related to them by biology and, as Matt says, by love. There are four sets of biological kin, given the number of parents involved. T.J. is Mama and I am Tata; Ken is Dad, Keith is Papa, and my brother remains "Johnny." Sometimes, Matt calls Keith "Puncle, because he's part Papa, part uncle." Our sons have a rich language for kinship and many adults in their lives of all ages, backgrounds, orientations, and beliefs who have two things in common— these adults have *chosen* the way in which they conduct their intimate lives, and they have a fierce commitment to ensuring the well-being of these boys.

We have worked out relationships of which we are proud, owing in part to our personal strengths and the resources we have as educated, privileged professionals: My partner is a family therapist, and I am a professor of family studies. We have access to theorized accounts explaining the innovative complexities in lesbian and gay kinship (Weston, 1991) and the development of postmodern families in the late 20th century (Stacey, 1990). The descriptive language in Stacey's (1990) feminist ethnography of a "divorce-extended family" has served as a reminder that the families headed by women today are "sprouting some odd branches" in the family tree. For example,

> serving as the official wedding photographer was Pam's ex-husband Don Franklin, who was accompanied by Shirley Moskowitz, his live-in lover and would-be third wife. All of the wedding attendants were stepkin and step-in-laws to the groom. . . . More than half of the pews were filled with members of four generations from the "confusing tangle" of former, step-, dual, and in-law relatives of Pamela and Al's divorce-extended family. . . . And of the friends. . . most were fictive kin and former or current housemates to members of the wedding party. (p. 64)

As family professionals, we have learned to use language that can describe our personal family complexity to outsiders, and we have access to knowledge that we are part of a broader trend toward increasing family diversity (Cheal, 1991; Stacey, 1996).

Yet despite our privileged status as middle-class professionals, there are obvious challenges to our safety that are linked to the heterosexism of our society. Heterosexism, like sexism, racism, and classism, is a type of bias evident by "conceptualizing human experience in strictly heterosexual terms and consequently ignoring, invalidating, or derogating homosexual behaviors and sexual orientation, and lesbian, gay, and bisexual relationships and lifestyles" (Herek, Kimmel, Amaro, & Melton, 1991, p. 958). Heterosexism reflects beliefs and practices that only heterosexuals are normal; it is usually accompanied by either overt or subtle homophobia, which refers to the irrational fear of those who are gay (Pharr, 1988). These fears are rooted in the myths that accompany a stigmatized identity. Although there is some agreement in our society that racism and sexism should be legally prohibited and that people need to be liberated from their prejudice through education, it is still acceptable to espouse negativity regarding a gay sexual orientation, as recent legislation against gay marriage and equal employment protection demonstrates. Myths about gay people, such as, that they molest children (Falk, 1989; Jenny, Roesler, & Poyer, 1994), flaunt their sexuality (Savin-Williams, 1993), and are genetically inferior or sick (Kirsch & Weinrich, 1991), continue to be believed despite scientific evidence and personal experience disputing these myths.

People who are presumed to be heterosexual have a particular privilege that is difficult to appreciate unless one no longer has it. Recently, I completed a continuing education program in my community. I was struck by the number of times male instructors mentioned their wives. One situation was so pronounced that I made hatch marks each time the teacher referred to his wife. During a lecture on a topic completely unrelated to his family, he referred to his wife more than 50 times. I sat there knowing that if I mentioned my female partner only once, that one comment would be one time too many for most people's comfort. I did not understand heterosexual privilege until I relinquished it (Allen, 1995).

Despite the benefits of living in a loving family, gay adults face daily reminders of second-class citizenship. Gay men and lesbians are legally barred from the protection and sanctity of marriage in every state (Eskridge, 1996). Major religious denominations enact formal policy to condemn gay marriage. School forms routinely include space for two parental identities only: father's name and mother's name.

I am a legal stranger to my second son, and despite the safeguards we have pieced together with the help of our lawyer, my relationship to him is not recognized or supported by the state in which I live. I cannot carry Zack or T.J. on my health care policy and must provide a substantial amount of money to compensate for their inaccessibility to a benefit I could give to a legal dependent. Local citizens in our community recently protested a billboard sponsored by our PFLAG chapter that read, "Diversity Enriches: Gay and Straight Citizens of Southwest VA." Within several hours after a newspaper article about the billboard appeared, more than 50 phone calls were received by the sign company, including death threats to the owners and threats to vandalize the company's property. These realities can provide a hostile environment in which to live, despite the personal security I feel in my partnership and my professional networks.

Reflexivity, Subjectivity, and Understanding in Research

What does all of this have to do with my research? What do these facts and feelings about my personal life have to do with the knowledge I construct? I describe these experiences to demonstrate the relevance of the life one lives to the subject matter one studies. As a feminist, I want to make explicit the connection between the personal and the political.

Following the interviews I conducted in 1995, I returned to full time teaching and to writing grant proposals to fund this research. As I was engaged in these activities and began to analyze the interview transcripts, several things happened that shook my faith in reflexivity. I feared that I had "gone native" (Bogdan & Biklen, 1982, p. 128) and become too subjective in my connection to the project. If reflexivity is the human capacity to reflect on one's thinking "from a standpoint that is relatively, not absolutely, outside" the self (Minnich, 1990, p. 30), I wondered about unknowingly reproducing my experience in the interviews and data analysis. I felt limited, rather than freed, by my subjective connection and social location in relation to the study. I became too self-conscious about this work to continue, a move that has affected many feminist scholars across disciplines (see Elam & Wiegman, 1995, for an exemplary set of essays interrogating feminist standpoint and postmodern theories in the context of feminist literary criticism).

First, I will describe this reactive attempt to distance myself from the role of participant-participant (Bogdan & Biklen, 1982) in my research project. Second, I will speculate about how research is compromised unless we do find ways to make the best use of our personal experience to show, scrupulously and self-consciously, how we do, indeed, affect the process of research (Allen, 1994; Stacey, 1990; Stanley, 1990). My uneasy resolution of this dilemma is a renewed understanding of the tension between objectivity and subjectivity, between science and advocacy. Postmodern and feminist theorists refer to this tension as the necessity of engaging in both outer- and inner-directed activities. Scholars today are "caught between the desire to act and the resistance to action that threatens to reproduce . . . the economy of the same" (Friedman, 1995, p. 12). Relating this observation to research, we need both our subjectivity and the recognition of its limitations in order to construct more adequate knowledge.

I have long been an advocate of reflexivity in research and teaching, having written about its influence in my work for many years. Recently, however, I tried to distance myself from my own subjective identities. Because my teaching style incorporates unrelenting self-disclosure (see Allen, 1995; Allen & Farnsworth, 1993), I started to see what I had once considered a great strength as an impediment to understanding. Rather than viewing my scholarly and pedagogical style as liberating for students, I began to experience myself as sharing and soliciting information that was too personal, too vulnerable, too squeamish, too sensitive, and too private to share. Feminist writers, such as bell hooks (1994), came to my rescue in their texts, as I read about the inevitability of this crisis of confidence in other emancipatory scholars' work.

Lather's (1991) essays, as well, helped me to come to grips with the tentative nature of any research report. She exemplifies the choices that researchers must make by describing four ways to write a report:

a realist tale, a critical tale, a deconstructive tale, and a reflexive tale. She demonstrates that the imposition of the perspectives, biases, and values of the researcher, regardless of how much the researcher can admit or describe them, transforms the data and their messages depending on the slant taken by the researcher. Qualitative researchers have long been aware of this potential dilemma, and numerous remedies have been described. Depending upon the epistemological position of the researcher, some positivist, qualitative researchers have suggested ways to eliminate this so-called bias by following techniques that mirror quantitative reports (e.g., Rubinstein, 1994; Smith, 1987), whereas some postpositivists have attempted to embrace subjectivity to create multiple interpretations and deepen understanding of the phenomena under study (e.g., Jaffe & Miller, 1994; Kvale, 1994).

I experience a tension around the value of using personal experience to gain deeper access to meaning, deal with my own reactivity in relation to a topic, or discover new patterns in human behavior that cannot be seen when using prevailing paradigms. Yet I also know that it is my very desire to understand a topic close to my personal experience that is the creative energy that fuels my work. In other words, one's investment in a project, whether overt or unconscious, is of ongoing concern for a qualitative researcher. A range of opinion exists about what the personal connection means for the project goals and outcomes (see Gilgun, Daly, & Handel, 1992; Gubrium & Sankar, 1994; and Sollie & Leslie, 1994, for exemplars in the family studies, gerontological, and close relationships literatures, respectively).

Part of my story, then, concerns my ongoing struggle with self in the research process. The down side of reflexive understanding in one's research is that the use of self-knowledge can be perceived as mere vanity. This point is evident when perusing "how-to" books for getting funded—researchers are advised to avoid the personal. Often, I have followed that advice, but now, I agree that it is the passionate investment in research that allows scholars to contribute to basic research or its application in the real world (Game & Metcalfe, 1996).

My current resolution to this dilemma is postmodern, which is to say that I have no singular resolution, but rather a tentative, flexible, and dynamic truce with science and narrative work. I realize now that my use of reflexivity is sometimes a burden, sometimes a bonus, and sometimes an unknowable quality that just is. This has the unintended benefit of opening up new spaces in which to make use of increased reflection. The decision to move toward my anxiety by interviewing my own parents is an example of a new space opening.

Losing (and Reclaiming) My Faith in Reflexivity

I now understand that I got scared and questioned my methodology because of some criticism of me as a lesbian teacher and scholar. After receiving my university's award for teaching excellence, a group of students in my undergraduate class was annoyed by and protested the fact that I openly called myself a lesbian. Furthermore, I did not receive a grant for which I had applied because the topic (older parents of adult gay children) was considered too political, despite obtaining a high score for scientific merit. Personal and professional experiences such as these activated an intense wave of internalized homophobia in which I felt reactive to my own identity as a lesbian. My confidence that I could conduct a study so close to home diminished.

This crisis was about losing confidence in my methodological ability to generate and analyze valid data. I learned some lessons about reflexivity by going through this phase of severely doubting myself. I again feel strongly about the value of intense connection to one's research.

Taking on the role of my critics forced me to challenge and test my faith in reflexivity. In doing this, I gained a better understanding of its value in qualitative projects. It is ironic that I used my reflexivity, particularly my reactivity, to challenge the very subjectivity I use in my practice as a teacher and researcher, and I have come to a deeper understanding of how to complete this qualitative research. I now describe six experiences that contributed to this journey of challenge and reevaluation.

When the Researcher Becomes the Researched

As a lesbian mother, I am sometimes treated by others as "a phenomenon." My partner and I are frequently asked to be subjects in someone else's research project. I have been interviewed for a dozen student papers or projects on lesbian mothers. By taking on the role of interviewee, I encountered my own incredulity and distrust about the ability of an outsider to adequately represent my experience. I felt reactive if I perceived an interviewer's behavior to be judgmental or stereotyping toward me. I learned by reading the term papers and reports written by these students and investigators that I am not always perceived as I want to be, and I often think they have distorted and decontextualized my experience. I know the sting of someone referring to me by a label I dislike, such as "homosexual parent," or "the older one in a lesbian couple," or "a mother who thinks it is okay for her son not to live with his father."

Experiencing myself as an interviewee in more than one project provides a check on ways in which I, too, am capable of reducing participants in my study to "an object of study." I do not like being labeled, preferring to be asked how I want to be described, and I also object to seeing my sense of self fragmented in print. From this experience, I have gained more insight into how many qualitative researchers, including myself, can shortchange sample size and finish prematurely before saturation is achieved.

When the Researcher Is More Marginalized Than the Participants

As Lather (1991) points out, by sharing an experience with a marginalized group, the researcher is in the pivotal position to be a catalyst. As a catalyst, researcher and participant co-create meaning through conversations about their own lives. When a researcher shares or exceeds a participant's marginalized status, a space is opened for participants to reveal deeper aspects of themselves. As I interviewed the parents in my current study, one thought recurred: "Do they feel less marginal than I feel because I am gay and they are straight?" I felt my stigmatized identity reversing the normative power differential as a researcher. As an out lesbian, I upset the relations between "town and gown" by being from a more marginalized group than my participants.

This was an unanticipated discovery that gives me insight into the ways in which invisible power operates in a qualitative research context. I had merely expected that participants and I would be sharing the experience of otherness. This sharing allows the researcher to decode the invisible barrier that typically separates her from the "subject." Ironically, a new possibility opened up, in that I became aware that some of the parents may have felt more social power than me. I intend to pursue in future interviews how this power or status differential may affect the degree to which they share information with me. My hunch is that my more stigmatized location may be an advantage in securing greater disclosure.

When Transcripts Are Scrutinized by Other Researchers

In developing the analysis for the pilot data that I describe here, three colleagues, all senior researchers, read the transcripts. The transcripts were quite lengthy and scrupulously transcribed by a graduate student with whom I work. Initially, they included every "uh-hum," "yeah," and "right," and I wanted to "clean them up" before I presented them to my colleagues. Although I have echoed Stanley's (1990) caution of not cleansing the data in other studies I have published (see Allen & Walker, 1992), my colleagues pointed out that the version of the transcripts they received was like a script—almost too neat and tidy. Although the content was fine, the loss of conversational style in the hygienic transcripts left my readers feeling devoid of the context going on at the time of the interview. From this I learned that in trying to solve one problem (too many pages to copy, mail, and read), I created a new problem. Although I deleted only "ahs" and "hmmms" and repetitious "yeahs" and "rights," this decision had a distracting effect on my readers.

Another reason that I cleansed the transcripts was because many of the parents asked for copies of their interviews. Ironically, nearly all of the parents expressed self-consciousness about their choppy sentences and repetitions. What was too cleansed for my peers was too choppy for my participants. This experience raises an important dilemma for researchers who wish to involve their participants in reflecting on the research process (see Acker, Barry, & Esseveld, 1983; LaRossa, Bennett, & Gelles, 1981).

Benefitting from the observations of peers and participants, I relived several old lessons about qualitative data. First, even minor changes can alter the meaning and context of data. Second, participants are rarely satisfied with seeing their words in print, and the discovery of self through the researcher's eyes can be uncomfortable, even risky (LaRossa et al , 1981). Although it is so important to provide respondents with the opportunity to read either the transcripts or the written reports, researchers must be prepared for unintended reactions. Working with a collaborative team was valuable in learning that these minor, almost imperceptible changes altered the data. Stanley's (1990) caution against even minor changes was brought home by this experience.

When Unresolved Issues With My Own
Parents Challenge My Perspective

Part of my story since I came out has featured conflict and distance in my relationship with my parents. After many years of being defensive and reactive to them, despite our mutual efforts to stay connected through letters, telephone calls, and holiday visits, I was unprepared for a recent turn of events. In the past year, my mother was invited to join a task force at her church in which they studied the call to become an open and affirming congregation to gay and lesbian people. My parents spoke to the congregation about having two gay children. Although I live 600 miles away, my gay brother lives in their community, and they began to attend PFLAG meetings together.

I was surprised to learn, about myself, that my parents' resistance to me was easier to take than their change of heart. Initially, I did not share my gay brother's welcome of their new acceptance. I found it easier to hold on to the past than to see the present and our future as something in which change was possible. I balked, as if too much had been said and done to forgive the past.

I struggled intensely with the irony that although I was trying to investigate strategies that parents develop to accept having a gay child, I could not embrace this change in my own parents. Here I was inquiring about other parents' strengths and stressors, but when faced with the opportunity to see my parents in a new light, I resisted. Their movement toward me, and toward acceptance, was a catalyst for me to examine the story about them that I had reified within my own coming out story about their lack of acceptance of me. I was forced to change this story. In doing so, an unanticipated consequence occurred that had an impact on my research: I now saw increasingly multiple ways in which to interpret data from my study.

When Questions About Ownership of the Data Emerge

Ownership of data and who will benefit from the product of the research are important issues for qualitative methodologists (Small, 1995; Stacey, 1988, 1990; Walker, 1994). Feminists advocate the value of sharing the data with participants (Acker et al., 1983) as a way for them to ensure trustworthiness of the data (Lather, 1991). Some researchers involve participants in the benefits of the product, sharing authorship or including marginalized groups in research grants (Fonow & Cook, 1991). Although many feminists recommend that research be conducted *for* the participants whose lives are studied, typically only the scientist reaps the major financial benefits and prestige from the research. Feminist practices are improvements over the false belief that quantitative research is nonintrusive, but these innovations do not absolve the researcher of the fact that he or she is the major beneficiary of the research product.

In the present project, the interests I share with my participants to educate and inform about family diversity have not been a problem. I share my academic and personal skills with them whenever asked. For example, I gave participants copies of their transcripts, and I gave or loaned books to participants who requested them. I am also an active participant in organizations that benefit gay people and their families. The dilemma I feel about ownership, ironically, is not about my participants, to whom I have been reciprocal in returning services. Rather, because I have involved others to share in the work, the nonhierarchical, feminist style to which I am committed has been time consuming, an experience Walker (1994), too, has described. Ownership of the data, sharing publications, and managing the intellectual products with a variety of people have been unanticipated challenges of this project. At the same time, there have been many benefits. For example, this project has required an emotional clarity and maturity of all team members in order to deconstruct issues around professional responsibilities and rewards.

When Reactivity Happens

Finally, I would like to reflect upon my realization that in spite of the strategies I use to avoid doing so, I still impose myself on the data. This realization came to me as I was working on a different but related project with another colleague not involved in the older parents study. As I reread an initial analysis I had completed for that project, the same concept of "journey" appeared. I found myself describing a pathway toward resiliency that seemed remarkably similar to the way in which I describe my own journey in life: I had a certain identity as a heterosexual with its invisible privilege; I lost that identity and privilege by taking another journey as a lesbian; and I went through a transformation process in which I felt victimized, vulnerable, and ultimately triumphant in becoming a person with increased self-respect. The journey of resiliency that I found in those data seems like the personal journey of resiliency that I have taken in my own life. And this journey of resilience is similar to the parental resiliency I describe in this chapter.

To what extent have I merely reproduced my own narrative onto the data of the older parents in my study and the participants in another study in which I am collaborating? How can I demonstrate that I did not just find what I set out to find? This was the main question my teachers asked me in graduate school. This is also the question that qualitative researchers are forced to deal with in justifying their research. In some ways, I am alarmed that I still have to ask myself that question, even after a dozen years of conducting qualitative studies. On the other hand, I can just as easily ask: To what extent did my experience of marginalization prompt me to do this work? To what extent do students who have experienced marginalization seek me out as an advisor to guide them through the dissertation process? To what extent does my experience of difference improve this research? To what extent does research on marginality and resilience require a researcher who knows about marginalization firsthand? Cannon, Higginbotham, and Leung (1991) state that research on minority women must include minority women on the team so that majority group members are not conducting research *about* minority group members.

My way of dealing with this dilemma is to resist the desire to dichotomize and instead pursue a both/and approach. I recognize that my initial description of the resilient pathway is redundant to my personal journey in life. I recognize that I do impose this narrative onto the data I collect and analyze. Part of the reason is personal and part is due to my theoretical allegiance to the notions of change and developmental pathways in life course theory (Bengtson & Allen, 1993). At the same time, my experience of marginalization allows me to gain access to others' marginalization; to even know and see that some people are marginalized; and to be a catalyst for giving voice to it, with the goal to change and alleviate the condition of marginalization.

I can challenge the imposition of self onto the data by using reflexive questions and conducting additional interviews. The concern about imposing oneself onto the data can be checked through the qualitative process of theoretical saturation (Glaser & Strauss, 1967). For example, I need to interview more parents who are not dealing well with the experience. I can also use my reflexive understanding of self—my own struggle to embrace my parents as accepting at this point—to help me probe further when I do conduct subsequent interviews.

This reflexive approach is enhanced by collaborating on a team with other researchers. By viewing data I have collected from the viewpoints of multiple others, I can see that the story line I have written, "from marginalization to transformation to resiliency," is not just my story, but indeed, one of the metanarratives available across disciplines in the academy today (White, 1991). I must now use my reflexivity to resist just seeing myself or what I "know how to see" in the data. In standard qualitative research, grounded theorists (Strauss & Corbin, 1990) recommend the need to find a "story line" to use as a way to write up the findings. However, feminists have shown that just one story collapses the diversity and dissension into a falsely unified voice. Feminist postmodernists are trying to find ways to represent the multivocality of participants. There is not just one story to tell. Rather, it is possible to tell participants' stories through the use of analysis and their own words without having to fit into a singular story line. The narrative turn in qualitative feminist investigations is to show varying directions in participants' lives as well as the impermanence of how participants resolve life dilemmas.

Because we often study experiences we have shared in our own lives, it is helpful to have collaborators who will question the data (Blaisure & Allen, 1995; Farnsworth & Allen, 1996). At the same time, it is impossible to get such rich and deep perspectives without sharing some commonality or status with participants. I would not be able to gain access to a sample of older parents if I did not have the insider's knowledge that allowed me to enter their lives and hear the complexities that they would not share with a nongay person. I am convinced that it helps to be a person who has experienced the marginalization under study or who has experienced a related type of marginalization that is similar in its complexity.

New research questions guide my future work in an attempt to open my perspective to plural understandings: In what ways is the capacity to empathize with another person's marginalization dependent upon having experienced a similar type of marginalization? In what ways does that shared marginalization facilitate deeper access to a respondent's thinking and feeling about a complex issue? Conversely, to what extent is the data analysis compromised or distorted when the researcher shares a similar experience with the respondent?

In asking these questions, I do not mean the naive sense of "objectivity" that some researchers use to reject qualitative reports. Rather, I am concerned about the potential rigidity of private experience and how it can inhibit a qualitative researcher's ability to "hear" a story in a new way. This is a different question from the belief in an allegedly objectivist neutrality that is taken at face value in quantitative research (Lather, 1991). To pose this question to myself, with renewed understanding about my own limited vision and unresolved issues, I now ask: How well can I hear an older parent's story when it intersects with my personal experience with my older parents? Through this questioning, I affirm the importance of reflexivity in my work. This process brings new research questions to the forefront. These questions, in turn, open up additional avenues for theorizing that allow the researcher to probe the depths of private experience and inquire about topics that are considered taboo. What if an additional factor in resilience is the fierce love that some parents have for their children? Perhaps, despite everything, parents of gay children eventually get over their child's difference and come into an acceptance that was unknowable until they had to deal with such a strong "test" of their love. Personal experience tells me that a gay child can change, too.

Families with lesbian and gay members eventually come to view their lives from a new perspective. The safe characterizations handed down to the majority culture no longer apply to families touched by this issue. Parents are forced to give up the rose-colored glasses and deal with the complexities that their children bring in adulthood (Ryff et al., 1996). All of the family members I interviewed said that they replaced platitudes about family harmony with "real relationships." For example, last summer, one family was actively engaged in integrating a lesbian daughter into their lives when they got the news that their 40-year-old son, father of three children under the age of 6, was diagnosed with leukemia and had 2 years to live. Now, their lesbian daughter is transgendered and in the process of becoming a man. These parents describe themselves proudly as survivors. Like the resiliency found in other families facing adversity, these parents demonstrated a bedrock of acceptance toward their children despite very challenging events (McCubbin et al., 1996).

Conclusion

Being a reflexive, qualitative researcher requires the capacity to probe another's history in a more rigorous way than through everyday conversation. This capacity is honed by a genuine interest in self-understanding and the ability to handle intense emotions in oneself and others. It is also honed by letting go of the need to control another's belief system or insist that they see things your way (Ewing & Allen, 1996). The capacity to analyze complex situations and to make wise decisions for ethical behavior and responses, often at a moment's notice, is also required. Coming to one fluid or unitary story is not the outcome of good qualitative research. Rather, representing multivocality is more important than providing a singularly coherent resolution to one's research questions.

Although there cannot be a singular voice that speaks for all of us, Lather (1991) concludes that we can share the common goal of creating more adequate knowledge "in an unjust world." Feminists assume that all things are not equal in this world and that some have greater access to resources and power than others. Reflexive research requires the judicious use of insider and outsider perspectives (Collins, 1990; Friedman, 1995). I tie these ideas together with the concept of marginalization—the substance of my research program on family diversity, which includes past investigations of older never-married women, older black women, and aging mother-daughter dyads. The possibilities for positive change that occur in parent-child relationships that are initially characterized by a fear of stigma suggest exciting new avenues for future research into the complexity of adult kin relationships (Allen & Demo, 1995; Demo & Allen, 1996). Older parents of lesbian and gay adults are grappling with complexities that challenge normative models of adult child/aging parent relationships.

Note

1. Presented at the conference Resiliency in Families: Qualitative Approaches, sponsored by the Center for Excellence in Family Studies, University of Wisconsin--Madison, June 16-18, 1996. I thank Karen Wilcox for her research assistance on this project and insightful comments on the preparation of this manuscript. I also thank David Demo, Jo Futrell, Judith Stacey, and Alexis Walker for their invaluable assistance.

References

Acker, J., Barry, K., & Esseveld, J. (1983). Objectivity and truth: Problems in doing feminist research. *Women's Studies International Forum, 6*, 423–435.

Allen, K. R. (1994). Feminist reflections on lifelong single women. In D. L. Sollie & L. A. Leslie (Eds.), *Gender, families, and close relationships: Feminist research journeys* (pp. 97–119). Thousand Oaks, CA: Sage.

Allen, K. R. (1995). Opening the classroom closet: Sexual orientation and self-disclosure. *Family Relations, 44*, 136–141.

Allen, K. R., & Baber, K. M. (1992). Ethical and epistemological tensions in applying a postmodern perspective to feminist research. *Psychology of Women Quarterly, 16*, 1–15.

Allen, K. R., & Demo, D. H. (1995). The families of lesbians and gay men: A new frontier in family research. *Journal of Marriage and the Family, 57*, 111–127.

Allen, K. R., Demo, D. H., Walker, A. J., & Acock, A. C. (1996, November). *Older parents of gay and lesbian adult children.* Paper presented at the annual meeting of the National Council on Family Relations, Kansas City, MO.

Allen, K. R., & Farnsworth, E. B. (1993). Reflexivity in teaching about families. *Family Relations, 42*, 351–356.

Allen, K. R., & Walker, A. J. (1992). A feminist analysis of interviews with elderly mothers and their daughters. In J. F. Gilgun, K. Daly, & G. Handel (Eds.), *Qualitative methods in family research* (pp. 198–214). Newbury Park, CA: Sage.

Allen, K. R., & Wilcox, K. L. (1996, November). *Becoming an activist: Older parents of adult gay children.* Paper presented at the annual meeting of the Gerontological Society of America, Washington, DC.

Baber, K. M., & Allen, K. R. (1992). *Women and families: Feminist reconstructions.* New York: Guilford.

Bengtson, V. L., & Allen, K. R. (1993). The life course perspective applied to families over time. In P. Boss, W. Doherty, R. LaRossa, W. Schumm, & S. Steinmetz (Eds.), *Sourcebook of family theories and methods: A contextual approach* (pp. 469–499). New York: Plenum.

Bernstein, R. A. (1995). *Straight parents/gay children: Keeping families together.* New York: Thunder's Mouth Press.

Blaisure, K. R., & Allen, K. R. (1995). Feminists and the ideology and practice of marital equality. *Journal of Marriage and the Family, 57,* 5–19.

Bogdan, R. C., & Biklen, S. K. (1982). *Qualitative research for education.* Boston: Allyn & Bacon.

Cannon, L. W., Higginbotham, E., & Leung, M. L. A. (1991). Race and class bias in qualitative research on women. In M. M. Fonow & J. A. Cook (Eds.), *Beyond methodology: Feminist scholarship as lived research* (pp. 107–118). Bloomington: Indiana University Press.

Cheal, D. (1991). *Family and the state of theory.* Toronto: University of Toronto Press.

Collins, P. H. (1990). *Black feminist thought: Knowledge, consciousness, and the politics of empowerment.* Boston: Unwin Hyman.

Demo, D. H., & Allen, K. R. (1996). Diversity within lesbian and gay families: Challenges and implications for family theory and research. *Journal of Social and Personal Relationships, 13,* 417–436.

Du Bois, B. (1983). Passionate scholarship: Notes on values, knowing and method in feminist social science. In G. Bowles & R. D. Klein (Eds.), *Theories of women's studies* (pp. 105–116). London: Routledge.

Editors of the *Harvard Law Review.* (1990). *Sexual orientation and the law.* Cambridge: Harvard University Press.

Elam, D., & Wiegman, R. (Eds.). (1995). *Feminism beside itself.* New York: Routledge.

Eskridge, W. N., Jr. (1996). *The case for same-sex marriage.* New York: Free Press.

Ewing, J. A., & Allen, K. R. (1996, November). *Reflecting on our process: Ethical issues in doing feminist research when participants are opposed to feminist ideas.* Paper presented at the Theory Construction and Research Methodology Workshop, annual meeting of the National Council on Family Relations, Kansas City, MO.

Falk, P. J. (1989). Lesbian mothers: Psychosocial assumptions in family law. *American Psychologist, 44,* 941–947.

Farnsworth, E. B., & Allen, K. R. (1996). Mothers' bereavement: Experiences of marginalization, stories of change. *Family Relations, 45,* 360–367.

Fonow, M. M., & Cook, J. A. (1991). Back to the future: A look at the second wave of feminist epistemology and methodology. In M. M. Fonow & J. A. Cook (Eds.), *Beyond methodology: Feminist scholarship as lived research* (pp. 1–15). Bloomington: Indiana University Press.

Friedman, S. S. (1995). Making history: Reflections on feminism, narrative, and desire. In D. Elam & R. Wiegman (Eds.), *Feminism beside itself* (pp. 11–53). New York: Routledge.

Game, A., & Metcalfe, A. (1996). *Passionate scholarship.* London: Sage.

Gilgun, J. F., Daly, K., & Handel, G. (Eds.). (1992). *Qualitative methods in family research*. Newbury Park, CA: Sage.

Glaser, B. G., & Strauss, A. L. (1967). *The discovery of grounded theory: Strategies for qualitative research*. New York: Aldine de Gruyter.

Goodman, P. (1991, May). *Supporting our gay loved ones: A Parents FLAG perspective*. Paper presented at the American Psychiatric Association annual meeting, New Orleans.

Griffin, C. W., Wirth, M. J., & Wirth, A. G. (1986). *Beyond acceptance: Parents of lesbians and gays talk about their experience*. New York: St. Martin's.

Gubrium, J. F., & Sankar, A. (Eds.). (1994). *Qualitative methods in aging research*. Thousand Oaks, CA: Sage.

Henderson, J. N. (1994). Ethnic and racial issues. In J. F. Gubrium & A. Sankar (Eds.), *Qualitative methods in aging research* (pp. 33–50). Thousand Oaks, CA: Sage.

Herek, G. M., Kimmel, D. C., Amaro, H., & Melton, G. B. (1991). Avoiding heterosexist bias in psychological research. *American Psychologist, 46,* 957–963.

hooks, b. (1994). *Teaching to transgress: Education as the practice of freedom.* New York: Routledge.

Jaffe, D. J., & Miller, E. M. (1994). Problematizing meaning. In J. F. Gubrium & A. Sankar (Eds.), *Qualitative methods in aging research* (pp. 51–64). Thousand Oaks, CA: Sage.

Jenny, C., Roesler, T. A., & Poyer, K. L. (1994). Are children at risk for sexual abuse by homosexuals? *Pediatrics, 94,* 41–46.

Kirsch, J. A. W., & Weinrich, J. D. (1991). Homosexuality, nature, and biology: Is homosexuality natural? Does it matter? In J. C. Gonsiorek & J. D. Weinrich (Eds.), *Homosexuality: Research implications for public policy* (pp. 13–31). Newbury Park, CA: Sage.

Krieger, S. (1991). *Social science and the self: Personal essays on an art form.* New Brunswick, NJ: Rutgers University Press.

Kvale, S. (1994). Ten standard objections to qualitative research interviews. *Journal of Phenomenological Psychology, 25,* 147–173.

LaRossa, R., Bennett, L. A., & Gelles, R. J. (1981). Ethical dilemmas in qualitative family research. *Journal of Marriage and the Family, 43,* 303–313.

Lather, P. (1991). *Getting smart: Feminist research and pedagogy within the postmodern.* New York: Routledge.

McCubbin, H. I., Thompson, A. I., & McCubbin, M. A. (1996). *Family assessment: Resiliency, coping and adaptation–Inventories for research and practice.* Madison: University of Wisconsin System.

McWhirter, D. P., Sanders, S. A., & Reinisch, J. M. (Eds.). (1990). *Homosexuality / heterosexuality: Concepts of sexual orientation.* New York: Oxford University Press.

Minnich, E. K. (1990). *Transforming knowledge.* Philadelphia: Temple University Press.

Pharr, S. (1988). *Homophobia: A weapon of sexism.* Little Rock, AR: Chardon.

Pillemer, K., & Suitor, J. J. (1991). "Will I ever escape my child's problems?" Effects of adult children's problems on elderly parents. *Journal of Marriage and the Family, 53,* 585–594.

Rafkin, L. (Ed.). (1996). *Different daughters: A book by mothers of lesbians* (2nd ed.). Pittsburgh, PA: Cleis.

Rich, A. (1976). *Of woman born: Motherhood as experience and institution.* New York: W. W. Norton.

Rich, A. (1980). Compulsory heterosexuality and lesbian experience. *Signs, 5,* 631–660.

Rubinstein, R. L. (1994). Proposal writing. In J. F. Gubrium & A. Sankar (Eds.), *Qualitative methods in aging research* (pp. 67–81). Thousand Oaks, CA: Sage.

Ryff, C. D., Lee, Y. H., Essex, M. J., & Schmutte, P. J. (1994). My children and me: Midlife evaluations of grown children and of self. *Psychology and Aging, 9,* 195–205.

Ryff, C. D., Schmutte, P. S., & Lee, Y. H. (1996). How children turn out: Implications for parental self-evaluation. In C. D. Ryff & M. M. Seltzer (Eds.), *The parental experience in midlife* (pp. 383–422). Chicago: University of Chicago Press.

Savin-Williams, R. C. (1993). Personal reflections on coming out, prejudice, and homophobia in the academic workplace. In L. Diamant (Ed.), *Homosexual issues in the workplace* (pp. 225–241). Washington, DC: Taylor & Francis.

Savin-Williams, R. C., & Cohen, K. M. (Eds.). (1996). *The lives of lesbians, gays, and bisexuals: Children to adults.* Fort Worth, TX: Harcourt Brace.

Small, S. A. (1995). Action-oriented research: Models and methods. *Journal of Marriage and the Family, 57,* 941–955.

Smith, M. L. (1987). Publishing qualitative research. *American Educational Research Journal, 24,* 173–183.

Sollie, D. L., & Leslie, L. A. (Eds.). (1994). *Gender, families, and close relationships: Feminist research journeys.* Thousand Oaks, CA: Sage.

Stacey, J. (1988). Can there be a feminist ethnography? *Women's Studies International Forum, 11,* 21–27.

Stacey, J. (1990). *Brave new families.* New York: Basic Books.

Stacey, J. (1996). *In the name of the family: Rethinking family values in the postmodern age.* Boston: Beacon.

Stanley, L. (Ed.). (1990). *Feminist praxis.* London: Routledge.

Strauss, A., & Corbin, J. (1990). *Basics of qualitative research: Grounded theory procedures and techniques.* Newbury Park, CA: Sage.

Walker, A. J. (1994). You can't be a woman in your mother's house: Adult daughters and their mothers. In D. L. Sollie & L. A. Leslie (Eds.), *Gender, families, and close relationships: Feminist research journeys* (pp. 74–96). Thousand Oaks, CA: Sage.

Weston, K. (1991). *Families we choose: Lesbians, gays, kinship.* New York: Columbia University Press.

White, S. K. (1991). *Political theory and postmodernism.* Cambridge, UK: Cambridge University Press.

4

Becoming Resilient

Skill Development in Couples Living With Non-Insulin Dependent Diabetes

Catherine A. Chesla

Diabetes affects approximately 7% of the population in the United States. Non-Insulin Dependent Diabetes (NIDDM) or adult-onset diabetes is the most prevalent form of the disease and accounts for approximately 90% of the identified cases. NIDDM is characterized by inadequate insulin production and disrupted glucose metabolism, which results in dramatic fluctuations in blood glucose levels. Care of NIDDM encompasses many routine daily habits, such as diet and exercise, as well as illness-specific treatments, such as medications and glucose monitoring. The aim of these treatments is to modulate fluctuations in blood glucose as a form of prevention of the sequelae of the disorder, which include microvascular and macrovascular diseases that affect every organ system.

Theoretical perspectives on the role of families in diabetes or other chronic illnesses have framed the family as a problematic context, as the unit burdened by the demands of the illness, or as one aspect of the patient's social support (Blechman & Delamater, 1993; Campbell, 1986; Cox & Gonder-Frederick, 1992). In this chapter, the Resiliency Model of Family Stress, Adjustment and Adaptation (McCubbin & McCubbin, 1993, 1996) serves as a sensitizing frame for an examination of couples' reports of their experience of living with the chronic illness of NIDDM. The chapter explicitly focuses on interpreting the skills apparent in couples' descriptions of their responses to living with NIDDM, captured in naturalistic interviews with both the Person With Diabetes (PWD) and spouse. Prior to a description of the study, I review aspects of the Resiliency Model that relate conceptually to the notion of couple skill. Second, my theoretical orientation to skill is described. Empirical work examining interrelationships between family processes and diabetes progress and management is briefly described, and an overview of ethnographic studies of diabetes is also presented. All of these comprise my pre-understandings that both structured the study and informed my analysis of the text.

Family Skills in a Resiliency Model

Skill can be conceptualized as encompassing the complex coping that arises every day in the life of a couple living with NIDDM. Skill entails being able to grasp and respond to a multifaceted situation and stay engaged rather than being disrupted or thrown into reflection. Skill includes the ways in which the person with diabetes (PWD) and his or her partner take up the issues and changes that diabetes presents in their lives. Skill might revolve around the ways that they anticipate, enter, and respond to, for example, a hypoglycemic episode, an elaborate banquet of "forbidden food," or encounters with health care providers.

In common parlance, and in some models of skill acquisition (Dreyfus, Dreyfus, & Athanasiou, 1986), several elements are necessary for skill development. As an individual or couple moves into a new or unfamiliar situation, knowledge about the territory is necessary. For example, for couples in which one partner is newly diagnosed with a complex disease like diabetes, learning about the disease, how it works, the medications, and other treatments required are important first steps.

To become skilled, couples must go beyond the facts about diabetes and learn primarily by experience *how* to incorporate these facts into their everyday habits and practices. Knowing that one should eat no more than 15 grams of carbohydrates at a single sitting is one level of knowledge, but knowing *how* to construct interesting, varied meals that incorporate this restriction requires a different kind of knowledge–what some have termed experiential or practical knowledge. Similarly, learning one's own (or a partner's) response to dietary restrictions takes practice. Living through many similar situations is required to learn the range of personal and physiologic responses to maintaining or ignoring dietary restrictions, exercise prescriptions, medication regimens, and glucose monitoring practices.

Models that address family resiliency in the face of difficult life events (McCubbin & McCubbin, 1993, 1996; McCubbin, McCubbin, Thompson, & Thompson, 1995), although not addressing family skill development explicitly, highlight family factors that may influence a couple's capacity to learn factual information about diabetes as well as learn experientially how to incorporate diabetes into their lives. Aspects of the Resiliency Model that seem conceptually important to an examination of a family's capacity to learn to cope with diabetes are highlighted here. Because it is reasonable to assume that the diagnosis of NIDDM in the life of a couple constitutes an impact requiring considerable reorganization, only the postcrisis or adaptation aspect of the Resiliency Model is addressed.

Several aspects of the Resiliency Model are relevant to a naturalistic examination of couple responses to diabetes. Adaptation within the model is conceived as a process involving the interaction of multiple factors, including the accretion of stress from living with a chronically challenging disease; the new patterns of living that have been instituted since the onset of the disease; the family's appraisal of both their situation and their capacities within the situation; resources available to the family, including social support; and the family's problem-solving or coping capacities. The examination of how couples respond and become skilled at coping with diabetes fits conceptually with the notion of coping with the disease. Although there are conceptual definitions of coping offered in the model, in this examination, categorical preconceptions are not utilized. Rather, the actual practices that the couples describe form the basis for discovering what was important to them in their life situation and how they managed.

Two additional aspects of the Resiliency Model that map closely onto the process of skill development with couples deserve discussion. First, the new patterns that couples establish in their day-to-day living with the disease are of interest. Second, the resources that the couple bring to the situation are also conceptually of interest in how they respond.

Family patterns that might shift in response to the chronic demands of diabetes involve many routine activities for a couple or family. Ideal management of diabetes would require reconsideration and reformulation of many aspects of family meals: the timing of the meal, regularity of mealtimes, content and balance of meals, and amounts served. Sleep and wake cycles may be reestablished to accommodate medication regimens, particularly if the PWD uses insulin. Other family patterns may need to be readjusted to accommodate a heightened need for regular exercise. Additionally, family patterns for coping with illness, such as sharing information about health status, changes in health status, and health maintenance activities may be heightened. For example, partners of people with diabetes may want to know what the doctor has said about the illness or about the results of regular monitoring of the adequacy of blood glucose control (hemoglobin A1C tests), but the PWD may not wish to disclose this information. New practices of disclosing personal health information may need to be negotiated in the couple.

Personal resources also figure, theoretically, in the responses of couples to diabetes. For example, intelligence, fund of knowledge, experience and comfort in coping with complex health systems are all qualities that might help the couple work well with the expectations of bio-medical prescriptions. Similarly, a sense that one can master challenges and that one deserves a good life in the face of a chronic illness may be important issues. Resources that are important for coping with the overall illness demands or the unique requirements of the disease, however, may be different. Perhaps a tolerance of ambiguity about one's future is as important in adapting well to NIDDM as is innate intelligence or education. Because most people with diabetes face eventual complications of the disease, the capacity to accept whatever the future may bring may make the present more tolerable or comfortable. The notion of resources for responding contained within the Resiliency Model is illuminating, although the actual resources necessary for adapting to NIDDM need to remain open ended.

Defining Skill

Defining skill as engaged practices for living with diabetes highlights the difference between *knowing how* and *knowing that*, a distinction discussed by Dewey. Know-how is the practical, everyday capacity that we have as humans for moving smoothly through our world, coping with everyday requirements without thought or deliberation. Know-how, or practical knowledge, supports engaged practical activity.

A second kind of knowledge for living is more deliberative. Dewey describes this as "knowledge *of* and *about* things, knowledge *that* things are thus and so, knowledge that involves reflection and conscious appreciation" (Dewey, quoted in Dreyfus, Dreyfus, & Athanasiu, 1986, p. 260). This second kind of knowledge is more removed from everyday comportment and is reserved for situations in which established habits and practices are not routine, worked out, and unproblematic. This second kind of knowledge is referred to as *abstract or theoretical knowledge.*

Once these two forms of knowledge are distinguished, it is possible to recognize how the majority of human living depends on *know-how*—how our getting through a day draws primarily and predominantly on our knowing how to navigate the practical dilemmas of our day, and how this functioning draws upon all of our experience and wisdom, but is not reflective. The distinction also allows us to see what a small part of life is spent in the "deliberate, effortful, subject/object mode of living" that draws upon knowledge *about* things (Dreyfus, Dreyfus, & Benner, 1996, p. 260). It is also remarkable that, because the latter mode of living attracts our attention, it is the mode that has been so examined by philosophers and social scientists.

From the writings of Dreyfus and Dreyfus (1996), I assume that skillful coping derives from both sources of knowledge for living, the practical and theoretical, knowing how and knowing that. They describe the interrelation of the two sources of knowledge for the development of skill:

> We [shall] argue that while practice, without theory, cannot alone produce fully skilled behavior in complex coping domains. . . , theory without practice has even less chance of success. In short, theory and practice intertwine in a mutually supportive bootstrapping process as [one] develops his or her skill. Only if both are cultivated and appreciated can full expertise be realized. (Dreyfus & Dreyfus, 1996, p. 29)

Capturing skilled activity in everyday life is problematic, because often the person can enact but cannot describe engaged practical activity. One way to access skilled actions is to have informants describe concrete, specific events that have arisen in their lives and detail their thinking, emotions, and action. This, along with participant observation, may be the best way to help informants disclose the practical, experiential knowledge embedded in their actions (Benner, 1994; Chesla, 1995).

Family Processes and Diabetes

Recent reviews suggest that several family characteristics are consistently found to be important in the management or metabolic control of diabetes (Blechman & Delamater, 1993; Cox & Gonder-Frederick, 1992). Most of the research has focused on young families living with insulin-dependent diabetes (IDDM) in children and adolescents; considerably less attention has been addressed to adult families with NIDDM. Interpersonal variables examined in relation to diabetes control include family organization, resources, and coping. Family conflict and limited resources have been associated with poor control in diabetes. In contrast, couple marital satisfaction, family cohesion, stability, distinct boundaries and lower conflict between members, and higher levels of adaptive functioning have been associated with good metabolic control (Blechman & Delamater, 1993; Peyrot, McMurry, & Hedges, 1988).

The mechanisms by which family factors influence metabolic control have received some attention. Family variables, including cohesion, adaptability, and marital satisfaction, as well as measures of support and knowledge of the diabetes regimen, were found to be indirectly related to metabolic control through their influence on an adolescent's diabetes regimen behaviors (Hansen, Henggeler, & Burghen, 1987). Time may be important, because the influence of family factors appears to decrease as the duration of the illness in adolescents increases (Hansen, Henggeler, Harris, Burghen, & Moore, 1989).

Communication strengths in families of children with IDDM may facilitate adjustment and self-care within the prescribed disease regimen. For example, mother-adolescent daughter communication skills (including information exchange, behavior management, and problem solving) were associated with better self-care diabetic practices. Problematic communications (confrontive, emotionally charged, negative interactions) were associated with poorer self-care practices (Bobrow, AvRuskin, & Siller, 1985). Similarly, families' skills at exchanging information; cooperating in an organized task; and mutually solving a relevant problem, conceptualized as effective communication, were positively associated with good metabolic control (Blechman & Delamater, 1993).

In a prospective study of families with children newly diagnosed with IDDM, family communication and cohesiveness proved important in the 4-year progress of the disease. Jacobson and colleagues (1994) found that family expressiveness and the encouragement to act openly and express emotions directly inhibited the deterioration of glycemic control commonly seen in the first 2 years of IDDM (Blechman & Delamater, 1993). For the boys in the study, family cohesiveness and conflict additionally predicted glycemic control; boys from less conflicted and more cohesive families showed less deterioration in glycemic control over time.

In summary, examinations of family structural and interactional characteristics have shown some consistent associations with self-care or metabolic control, particularly in young families. How these family patterns evolve and how they interrelate with the progress of diabetes over time remain in question. Also, because the majority of the studies have been conducted on families with children, the particular ways that adult families in which one member is ill cope with diabetes deserve investigation.

Meanings and Practices of Diabetes

Ethnographic studies of diabetes, although quite limited, suggest some consistent patterns and meanings in the responses of people with diabetes that inform any naturalistic study of personal or family responses to diabetes. Retrospective investigation of illness trajectories repeatedly trace an initial period where the PWD attempts tight control by strictly adhering to care prescriptions, followed by increasingly individualized responses to the illness and its demands. Over time, responses become more personally articulated (Kelleher, 1988; Peyrot et al., 1987; Price, 1989).

People with diabetes are more attentive to and concerned about controlling symptoms and maintaining a sense of well-being than maintaining metabolic control (Hamera et al., 1988; O'Connell et al., 1984; Peyrot et al., 1987; Price, 1989). People with both IDDM and NIDDM report using symptoms rather than blood glucose levels to monitor how they are managing their diabetes. Symptoms are thought to be good indicators of both high and low blood glucose levels, and they are triggers to corrective action. The relief of symptoms ends efforts to correct blood glucose (Hamera et al., 1988; O'Connell et al., 1984).

Additionally, ethnographic reports suggest that concern for managing diabetes is balanced with concerns for other life commitments and quality of life. A range of concerns that competes with biomedical prescriptions has been identified, including maintaining an identity uncontaminated by diabetes; keeping the restrictions of diabetes private (Jayne, 1993; Kelleher, 1988); and maintaining a quality of life and social commitments, even if this requires contradicting medical advice about illness management (Kelleher, 1988; Peyrot et al., 1987; Price, 1989).

The complexity of the demands and responses to diabetes has led researchers to examine relations between illness understandings, attitudes, and self-care behaviors in diabetes. Beliefs about the seriousness of the disease and the treatments needed predicted behavioral outcomes (Hampson, Glasgow, & Toobert, 1990). In one investigation, spousal beliefs in the importance of diabetic control proved more important than the beliefs of the PWD in predicting outcomes (Shenkel, Rogers, Perfetto, & Levin, 1986). Attitudes toward diabetes have differentiated those with better psychosocial adaptation (Nowacek, Anderson, Richards, & O'Malley, 1986; Nowacek, O'Malley, Anderson, & Richards, 1990) and those with high and low adherence on the most demanding aspects of NIDDM management: diet and exercise (Anderson, Fitzgerald, & Oh, 1993). However, the nature of the relationships between attitudes of PWDs, their self-care behaviors, psychological adjustment, and adequacy of control are far from clear (Wikblad, Wibel, & Montin, 1990). Although positive attitudes toward diabetes are commonly associated with positive adjustment and self-care behavior (Anderson et al. 1993; Nowacek et al., 1990), the inconsistency of the findings argues for continued investigation of the factors in self-care behavior.

Research Aims

This project is an exploratory interpretive investigation of couples' experiences with and understanding of NIDDM in the chronic phase of the illness. This chapter is drawn from a pilot investigation of 14 couples who were living with NIDDM that preceded a large-scale model testing and interpretive study of the personal, family, and provider influences on self-care in NIDDM (Fisher et al., 1994). General questions that guided this interpretive investigation included the following.

> 1. How do people with NIDDM and their spouses come to understand diabetes and its requirements in their everyday lives?
>
> 2. What demands does the illness (the disease, its management requirements, and the personal experience of living with the disease) place on the PWD and spouse and family?
>
> 3. How do PWDs and their spouses cope with the demands of the illness in their everyday lives?

This chapter focuses on an aspect of the third general guiding question and addresses the following:

> 3a. What skills do couples develop in negotiating the illness experience of NIDDM?

Method

Methodological Background

The method employed in this project is interpretive phenomenology, an approach that attempts to capture everyday skills, habits, practices, and concerns by eliciting narratives about the everyday events that occur in meaningful contexts. The particular interpretive tradition within which I work derives from the phenomenological work of Heidegger and Kierkegaard. Present-day interpreters of this existential phenomenology have articulated the philosophical underpinning of this approach and furthered the possibilities for its use in examining engaged practices (Dreyfus, 1979, 1991; Taylor, 1985). Benner (1994) provides a full discussion of the ways in which this form of interpretation articulates with and is shaped by an existential philosophy.

This study of skill development in couples was shaped by a pre-understanding of human action and engagement (Chesla, 1995). I want to discuss my pre-understandings because they directed my approach to the study of family skills, including the stance I and my research assistants took vis-a-vis the informants, the modes we used to capture the couples' concerns and action, and the approaches we used to interpret those narratives.

Pre-Understandings

At base, I understand that human lives are situated within meaningful activities, relationships, commitments, and involvements that set up both possibilities and constraints for living. Humans become situated within their worlds by being raised up and living within a complex of understandings about the world and ways of being and acting in the world in that particular time in history, in the culture, and in the family in which they find themselves. Being situated means that one is neither totally determined or constrained nor radically free in how one acts. Rather, one has situated possibilities, certain ways of seeing and responding that present themselves to the individual in certain situations, and certain ways of seeing and responding that are not available to that individual.

A second assumption is that the basic way that humans live in the world is in engaged, practical activity. Being fully and unreflectively involved in everyday action (Dreyfus, 1991; Heidegger, 1975) is the basic and predominant way that humans live their lives. However, this mode of existence is so commonplace, so taken for granted, that it is often ignored for the more abstract, disengaged modes of existence. Engaged practical activity is the smooth way that one moves through a day, cooking breakfast, dressing children, driving to work, all without deliberation or reflection on these actions. Additional ways that humans are involved in everyday activities are standing back and thinking about one's everyday activities, which is a more abstract, reflective mode of engagement (present at hand); and a middle ground of being disrupted but still involved in one's activity by an unexpected turn of the situation (unready-to-hand). The second mode of engagement is familiar but derivative of the first; an example is sitting down and reflecting on one's parenting after the children have been settled in bed. The third mode of engagement in everyday life is also common but arises only when one's taken-for-granted expectations of a situation momentarily fail, when one's skills falter, or when there is some breakdown in the smooth flow of the person acting within the situation. An example of the third form of involvement occurs when, while dressing a child for the day, a parent is startled to find that both pairs of the child's shoes are muddy and wet. Quickly, consciously reviewing the possibilities, the parent decides that slippers will suffice at the baby-sitter's that day, puts them on the child's feet, and reenters the taken-for-granted flow of the morning.

A third assumption is that the way that humans are engaged in their worlds is set up and bounded by what matters to them. Concerns, or those things that matter to the person, set up how people enter any situation, what they see or do not see, what attracts their attention, and what sets up their involvement. For example, two parents, one who is concerned about teaching fairness and another who is concerned about teaching generosity, will respond quite differently when their child is involved in an argument with a peer. Often, concerns that cannot be directly expressed because they are not readily conscious and available show up in the actions and responses of the individual within situations.

As family scientists, the experience of being situated patterns our work. First, being situated in everyday reality sets up the circularity of both our action and our understanding. Living is the working out of the existential possibilities that our background or situatedness provide us, and accommodating those possibilities in action. Similarly, understanding is the working out of the pre-understanding that we always, already have of a situation, but accommodating or correcting the pre-understandings as we act.

As researchers, we bring this pre-understanding or forestructure to any project we develop. Forestructure is composed of (a) our practical understanding of the world and humanness, which we share with those we study; (b) our understanding the phenomenon enough to be able to state the problem and formulate the research question; and (c) the theoretical or conceptual pre-understandings that we as researchers bring to the project. I will briefly describe my pre-understandings in all three realms because doing so allows the reader to evaluate the access that I had to the overall problem area, or, stated differently, how I entered the hermeneutic circle (Packer & Addison, 1991).

My practical understanding of couples with diabetes comes primarily from my detailed study of families with other chronic illnesses. Interpretive phenomenologic studies of families with two chronic illnesses, schizophrenia and Alzheimer's disease, have oriented me to the lived experience of families and chronic illness in mid- to late life. My practical, personal, and clinical experience with diabetes has been quite limited. My grasp of how to set up the problem to be studied comes both from my previous study of families in chronic illness and from my reading of the literature on the reciprocal relations between families and health. Additional theoretical pre-understandings were reviewed in the introduction.

Informants

Informants were recruited through two sources: a public service announcement on a local radio station asking for volunteers for a family diabetes study, and a recruitment letter and follow-up telephone call to a diabetes clinic-based group. Inclusion criteria for the PWD were (a) diagnosis of adult-onset diabetes for at least 1 year; (b) cohabiting with partner or spouse for at least 1 year; (c) no major complications of diabetes that would impede daily functioning, including proliferative retinopathy, amputations, any CVA (cerebral vascular accident), MI (myocardial infarct) within the last 12 months, and renal insufficiency; and (d) PWD and partner/spouse self-identify as White or Latino (from Mexico or Central America). Rationale for these sample characteristics was that we were trying to capture people in the chronic but not final phases of the disease. We delayed recruitment until the PWD had the illness for 1 year, assuming that that allowed for the initial phase of adjustment and diversification of response (Kelleher, 1988; Peyrot et al., 1987; Price, 1989). We restricted the sample to those who had not yet developed sequelae of the disease because this is the population we hope to treat preventively in subsequent intervention trials. Finally, we sampled Whites and Latinos because they comprise the two largest ethnic groups that present for care of diabetes in the State of California.

The sample included 14 couples, eight of whom were White and five of whom were Latino; in one couple, the wife was White and the husband was Latino. In the couples studied, the PWD was predominantly male (10 out of 14) and in a heterosexual relationship (13 out of 14). One lesbian couple participated in which one partner had diabetes. Ages of the PWD and partner were closely matched; mean age for the people with diabetes was 50 (30–67), and the mean age of the partner/spouse was 48 (30–68). Partners/spouses had been together for an average of 23 years (6–42). The mean duration of illness was 7.6 years (1–28), but half of the sample had been diagnosed with diabetes for 5 or fewer years. The majority of the sample had children (11 out of 14), but in only half of the families with children did the children live in the home. Economically, the sample was middle class.

Interpretive Interviews

The study was designed so that the PWD and partner were interviewed individually and in the presence of the other. The schedule of interviews included an individual interview with each spouse, followed by a second interview with the couple, and the third follow-up interview with each individual. Interpretation of interviews proceeded sequentially, so that Time 1 interviews were reviewed and additional interpretive questions were added to the Time 2 interview schedule before we met with the couple again.

In the initial interview, we explored informants' illness understandings: their grasp of the cause, nature, course, needed treatment, and expected outcome of the diabetes. We probed for informants' grasp of the impact of the illness on their lives and the ways in which they adjusted to those problems and impacts. In addition to eliciting their reflections on their experience, we tried to appreciate their direct experience, that is, their engaged practical activity that would evidence skill, by asking them to recall narratives about salient, difficult, or memorable episodes of care or adjustment to the diabetes. Full narratives of the episodes; preceding events; informants' emotions, thoughts, and actions throughout the episodes; and outcomes were elicited. Typically, each couple provided three to five experiential narratives in the course of the study, although there was variation in the informants' ability to tell stories of direct, concrete experience. Interviews lasted approximately 2 hours and were conducted in the participants' home. Each interview was audio-recorded and transcribed verbatim between each interview.

Actual interviews completed were determined in part by the quality of the data and the sense that further interviews were not immediately required. In the study, seven couples completed the full five interviews; three couples were interviewed three times (twice individually and once as a couple), and follow-up interviews were not sought because the couples' practices were thought to be adequately spelled out; two families were interviewed three times, and follow-up interviews were not arranged because of moves and life commitments; and in two families, only a first individual interview with the PWD was conducted because the spouse/partner refused, after initially consenting, to participate.

Data Interpretation

The aim of interpretive phenomenology is to explain the common and distinct patterns of meaning and action of those studied, taking into account their context, history, and concerns. The movement in interpretation is to provide detailed explanations of the varied patterns of the informants' understanding and action rather than a modal or group response. Work begins with a detailed interpretation of a particular case and proceeds with detailed reads of additional cases that are taken up in contrast and comparison with the whole first case.

Interpretation within and between cases comprised two interwoven processes: thematic interpretation and interpretation of exemplars. Three levels of thematic interpretation are used to uncover themes in the text: (a) a holistic approach, (b) the selective approach, and (c) the detailed or line-by-line approach. In the holistic approach, the whole text was read and described as a piece in an attempt to capture its fundamental meaning as a whole. This read occurred during data collection and was conducted by at least the interviewer and myself and often by the entire team that was working on data collection. In the selective approach, aspects of the text that stood out as essential or revealing of skill were the focus. A line-by-line, detailed reading was then completed in which the text was examined for what it revealed about experience. The latter part of the interpretation I did independently.

Interpretation of narratives occurred simultaneously to the thematic interpretation. In this analysis, the whole incident described by the couple was analyzed, and aspects of each narrative were interpreted together, including the informant's recollection of what preceded the episode, how it unfolded, emotions throughout, actions considered and taken, direct and indirect clues to the concerns that guided action, and the informant's retrospective reworking of the incident.

Limitations

In this, as in all interpretive work, the findings are the best working out of the data that is available to date. The study reported upon here comprises pilot data for a large-scale interpretive and model-testing study of NIDDM in couples. The interpretations offered are true to the data collected in the 14 couples studied. However, study of additional couples may refine and make more dense the interpretations offered here. Additionally, as the interpretation of other lines of inquiry that are being worked on in the data evolves (e.g., how couples pattern their larger relations around the diabetes), the skill story will become more comprehensible. A major limitation of this pilot project is the predominance of one gender relationship: the male with diabetes and the female spouse/partner. There were too few representatives of the alternate arrangement to discuss in any detail. Finally, the commonalities of experience between Latino and non-Latino White subjects are emphasized in this report. The culturally distinct ways in which couples of Mexican or Central American descent versus those of Euro-American descent manage diabetes will be investigated when more detailed data are available.

Findings: Skilled Habits and Practices

The skills that are described here involve ways in which couples manage the everyday habits and practices that must be transformed and maintained in living with NIDDM. In this data presentation, the major focus is upon the skills developed around the disease management requirements. This fairly represents the primary focus of the interviews. The focus on management strategies in couples may have resulted from the ways in which interviews were structured; this issue will be explored in continued interpretive interviews with couples. The presentation of the findings will begin with an overview of early findings about the relational context of skill development. Two exemplary cases of different kinds of couple relations are described. Next, the pattern of skills apparent in couples' narratives about living with NIDDM are outlined. Finally, the implications of these findings for resiliency concepts and for future research are reported.

Taking up the findings about how couples coped with NIDDM in terms of "skill" has proven problematic in one respect. During the interpretation of the interview texts, the valuative connotation implicit in the term became problematic. That is, identifying couples who are skilled in managing the diabetes and its demands implies that there are couples who are unskilled or at least less skilled. At this time, it seems sufficient to describe the varieties of ways that couples respond to the illness experience and to elucidate the prevailing habits and practices that couples acknowledge, but to not denote any particular pattern as superior or inferior to another. The field is too open, and understanding what is more or less problematic for couples in the short and long term is insufficiently understood to identify any pattern as optimal. At present, skill is better used in a nonvaluative way.

Skill development described in the following section is predominantly the skill of the partner of the PWD. When selecting narratives that focused on *couple*-negotiated, interactional rather than individual skills, most of the narratives were told by partners. Interviews with the PWD informed the interpretation of couples' skill development, but data from these interviews were much more focused on the self and actual illness responses. Partners, by virtue of their position vis-a-vis the disease, told more relational stories. In future work, I need to learn if the self-focus of the PWD is an artifact of the interview design, or whether further probing about relational issues will yield more interactional stories.

Relational Context of Skill Development

Two predominant patterns of how couples relate around the illness experience of diabetes are evident in this study. Interpretive description of the patterns of couple relations in NIDDM will be detailed in another paper. Here, they are briefly described as a contextual feature of skill development. The first pattern is one in which the couple works together to think about, learn about, and manage the diabetes. In this pattern, the couple works as a team to make the lifestyle changes required by the disease. In the exemplary case that will be presented, and in most of the couples who evidence this pattern, the female partner or wife is the captain of the team and is relied upon for setting up one key management issue–diet. Additionally, she is either explicitly or implicitly involved in monitoring and coaching some behaviors when the PWD's actions do not match her concerns. Variability in this pattern, apparent in the interviews, showed up as the degree of comfort that each partner has with this hierarchical relation. For some couples, the pattern is described in unproblematic terms and is acceptable and comfortable for each. In other couples, uneasiness with the pattern is evident for both. For the woman, there is a wish for the PWD to take more personal responsibility without coaching. For the PWD, there is ambivalence about externally applied rules and acknowledgment of purposefully breaking rules, at least in part, to disrupt the power relations.

In a second predominant pattern, the PWD maintains within his or her own sphere the knowledge about and management of the disease. In this pattern, the partner is much less involved in the day-to-day management of all aspects of the disease. Given this relational context, the skills developed are different from those in couples who manage diabetes as a team. Variability in comfort or satisfaction with this relational pattern is also apparent. Several couples express contentment that the PWD manages independently. Some of these partners are unhappy about the centrality of the diabetes in their partners' lives but are satisfied with their place in the management. There is a second group of partners that perceives that it is excluded from the management process by the PWD; these partners wish for greater involvement and information primarily because they believe they could effect better disease management. However, at the present time, most of the disease management is out of their reach, and thus their skills must develop at a distance from the diabetes.

I will begin by presenting two couples who exemplify patterns of couple skill development that I observed in this study. The exemplary case of satisfied teamwork is a Latino couple who have been married 20 years and have two daughters, ages 14 and 15, and a son, age 20, who all live in the family home. At the time of the interview, Mr. A. had been diagnosed with NIDDM for 2 years. He manages his illness with oral agents, diet, and exercise.

Initial symptoms that brought the disease to the couple's attention were the classic diabetic symptoms of thirst and frequent urination. What brought Mr. A. to visit a physician were frequent urinary tract infections. The disease was diagnosed in the first visit, and oral hypoglycemic medications were prescribed. However, Mr. A. delayed about a year before taking any action to manage the diabetes. During this time, Mrs. A., who knew the diabetic regimen from watching her mother-in-law manage the disease, tried to coach Mr. A. into action.

> At that moment [of diagnosis] you know, one gets sad. . . . And to try and convince him that he has to take care of himself; and see the problems that the people that have this disease have; and take care not to injure himself, his eyes, because people lose their sight.

Mrs. A. employed many of the same strategies as other spouses who were trying to raise the awareness of the PWD: She tried to argue rationally with her husband that he needed to take better care of himself, revisit the doctor, and take the prescribed medicine so that he could live longer and not damage his vital organs.

In this case, a turning point in the awareness of the PWD came when a male friend, who also had diabetes, offered to check Mr. A.'s blood glucose on his home monitor. The reading was very high, and the friend told him, "You are dying." The event motivated Mr. A. to reschedule a visit with his health care provider, take diabetes education classes, and begin taking oral hypoglycemic medications. At the time of the interviews, Mr. A. had been taking these more active measures for approximately 1 year.

Mr. A. describes his relationship with his wife regarding diabetes as clearly hierarchical. He explicitly refers to her as "the boss," a "mother figure" as well as "the perfect wife," in describing her role in setting limits on his eating and in coaching him on his diabetic restrictions. He also volunteers that he is extremely happy with this arrangement. He says, "She's helping me a lot," and he sees the relationship that they have around his diabetes to be similar to, but a more extreme form of, their relationship prior to the diabetes. For example, he says that earlier in their 21-year marriage, she "domesticated me," that is, turned him from a rough military man to a softer, more educated man. In the couple interview, she agrees that she always "cared for" him in this way, but her care intensified with the diabetes because of the health risks associated with the disease.

A second couple, whom I will call the Z. family, had a much less unified approach to the disease. Mr. Z. had been diagnosed with diabetes for 9 years and the diagnosis preceded his relationship with his female partner of 6 years. Mr. Z. is driven by a need for information about his illness and actively uses this information to attempt tight control over his blood sugars. He has progressed, in part by his own preference, to the use of insulin; he monitors his glucose and administers the medication four to six times per day.

Although Ms. Z. is a health care professional, she is relatively uninvolved in the day-to-day concerns about the disease. She describes this as a conscious choice:

> I think that an outside person has a better influence, sometimes, than an inside person. And I think that that's really good. And a lot of times I'd rather him hear things from people other than myself, particularly if it's bad news. Even if it's good news, it's just a lot easier. So I try to let him have appropriate medical management outside of our relationship. And our relationship is our relationship.

The distance that exists between Mr. and Ms. Z. about diabetes management may have resulted from the fact that the disease was part of his life before she was, but it seems to result more from the conscious wish of both to keep the disease in the hands of the PWD.

> *Ms. Z.:* The only real concern I have is when his blood sugar starts to get low, he'll sit there and pop candies. It drives me wild. Eat something! But, I mean, I've really taken an effort that I can't be a nagging person and I can't be the one who's telling him how to control his life. And I think that that's what makes our relationship worth a lot. We kind of accept a lot of things in each other.
>
> *Interviewer:* So was that something that you had to work out, or was that your style?
>
> *Ms. Z.:* I think it's because we were older when we got together. We were both really established. And we both keep some of our independence now.

The degree of separation that they have about the diabetes is evident in the couple interview, when they are asked about responding to bad news about his diabetes.

> *Interviewer:*   [When you get bad news about your microalbuminuria] what kinds of things are helpful to you in terms of your relationship?
>
> *Mr. Z.:* Nothing in terms of the relationship. For me, probably what helps the most is getting into seeking out the information about it, researching it, finding out what other professionals and other diabetics know about it and putting it into a perspective.
>
> *Ms. Z.:* I'm totally useless. . . .
>
> *Mr. Z.:* It's not true. Just marginally. . . (laughing follows by all). If I want to know how to cook something, I'll come to you. But no, it's a matter of, I'm very certain that information, education, and in my case personal education about that issue is what I need. And that helps to calm me down and so forth. And if (partner) has that information, that's terrific, but it's awfully specialized, you know she's not a diabetologist.

I will use the case of the "A." and "Z." families to describe skills that were apparent in many of the couples interviewed. These couples present good examples of these skills, that is, they present a strong and clear instance of the pattern of interactions that other couples also displayed. The particular ways in which these skills were worked out varied in other cases, and these variations will be discussed throughout.

Learning the Rules: Acquiring "Theoretical" Knowledge

Couples described variable experiences regarding the sharing of information about the diabetes at the beginning of the disease. For most, the PWD was informed in private by a physician and was given pamphlets about managing the diet for the NIDDM. For example, Mr. A. went alone to his physician visits, met with the dietitian alone, and was given diabetic instruction and information in English. (Mr. A. is bilingual but more comfortable speaking in Spanish. Mrs. A. uses Spanish exclusively.) Mrs. A., like many partners of PWDs, sought information independently.

> Because when he went to the nutritionist, I told him that I wanted him to bring back the papers that she gives you, so that in that way I could guide myself with the food. [I'm] trying to do it by the book.

All couples reported active efforts to seek information early in the disorder. However, only a few partners benefited from contact with health care providers or dietitians regarding disease management information. One woman insisted that she attend the diagnostic interview, whereas another went to multiple consultations with the dietitian, some without her husband present. For most, who relied on printed materials, practical wisdom and advice that could contextualize "the rules" were lost, as was the opportunity to ask specific questions. The pattern of information seeking was similar in couples who practiced teamwork and those who managed in separate spheres, except the degree of effort was less and the use to which the information was put was more personal in the latter group.

Negotiating Diet

In most of the couples studied, the female partner was primarily responsible for meal planning and preparation. When diabetes was diagnosed, the pattern of responsibilities around food did not change, and therefore, the female spouse became a key person in managing one of the most essential aspects of the NIDDM regimen: diet. This was true in all but two of the couples studied. As Mrs. A. said,

> In the matter of food, since I'm the one that cooks, I shop, he takes me, but I'm the one that decides what we're all going to eat, the one that makes the menu, daily.

In the few instances in which the woman was the PWD, the woman most commonly handled the family diet: meal planning, shopping, and preparation of food.

Restricting Sugars

Most couples describe an almost immediate modification of their diets to accommodate what they took to be an important diabetic restriction: the elimination of sugar.

> *Mrs. B.:* So, I had to kind of alter a few things, and then no more sugar in the house. (Both laugh). There's diabetes sugar and there's a little fructose, but there is no real sugar . . . . because I don't need it.
>
> *Interviewer:* You didn't really miss it.
>
> *Mrs. B.:* No, no, and then if we have people over for dinner, well, there's fresh fruit for dessert, there's no dessert. And I just don't feel like saying, you can have it, while he sits there and [cannot]. I can't do that, and so people have come to know, and it's acceptable.

This comment reflects a concern not only for restricting sugars but also for protecting her husband from social losses. She protects her husband from the social and emotional strain of having to sit at the table and not participate. It alters her diet, whose importance she downplays, and the diet of guests in the home, which she sees as an acceptable change.

Many women traced how their diet management became more refined over time. They began to see the interrelationships between foods in the diet and moved beyond the simple elimination of sugar. For example, they began to reduce fats, balance the amount of protein and carbohydrate, and attend to the amounts of foods consumed at each meal. This skilled understanding came from experience and from further reading of books on diabetes, diabetic cookbooks, magazine articles, and pamphlets available in the community. Although few complained, the factual information available was less than ideal. For example, Mrs. A. never found information in Spanish, and no one in the Latino sample was offered dietary guides with culturally specific foods as examples. In addition, even after years of managing the diabetes diet, many women had not spoken with a health professional or dietitian about optimal diets or about practical strategies for maintaining optimal diet practices.

Introducing Dietary Restrictions Into Meal Practices

The dietary restrictions that were introduced for the PWD were generally introduced into the major household meals. Couples identified this as a benefit to the overall health of the family because to them, the restrictions comprise a healthy diet–more fresh fruit and vegetables, smaller meals, and meals less concentrated in sweets and fats.

Partners of some of the PWDs developed multiple ways to highlight for their partner appropriate responses to situations that called for following the restrictions. Some of the actual skill in this negotiation is only alluded to by the informant. That is, although a family therapist or health care provider observes in these interactions a skilled and careful negotiation of couple behavior change, the women presented the changes as normal, expected, or unremarkable. Women acknowledged using a gradual, gentle, and non-confrontational approach to diet change, particularly in the beginning. They recognized that dietary changes represented significant losses and attempted to introduce the restrictions in a less charged way. Gentle introductions to dietary restrictions, along with creative meal planning to keep meals interesting and searching for dietetic alternatives, were some practices employed by wives to protect their husbands from experiencing negative consequences from dietary restrictions.

> *Mrs. B.:* I didn't do it really abruptly, that I said you can't have this anymore. No, I just, you know, very diplomatically.
>
> *Interviewer:* You worked your way around it, yeah.
>
> *Mrs. B.:* Oh, yeah, in a way that he, it was only for your good, and you know, and you have to do it this way. He's not stubborn.

Women developed a host of options for increasing the spouse's adherence to the diet. They used humor to cajole changed behavior, and they highlighted the negative outcomes of uncontrolled diabetes for the PWD and for the family. Mrs. A., for example, noticed that her sexual relations with her husband were less frequent when his blood glucose was poorly controlled. After a period of time, she would tease him, ask him to check his sugars, to see if he could get interested in sex. Another wife, when preparing breakfast, would casually ask her husband for his morning glucose reading. If it was below some mutually agreed-upon level, then he could have raisins on his oatmeal; if above that level, "no raisins."

One woman described a dramatic and successful example of reorienting her husband to the dietary restrictions.

> *Mrs. B.:* I tried to tell him, that he shouldn't have this. And he said, "Oh no, no, it's OK." And I knew I wasn't going to get it this way, and I said, "OK, give me your finger, I'm going to cut your finger off right now. You're going to lose it anyway."
>
> *Interviewer:* Oh.
>
> *Mrs. B.:* Mm hum, because I was trying to remind him of his father. They took several fingers off him. And I said, think about it. (He said) "Oh, you're right." (Laughs.) But later on he told me it was cruel of me to say that. And I said, "That was. I'm sorry. But you didn't, there was no other way that you really stopped and thought about it." You know, this was the only time that I did do that. (Laughs.)
>
> *Interviewer:* So he told you were cruel. (Laughs.)
>
> *Mrs. B.:* That was cruel. (Laughs.) Well, I think this made him even more aware of the fact that he really had to watch it, and had to live by what the doctor tells him.

For couples in which the PWD managed more independently, coaching appropriate eating was much less evident. In the exemplary case, Ms. Z. acknowledged that she actively attempted *not* to interfere.

I think the negative part is remembering to take all the stuff with us that's got to be—that you have to be conscious about when we're going out for dinner, to make sure he's taken his insulin and everything with him, that he has his stuff with him. Because sometimes if we just go somewhere and we're not conscious of it. . . so some spontaneity in things is gone. But, as a general rule, no, it's not a real event. Besides, I kind of let him take care of it himself.

Eliminating Restricted Foods From the Household

Most partners supported the PWD in the dietary restrictions by eliminating from the household foods that should not be eaten. Mrs. A., for example, converted the entire household to diet soda; reportedly decreased the household intake of sugar from 25 pounds a month to one; and purchased a kind of bread that she thought was more healthy, particularly because her husband did not like it. Even in couples where the diabetes was managed separately, the household items changed. As Ms. Z said,

> It's kind of a little bit of a bummer because I like to bake a lot. So I don't bake very much anymore because [Mr. Z.] doesn't like. . . . I mean, I understand that's kind of a little bit of a torture. [Mr. Z.] used to—claims to have been a real sweetaholic, and now he can't have it. So it's very hard for him. So he doesn't like to have it in the house. So I don't, you know, normally keep things in the house. But, I have this little stomach here so, I mean, it's not like I'm being deprived.

Balancing Restrictions With Family Needs

Particularly in families like the A.s, who have children, a tension develops around planning a diet that takes into account the well-being of the PWD and the health and enjoyment of other family members. Mrs. A. tells the following story about the family's struggle over how to cope with dessert items.

> *Mrs. A.:* For example, when we buy ice cream, I tell him, don't serve yourself so much. "Yes, only a little bit," he answers. Then I say, it's too much, I'm going to buy sugar-free then. No, he'll say, because it doesn't taste good. Then eat only a little bit [I say], but later, when I go to bed, [he stays up] watching TV. Next morning it is empty.
>
> *Interviewer:* Aha, empty?

> *Mrs. A.:* Yes, he eats more. So then I tell him, I'm not going to buy any more ice cream. And for a while, we didn't buy any more. But how could I [do that] to the children? *How could I also punish them?* (Emphasis added.) I'll buy it and the same thing happens. He knows that it hurts him. And he eats it.

At the time of the interviews, Mrs. A. had not totally resolved this dilemma but, overall, maintained restrictions rather than address the range of needs of the children. She did admit buying things for the children and hiding them from her husband. Other strategies used were to allow nondiabetic family members to eat treats outside of the home or when the PWD was not present.

In some couples, the partner reduced but did not eliminate the restricted food. They would eat desserts, for example, at home and when out. As Mrs. Z. explained,

> I have been known to order dessert in restaurants. And he sometimes gives me a hard time about it but mostly he's fine.

Altering Food Rituals

Over time, some rituals around food that were harmful for diabetes were altered or eliminated. For example, Mr. A. was accustomed to a large breakfast of eggs, sausage, and bread, and he described having to relinquish this meal as "ripping out a wall" inside him. Mrs. A. dealt with the tension by ceasing to make breakfast for the family. Instead, she prepared coffee and set out bread that family members could prepare for themselves. Mr. A. began to cook for himself (when his wife was in the shower), and the children would run and tell her how much their father was eating! She eventually stopped buying all but a few eggs per week to discourage his consumption and reported that he changed his breakfast to toast only. In a similar fashion, Mrs. A. dramatically decreased the amounts that she cooked for each meal to discourage Mr. A. from eating large amounts at each dinner. She no longer cooked enough for leftovers because she could not, with her coaching, keep him from eating the remaining food.

Negotiating Diabetes Practices

General prescriptions for care of NIDDM include a four-fold approach: dietary changes, medication management, exercise, and glucose monitoring. It is striking how much couples focused on the dietary changes in both their individual and couple interviews to the relative exclusion of other management issues. Although there were references to negotiations around other aspects of the diabetes regimen, diet predominated.

Almost all of the people with diabetes in this study were prescribed medications to manage their diabetes. In a few instances, the partner of the PWD became involved in medication management by coaching the PWD to take the pills each day or by refilling the prescription in time to prevent lapses in medication-taking. However, the majority of the partners had only abstract knowledge of their partners' medication prescriptions and habits.

There is acknowledgment in the diabetes literature that in diabetes education, teaching about the role of exercise and exercise "prescriptions" are less well attended to than is diet. Concern about exercise and actual exercise practices comprised a relatively central place in diabetes management for a few couples, were acknowledged but not important to a few more couples, and were barely recognized in the remainder of the 14 couples. When exercise was identified as an important practice in the interviews, it was most often described as a practice the couple shared. In the exemplary case, Mrs. A. raised concerns with her husband about his exercise during our couple interviews. In good humor, she told him she would "sacrifice herself" by walking with him around a large neighborhood park when he returned from work each day. This never came to pass, but Mr. A. dramatically increased his exercise during the study period from almost none to walking several miles per day. In the Z. family, Mr. Z. began exercising vigorously when the couple joined a gym and exercised together. Several months later, Ms. Z. stopped going because of her work schedule, but by then Mr. Z. had become an avid proponent of exercise benefits, and he continued almost daily workouts. For the few families in which exercise was a serious part of the regimen, partners seemed to have negotiated ways to make the exercise a mutual concern or practice rather than a burden that the PWD took up alone.

Monitoring the Person With Diabetes for Health Practices

One clear and immediate marker of how well the PWD is actually managing the diabetes is the blood glucose level at various times during the day. In some couples, the PWD did not test regularly, or did so in private. In other couples, the readings were shared occasionally and casually and served as a basis for meal planning. There was a third, much smaller subset of people who diligently checked their glucoses several times a day for self-monitoring, but in none of these cases was the information regularly disclosed to their partner.

It should be acknowledged that for those who took insulin, regular glucose monitoring was a requirement to titrate the medications and to ward off the very uncomfortable state of hypoglycemia. Disclosure or nondisclosure of blood glucose readings was an issue about which many couples openly or covertly argued. Most spouses wished that the PWD would test more regularly and/or tell them the results more regularly. Perhaps because the reading could be understood as an evaluation of how well or poorly the PWD was doing overall, the PWD managed the information in a guarded fashion. Of course, the issue was not universal. For example, in the Z. family, Ms. Z. was happy to have her partner monitor his glucose levels independently unless there were signs of disregulation. In part because of lack of access to the regular blood glucose readings, partners of PWD monitored their partners' well-being through symptoms and personal readings of well-being rather than by using "the numbers."

Some partners of PWDs became personally invested in how their partner took up the diabetes regimen, particularly around food intake, and became quite vigilant of the partner's behaviors. Mrs. A. exemplifies this pattern, in an extreme, but recognizable form. For example, she dishes the food on her husband's plate, is aware of whether he takes second servings, and monitors his eating in the home indirectly by noting what food is missing each day. In addition, she packs his lunch for work and guesses whether or not he has eaten additional foods from the cafeteria by what remains in the lunch box. Both Mr. and Mrs. A. rely on her awareness in maintaining the limits of the diabetes. She gains some sense that her efforts are working, and he gains a sense of external monitoring and control. Evidence that this helps him in his efforts comes from the fact that they acknowledge that she serves as his "confessor" at times that he deviates; he admits to her his excess eating after the fact.

A quite different pattern was evident in the Z. family, where Ms. Z. claimed disinterest in her partner's daily eating and exercise patterns.

> *Ms. Z.:* Well, actually, it's OK with me if he doesn't go to the gym, but then he shouldn't have the ability to complain to me that his blood sugar is high. That's kind of how I feel about it.
>
> *Interviewer:* Does he complain to you about it, or. . . .
>
> *Ms. Z.:* He more laments about it.

What constitutes skill in monitoring diabetes as a couple is complex conceptually and practically, and what works to support healthy diabetes practices may be quite unique to each couple. For example, in the two excerpts above, even the practices acknowledged by the couple as helpful may not, in the long term, be the most supportive of healthy regimens. If Mrs. A. did not monitor her husband's actions so vigilantly, he might make a greater personal investment in self-monitoring. Additionally, if she stopped allowing him to "confess" incidents of going off a strict diet, he might experience more emotional motivation to maintain practices and avoid personal feelings of guilt. One important part of close monitoring is that if the couple have joint concerns that they are trying to work out, there must be some means for the PWD to communicate to his or her partner relevant information about how the plan is working. Particularly for couples who work as a team, the partner of the PWD needs ways to learn directly or indirectly about the fruits of his or her efforts.

Monitoring the PWD for Evidence of Disregulation

Many partners who are involved in a team approach to diabetes, or in a more distanced way, play a role in monitoring the mood and expressions of the PWD for evidence that the blood glucose is either too high or too low.

> *Mrs. A.:* When I see that there is something in him, like his character, that I say to him . . . or that his head hurts, or that he feels tired. . . . So then I ask him, why don't you do the test, to see if it's the sugar? Maybe it's too low, maybe you have it too high. In that respect, yes, I notice it. He says that almost always I can notice that his level of sugar is a little high.
>
> *Interviewer:* Then, you notice almost before the machine [chuckling by both]?
>
> *Mrs. A.:* Yes, one does suspect, true? That there is something wrong.

In the instance of hyperglycemia, there is no quick remedy to the situation, particularly for those who do not take insulin. Although some people can reduce their blood glucose by strenuous exercise. The monitoring of unusual behavior in this instance serves to inform the PWD that his or her behavior is out of the norm. At times, it serves to prevent people with diabetes from embarrassing themselves or helps them to temper their behavior in social settings.

In instances of hypoglycemia, the partner's warning of the altered mood or behavior may have a life-saving function. Several people with diabetes admitted that they rely on their partner for early warnings that their blood glucose is out of normal range. They recognize that the partner can sense danger long before they themselves feel it. Also, the partner offers a suggested action, to check the blood glucose, whereas the PWD may already be experiencing impaired judgment about taking this action. Mr. Z. notes:

> And it was late at night, I was working at the computer, I signed off the computer, and I went to bed. I took my NPH about an hour before and I went to bed. I felt funny but my blood sugar an hour before had been 100-110, something like that, and I took my NPH and went to bed. And I felt funny.

> And luckily Ms. Z. was still a little bit awake and asked me something. She said you're all sweaty. I said, yeah, I don't feel well. She said go check your blood sugar. I am too logical. It had never occurred to me it could be a blood sugar problem because an hour before I was 110. I hadn't taken any fast acting insulin, so what the hell was going on, you know? It made sense to me that it was not my blood sugar, but sure enough, when I checked, it was 38. So I drank orange juice, I ate crackers, and in the morning I was like, normal again, 120 or something.

Different "levels" of attentiveness were evident in the partners of PWDs in the monitoring of health practices and for glucose disregulation. Skilled attentiveness was apparent in Ms. Z.'s way of attending to her partner's irritability, mood, and need for more careful monitoring. Both she and Mr. Z. admitted relying on her assessment of his mood as the first sign that things were going awry in his blood sugars, and in coaching him to take appropriate action. Mrs. A. exemplifies a high level of vigilance because she was so attentive to the disease, her husband's mood, and all cues to his health behavior. When asked what percentage of her time she spent thinking, worrying about, or working on the diabetes, she admitted spending 100% of her time in disease-related activities. The emotional and attentive energy she expended was far greater than what her husband expended and could be assessed as vigilant beyond actual necessity.

Attunement With the Partner's Concerns About Diabetes

A final skill to be discussed is a relational quality of attunement about the diabetes and the diabetes-related work in the life of the couple. Partners who are attuned to their partners' concerns about the diabetes in their lives approach behavior change in a way that has a greater emotional (and perhaps) real behavioral impact. The A.s are an excellent example of attuned communication and coaching regarding the illness.

There is a symmetry in the couples' individual interviews about the importance of the children in their lives. They take various actions to protect the children from emotional stress by always taking their arguments to their own room; additionally, they structure their lives around the educational and emotional needs of the children. In managing symptoms of the illness, Mr. A. also protects his children. He related incidents when his diabetes was less controlled, and he would distance himself from his children by going to his own bedroom rather than take the chance of losing his temper with them. In many implicit and explicit ways, Mr. A. acknowledges that he would "die for" his children.

Mrs. A., who shares her husband's devotion to the children, captures her husband's attention by using his concerns about the children and about the family "needing more life from him." The story comes from Mr. A.'s perspective:

> Oh, she was all the time telling me that I have to pay attention, and she doesn't want to be a young widow. . . . That you have your kids to live for. You have to take care yourself. Not for you, because we have kids and we have to help them to go ahead, and you have to be careful with yourself.

In an earlier example, Mrs. B.'s attunement with her husband's concern prompted her to use a strong and compelling picture of the eventual outcome of her husband's eating discretions: She offered to cut off his finger on the spot. For some partners, this communication would have been merely repulsive. For Mr. B., the communication was "cruel" but effective, because it addressed head on the concerns that had been set up by his father's experience with diabetes: amputations of his fingers.

In couples where the diabetes management is in the sphere of influence of the PWD, attunement takes a quite different form. At least for Ms. Z., attunement to her partner's diabetes came in accepting that she had little or no role to play in providing either information or comfort. She was attuned to her partner's need for information and personal control and had scaled back her responses accordingly.

> *Interviewer:* How is that for you [that PWD doesn't talk with her about downturns in the disease]?

> *Ms. Z.:* There's nothing I can do about it, right? Sometimes, I would like to be able to help, but I realize probably the best thing I could do is nothing. And a lot of times, he doesn't like to take advice from me, even if I give him the same advice somebody else does later.

> But I think you kind of adapt. I do. He likes to get all his information. But I think it's okay. I don't take it personally anymore. I used to. I used to feel shut out, but I don't feel that way anymore.

Interviewer: So it's something that you kind of have worked out in your relationship.

Ms. Z.: It's just the way he deals with things. Yeah, it's more like you come to accept people, and you realize that it's not a personal thing, it's the way they deal, and that it's okay.

Discussion

The aim of this work was to explore the skills that couples develop in living with the illness of diabetes. The term "illness" is used to include the disease, its management, and the personal experience of living with the disease. The interpretation that I have presented has focused most centrally on the practical knowledge and skill that couples developed around the management of the disease regimen. In the discussion of attunement, skill in knowing and responding to the other's illness concerns was also addressed.

This work was designed to overcome one bias in the literature on diabetes: the examination of the illness experience of the individual in isolation from the social or family context. By opening up the question to how couples negotiate illness management and where they place diabetes in their lives, significant couple influences in managing diabetes became evident particularly in those couples who took up management as a team. Even in couples where the PWD managed the illness more individually, serious couple issues arose that needed negotiation.

The major focus on the dietary aspect of disease management in couples' interviews can be interpreted in several ways. First, diet may be fundamentally important in the couples' lives, and thus, food and limits on food become a large focus of their work together in managing the diabetes. A second interpretation is that food regulation in a household demands negotiation, more so than any other aspect of disease management. It would be very unusual for a couple to split off that area of their lives into individual management: to shop separately, eat separately, and separate their social eating from the couple's other activities. In contrast, medication management and glucose monitoring are medical regimens that impinge little on everyday couple routines and household habits, and thus might be handled independently and without negotiation with the spouse. This was apparent in the couples studied; medications and glucose monitoring were handled primarily by the PWD, separate from the spouse.

Another possibility for why food and food management predominated in the interviews is that the couples interviewed are still evolving their skills around food regulation, and thus, it became a large part of their narrative. In a prior study of skill development in nurses who worked in intensive care (Benner, Tanner, & Chesla, 1996), we found that nurses at various levels of skill development told stories about their learning edges. That is, their smooth-flowing skills, those they had well in hand, fell to the background. Instead, nurses told about their current challenges, the aspects of practice that comprised their current practical professional development "work." It seems very possible that, for example, medication management fell to the background because it is an easily acquired skill and required little negotiation. Regarding the larger issues of exercise and glucose monitoring, these were, I suspect, simply not salient enough in the lives of those interviewed to become a focus. Or, these may have been emphasized less than diet and medications by health care providers, and thus, the couple did not work as much on these habits together or mention them as consistently in the interviews. Health care providers place relatively less attention on exercise in diabetes care (Krug, Haire-Joshu, & Heady, 1990), and thus, PWDs and their spouses may do so as well.

A final reason why discussions of diet may have been a major theme in the interviews is that women primarily provided information on couple negotiations and skills around diabetes. As noted earlier, 11 of the 14 informants with diabetes were male, and in the current study, stories about *couple*-negotiated skills came primarily from the spouse/ partner of the PWD, who was predominantly female. DeVault's (1991) excellent exegesis of women's care through feeding the family points to the focal nature of food in the ways women constitute their lives as mothers and spouses or partners.   Most of the women in this study described their ways of negotiating diabetes care—centrally through diet—as an extension or intensification of their responsibilities for food and feeding of the family prior to the onset of the disease. In this respect, their involvement in diet management of the diabetes constituted a refined skill rather than a newly developed skill.

Skilled Practices

Recognizable skills, defined as "smooth flow" in taking up and managing a situational demand of the diabetes, were evident in couples in this study. Although this interpretation is based on a small sample of informants, initial discussion can begin about how skilled practices in couples working with diabetes can contribute to theories of resiliency in families. In the findings of this study, the couple's relationship was presented as a contextual feature of skill development. In foregrounding skilled practices around diabetes, couple relationship patterns were placed in the background, as if they were a stable structure. Obviously, this was not always the case and was simply a useful device for examining the skill data. However, the Resiliency Model, and couples' statements about themselves, suggest that patterns in couple relationships revise the ways that they take up specific problems or issues that arise in the illness, just as the introduction of new problems and issues from the diabetes revise relationship patterns.

The central contribution that the study of skill might bring to the study of resiliency in families is an appreciation of the open-ended nature of couples' responses to chronic illness. This naturalistic study of skill assumed that families learned *practically* from their experience with the disease, and therefore acquired not only better understandings of the disease over time but also more evolved practices for dealing with each other in the disease. Although longitudinal data would be required to adequately tap changes in skill level over time, couples retrospectively highlighted areas where they had changed or improved their responses to the disease.

The one caution in studying and detailing skill is that the concept might be reduced to mean the rational management of a clearly defined problem, that is, technical skills. Such a reduction might lead to efforts to generate decontextualized lists of skills that couples with diabetes might develop. The risk in this move is that further conceptualization about and eventual development of interventions with families would continue from this abstract position. Rather, I am arguing for a notion of skill that takes into account the actual personal meanings and concerns of the couples involved in responding to the diabetes. The importance of maintaining the couple's meanings and concerns as part of the conceptualization is evident from even a surface consideration of the two exemplary couples presented. The concerns that structure the A. family's habits and skill development are dramatically different from those that structure the action of the Z. family. Although both are seeking long-term health, the ways that the couples negotiate new practices are dramatically different. In managing diet, for example, Mrs. A. develops skills of careful vigilance, coaching, and limit setting with her quite responsive husband. In contrast, Ms. Z. learns that the most helpful response she can make to her partner's diabetes management is to change the household baking and shopping practices, but to otherwise remain uninvolved in his dietary practices.

Outlining areas of skills that have proven important in couples coping with diabetes could help focus further conceptualization and, perhaps, clinical work with these couples. But the nature or "content" of these skills could not be specified, except according to the particular needs and concerns of a particular couple. For example, a conceptual appreciation that renegotiating diet and food practices seemed central to the couples in this study might focus researchers and clinicians on this area of habits and skills in the future. However, to specify certain practices as optimal is a wrong move and diminishes the power of the concept of a skill in the overall understanding of responding to chronic illness.

References

Anderson, R. M., Fitzgerald, J. T., & Oh, M. S. (1993). The relationship between diabetes-related attitudes and patients' self-reported adherence. *Diabetes Educator, 19*, 287–292.

Benner, P. (1994). *Interpretive phenomenology: Embodiment, caring, and ethics in health and illness.* Thousand Oaks, CA: Sage.

Benner, P. E., Tanner, C. A., & Chesla, C. A. (Eds.), (1996). *Expertise in nursing practice: Caring, clinical judgment and ethics.* New York: Springer.

Blechman, E. A., & Delamater, A. M. (1993). Family communication and Type 1 diabetes: A window on the social environment of chronically ill children. In R. E. Cole & D. Reiss (Eds.), *How do families cope with chronic illness?* (pp. 1–24). Hillsdale, NJ: Lawrence Erlbaum.

Bobrow, W. S., AvRuskin, T. W., & Siller, J. (1985). Mother-daughter interactions and adherence to diabetes regimens. *Diabetes Care, 8*, 146–151.

Campbell, T. L. (1986). Family's impact on health: A critical review. *Family Systems Medicine, 4*, 135–328.

Chesla, C. A. (1995). Hermeneutic phenomenology: An approach to understanding families. *Journal of Family Nursing, 1,* 68–78.

Cox, D. J., & Gonder-Frederick, L. (1992). Major developments in behavioral diabetes research. *Journal of Consulting and Clinical Psychology, 60,* 628–638.

DeVault, M. L. (1991). *Feeding the family: The social organization of caring as gendered work.* Chicago: University of Chicago Press.

Dreyfus, H. L. (1979). *What computers can't do; The limits of artificial intelligence.* New York: Harper Colophon Books.

Dreyfus, H. L. (1991). *Being-in-the-world: A commentary on Heidegger's being and time, Division I.* Cambridge: MIT Press.

Dreyfus, H. L., & Dreyfus, S. E. (1996). The relationship of theory and practice in the acquisition of a skill. In P. Benner, C. Tanner & C. Chesla, (Eds.), *Expertise in nursing practice: Caring, clinical judgment and ethics,* (pp. 29–47). New York: Springer.

Dreyfus, H. L., Dreyfus, S. E., & Athanasiou, T. (1986). *Mind over machine: The power of human intuition and expertise in the era of the computer.* New York: Free Press.

Dreyfus, H. L., Dreyfus, S. E., & Benner, P. (1996). Implications of the phenomenology of expertise for teaching and learning everyday skillful ethical comportment. In P. Benner, C. Tanner, & C. Chesla, (Eds.), *Expertise in nursing practice: Caring, clinical judgment and ethics,* (pp. 258–279). New York: Springer.

Fisher, L., Chesla, C., Bartz, R., Gilliss, C., Lutz, C., & Kantor, R. (1994). *Person, provider and family factors in NIDDM.* Grant submitted and funded through NIDDK, NIH, 1995–1998.

Hamera, E., Cassmeyer, V., O'Connell, K. A., Weldon, G. T., Knapp, T. M., & Kyner, J. L. (1988). Self-regulation in individuals with Type II diabetes. *Nursing Research, 37,* 363–367.

Hampson, S. E., Glasgow, R. E., & Toobert, D. J. (1990). Personal models of diabetes and their relations to self care activities. *Health Psychology, 9,* 632–646.

Hansen, C. L., Henggeler, S. W., & Burghen, G. A. (1987). Model of associations between psychosocial variables and health-outcome measures of adolescents with IDDM. *Diabetes Care, 10,* 94–100.

Hansen, C. L., Henggeler, S. W., Harris, M. A., Burghen, G. A., & Moore, M. (1989). Family system variables and the health status of adolescents with insulin-dependent diabetes mellitus. *Health Psychology, 8,* 239–253.

Heidegger, M. (1975/1982). The basic problems of phenomenology. (A. Hofstadter, Trans.). Bloomington: Indiana University Press.

Jacobson, A. M., Hauser, S. T., Lavori, P., Willett, J. B., Cole, C. F., Wolfsdorf, J. I., Dumont, R. H., & Wertlieb, D. (1994). Family environment and glycemic control: A four-year prospective study of children and adolescents with insulin-dependent diabetes mellitus. *Psychosomatic Medicine, 56,* 401–409.

Jayne, R. L. (1993). *Self-regulation: Negotiating treatment regimens in insulin-dependent diabetes.* Unpublished doctoral dissertation, University of California, San Francisco.

Kelleher, D. (1988). Coming to terms with diabetes: Coping strategies and non-compliance. In R. Anderson & M. Bury (Eds.), *Living with chronic illness: The experience of patients and their families.* London: Unwin Hyman.

Krug, L. M., Haire-Joshu, D., & Heady, S. A. (1990). Exercise habits and exercise relapse in persons with non-insulin dependent diabetes mellitus. *Diabetes Educator, 17*(3), 185–188.

McCubbin, M. A., & McCubbin, H. I. (1993). Families coping with illness: The resiliency model of family stress, adjustment and adaptation. In C. Danielson, B. Hamel-Bissell & P. Winstead Fry, (Eds.), *Families, health and illness,* (pp. 21–63). New York: Mosby.

McCubbin, H. I., McCubbin, M. A., Thompson, A. I., & Thompson, E. A. (1995). Resiliency in ethnic families: A conceptual model for predicting family adjustment and adaptation. In H. I. McCubbin, E. A. Thompson, A. I. Thompson, & J. E. Fromer (Eds.), *Resiliency in ethnic minority families. Volume I: Native and immigrant American families*, (pp. 3–48). Madison: University of Wisconsin System.

Nowacek, G., Anderson, R. M., Richards, F., & O'Malley, P. (1986). The relationship of self-concept, to personal meaning and psychosocial adaptation in diabetes. *Diabetes, 35*, 22A.

Nowacek, G. A., O'Malley, P. M., Anderson, R. A., & Richards, F. E. (1990). Testing a model of diabetes self-care management: A causal model analysis with LISREL. *Evaluation and the Health Professions, 13*, 298–314.

O'Connell, K. A., Hamera, E. K., Knapp, T. M., Cassmeyer, V. L., Eaks, G. A., & Fox, M. A. (1984). Symptom use and self-regulation in Type II diabetes. *Advances in Nursing Science, 6*, 19–28.

Packer, M. J., & Addison, R. B. (1991). *Entering the circle: Hermeneutic investigation in psychology*. Albany: SUNY Press.

Peyrot, M., McMurry, J. F., & Hedges, R. (1987). Living with diabetes: The role of personal and professional knowledge in symptom and regimen management. In J. R. Roth & P. Conrad (Eds.), *Research in the sociology of health care: The experience and management of chronic illness*, (Vol. 6, pp. 1–31). Greenwich, CT: JAI.

Peyrot, M., McMurry, J. F., & Hedges, R. (1988). Marital adjustment to adult diabetes: Interpersonal congruence and spouse satisfaction. *Journal of Marriage and the Family, 50*, 363–376.

Price, M. J. (1989). Qualitative analysis of the patient-provider interactions: The patient's perspective. *Diabetes Educator, 15*, 144–148.

Shenkel, R. J., Rogers, J. P., Perfetto, G. M., & Levin, R. A. (1986). Importance of "significant others" in predicting cooperation with diabetic regimen. *International Journal of Psychiatry in Medicine, 15*, 447–468.

Taylor, C. (1985). *Human agency and language: Philosophical papers I.* New York: Cambridge University Press.

Wikblad, K. F., Wibel, L. B., & Montin, K. R. (1990). The patient's experience of diabetes and its treatment: Construction of an attitude scale by semantic differential technique. *Journal of Advanced Nursing, 15*, 1083–1091.

5

Resiliency in Families With a Member Facing AIDS

Elizabeth A. Thompson

Since the onset of the Acquired Immunodeficiency Syndrome (AIDS) crisis in the early 1980s, AIDS-related social science research has attempted to identify and address the numerous stressors faced by Persons with AIDS (PWAs). Although significant attention has been paid to the role of social support in coping with AIDS-related stressors, including physical and mental health concerns and social stigmatization, much of the research has focused on an individualized analysis of the social support needs of PWAs without an adequate understanding of the social contexts in which they live. Families of origin, families of procreation/choice, significant others, friends, and communities have all been identified as potential sources of social support for PWAs, but the research on the constructions of meaning by those potential sources of social support around the issue of an HIV/AIDS diagnosis, and their perceptions of and willingness to fulfill social support needs, has been limited. The stigma that has surrounded the social construction of meaning for the human immunodeficiency virus (HIV) and AIDS presents a unique challenge to family studies. Much of the early social science research on people with HIV/AIDS has reflected the social stigma of the disease and has evolved from a "blame the victim" model (Anderson, 1992; Geis & Fuller, 1986). As such, PWAs as individuals became the focus, and the effects of HIV/AIDS on families were overshadowed.

Research is needed to examine the many diverse relationships affected by the AIDS crisis. The experiences of families of origin, families of procreation/choice, significant others, friends, and communities in response to the diagnosis and progression of HIV/AIDS, and the relationships between these various and often interconnecting sources of support, have not been addressed adequately. All of these potential sources of support deserve in-depth attention to illuminate the distinctive roles they play in the lives of PWAs. This study focuses on the mothers of adults living with AIDS, and the mothers' constructions of meaning around the issue of their adult children's HIV/AIDS diagnosis.

The issues presented in this chapter represent data from interviews conducted with 13 mothers of adult PWAs. The participants for this project were recruited in collaboration with two metropolitan AIDS service organizations in the Midwest.

Previous Literature on Families of PWAs

Little focus has been given to the involvement of families of origin in the social support and care of adult PWAs. The previous literature on family of origin has cited abandonment by the family of origin as a common experience for PWAs (Bennett, 1990; Christ, Siegel, & Moynihan, 1988; Weitz, 1990) without examining the experience of AIDS from the perspective of the family.

Within the issues pertaining to the PWA's family of origin, the active support and caregiving role of the PWA's mother has often been discussed. In interviewing patients with AIDS about the stressors related to HIV/AIDS, patients named disclosure to family of origin as the second most severe stressor of living with AIDS, and PWAs reported that informing their mother of the diagnosis was "the most dreaded" aspect of disclosure (Duffy, 1994). O'Donnell and Bernier (1991) found that mothers and other female relatives were more willing to assume the active support and caregiver role for an adult child with AIDS. In a qualitative study with 25 male and female PWAs, Laryea and Gien (1993) found that all of the male PWAs interviewed (n = 19) reported rejection or distancing by their male relatives, but the male PWAs all reported that female relatives were generally more willing to provide emotional and practical support. All of the PWAs interviewed reported attitudes of acceptance from their mothers (Laryea & Gien, 1993). Brander and Norton (1993) found that female caregivers to PWAs "viewed their involvement as inevitable, rather than a deliberate choice to care" (p. 53).

Contradictory findings about the family of origin's involvement with the PWA have emerged in the literature. Stuhlberg and Buckingham (1988) assert that the majority of families of origin are involved in providing social support on some level, whereas another study of 42 PWAs found that 26 of the participants had minimal or no contact with their family of origin (Christ et al. 1988). In addition to finding a lack of family of origin network support for PWAs, Christ et al. (1988) found that the families of origin were unreliable sources of emotional and instrumental support. Clearly, the level of network support and the degree to which the family of origin is involved with the PWA varies significantly.

If the family of origin has a high fear of contagion or reflects high levels of AIDS stigma based on lifestyle/group criteria (i.e., homophobia or moral censure of IV drug use), their willingness to embrace the PWA as a valued and esteemed network member may be limited (O'Donnell & Bernier, 1990; Rowe, Plum, & Crossman, 1988; Takigaku, Brubaker, & Hennon, 1993). The literature has cited many examples of PWAs whose families felt torn between a feeling that they should provide network connections for the ill member and a feeling that they should reject the ill member to protect other family members from exposure (Bennett, 1990; Weitz, 1990, 1991).

The isolation of the PWA from network support provided by the family of origin is often cited as an additional stressor for PWAs (Bennett, 1990; Robinson, 1994; Weitz, 1990). Some have argued that the prevalence of AIDS among IV drug users and homosexual men increases the possibility that some PWAs may have been previously estranged from family of origin network support (Raveis & Siegel, 1991; Tiblier, Walker, & Rolland, 1989). Isolation is associated with feelings of shame, guilt, helplessness, and loneliness for the PWA (Bennett, 1990; Crandall & Coleman, 1992; Nicholson & Long, 1990; Robinson, 1994; Zich & Temoshok, 1987). Crandall and Coleman (1992) found that PWAs who reported a postdiagnosis loss of network support also reported higher levels of AIDS stigma, anxiety, and depression. Crandall and Coleman (1992) assert that AIDS-related stigma is a primary factor in the social isolation of the PWA. They suggest that the shame related to the stigmatization of AIDS can cause PWAs to withdraw socially. Furthermore, they contend that "the loss of support may be a self-fulfilling prophecy in some cases, where the expectation of no support causes an infected person to withdraw from the source of support in anticipation" (p. 165).

The isolation of the family of origin in coping with the diagnosis of AIDS has also been frequently cited in the literature (Christ et al. 1988; Roberts, Severinsen, kuehn, Straker, & Fritz, 1992). Some families of origin isolate themselves due to the fear of possible social repercussions that might follow from a disclosure of AIDS (Aranda-Naranjo, 1992; Kelly & Sykes, 1989; Raveis & Siegel, 1991; Rinella & Dubin, 1988). In a study of caregivers to PWAs, Brown and Powell-

Cope (1991) found that biological familial caregivers cited the risk of public disclosure as both a personal and a social issue. Kelly and Sykes (1989) found that families of PWAs feared social rejection due to the stigma associated with AIDS, and parallel to findings for PWAs, the families reported isolating themselves so as to not be socially ostracized. Parental caregivers reported the experience of discrimination due to their association with the PWA, and they expressed fear over a "guilt by association" reaction from members of their social groups (Brown & Powell-Cope, 1991). The isolation of the family, and the inability of familial caregivers to acquire social support in coping with their own experiences of stress, may have an impact on the family of origin's ability or willingness to provide adequate social support to the PWA (Raveis & Siegel, 1991; Rinella & Dubin, 1988; Roberts et al., 1992). Atkins and Amenta (1991) contend that the stigma associated with AIDS additionally served to discourage family members from offering network support to PWAs.

The role of the family of origin in providing instrumental support to the PWA may be limited by several factors. First, the family of origin's available resources (financial resources, ability to perform tasks, etc.) may not be sufficient to meet the PWA's instrumental needs (McDonnell, Abell, & Miller, 1991). Second, the family of origin who possesses instrumental resources may not be willing to commit those resources to the PWA because of interpersonal conflicts with the PWA or a hesitancy to strain the family's resources for the PWA's care (Bonuck, 1993; McDonnell et al., 1991). Frierson (1987) posited that fear of contagion may also be a determinant in whether or not the family of origin is willing to offer nonfinancial and task-oriented instrumental support (i.e., housing, doing housework, doing laundry, etc.). An additional consideration in determining whether or not the family of origin is a viable source of instrumental care is their geographical proximity to the PWA (Bonuck, 1993; Kubler-Ross, 1987).

Although prediagnosis discord in the family of origin is cited as a possible deterrent to the family of origin's willingness to provide instrumental support to the PWA, it is not a universal predictor. In a qualitative study of PWAs, Weitz (1990) presents, for example, the case of a homosexual PWA whose fundamentalist Christian family of origin, despite their disapproval of his lifestyle, "provided him with housing, money and emotional support once they learned of his illness" (p. 24). Some authors have suggested that when the family of origin is faced with an ultimately terminal illness, they may be able to focus on the illness and hardship facing the PWA rather than on preexisting family conflicts (Kubler-Ross, 1987; Levine, 1990). In cases where the family of origin disapproves of the PWA's lifestyle or sexual preference, the reality of losing a family member may outweigh their feelings about that member's lifestyle.

The literature suggests that the family of origin may assume an active role in caregiving out of affective ties to the PWA or out of a sense of familial obligation to care (Takigaku et al., 1993). Caplan (1974) asserted that family-based support systems are not always developed through affective ties but rather "most cultures develop definite rules that legislate the reciprocal obligation that bind kinsfolk together, irrespective of their individual feelings about each other" (p. 8). The consideration of the social pressure on the PWA's family of origin to provide care has been negated in the literature by a focus on the social pressure *not* to care that has been communicated through AIDS stigma (O'Donnell & Bernier, 1990). Some have argued that AIDS stigma has overshadowed the expected familial sense of obligation to provide care for an ill member (O'Donnell & Bernier, 1990; Takigaku et al.).

Social Constructionist Theoretical Perspective

The focus on an individual's feelings, experiences, and perceptions of an event is consistent with a social constructionist theoretical perspective. Berger and Luckmann (1966) posited that knowledge must be understood as a subjective reality "developed, transmitted and maintained in social situations", and as such, knowledge must be understood as the "processes by which this is done in such a way that a taken-for-granted 'reality' congeals in the street. . . . The sociology of knowledge is concerned with the analysis of the social construction of reality" (p. 3). Guba and Lincoln (1994) assert that constructivism is best understood as a relativist perspective, and the emergent and alterable reality is a social and material construction. Schwandt, citing the work of Gergen, set forth that the world must be understood in terms that are "social artifacts, products of historically situated interchanges among people" (Schwandt, 1994, p. 127).

A constructionist perspective maintains that individuals are meaning constructors, and the significance of those meanings must be understood as contextually embedded. Schwandt (1994) contends that the construction of knowledge must be understood as an active process in which the individual meaning constructor invents "concepts, models, and schemes to make sense of experience and, further, we continually test and modify these constructions in the light of new experience" (pp. 125–126).

Additionally, as asserted by Guba and Lincoln (1994), the use of a constructionist perspective in social science inquiry acknowledges the relative nature of an individual's construction of meaning: A social constructionist perspective (Guba & Lincoln, 1994, p. 111) assumes that,

> realities are apprehendable in the form of multiple, intangible mental constructions, socially and experientially based, local and specific in nature. . . and dependent in their form and content on the individual persons or groups holding the constructions. Constructions are not more or less "true," in any absolute sense, but simply are more or less informed and/or sophisticated. Constructions are alterable, as are their associated realities.

Therefore, the goal of social constructionist inquiries is not to uncover the "truth" but rather to uncover the significance and meaning of an event for the individual who is experiencing it (Schwandt, 1994). A social constructionist perspective accepts the possibility of multiple meanings attributed to the same event, dependent on the previous experiences and knowledge brought to the event by the meaning constructors. Furthermore, the social constructionist perspective acknowledges that an individual's construction of meaning of a single event is not necessarily constant and unalterable, and an individual's construction of meaning around the event must be understood as contextually embedded and located in a specific period of time. For example, an individual may construct one meaning of an event at the time the event happens (e.g., initial meaning of the event), but he or she may attribute a different or more interpretively complex meaning to the event at a later time (e.g., influenced by additional experience gained since the event or influenced by the experience of processing one's reactions to the initial event). Guba and Lincoln (1994) set forth that the goal of inquiry from a constructivist perspective is "understanding and reconstruction of the constructions people (including the inquirer) initially hold, aiming toward consensus but still open to new interpretations as information and sophistication improve" (p. 113).

Methodology

In order to uncover the significance and meaning of an AIDS diagnosis and progression for mothers of PWAs, this project uses a semi-structured, in-depth interview method. Three primary forms of interviews can be identified: structured, unstructured, and semi-structured. The structured interview, as defined by Fontana and Frey, refers to an interview wherein the questions and possible range of responses are preset, and "there is generally little room for variation" (Fontana & Frey, 1994, p. 363). Structured interview techniques are seldom used in qualitative methods, because this technique assumes that, as May (1991) asserts, "the investigator already knows the salient parameters of the topic," and this assumption violates the "underlying philosophy and the major goal of discovery" of qualitative research (May, 1991, p. 191). The unstructured, or unstandardized, interview does not rely upon fixed interview questions (Berg, 1989). The assumption underlying the unstructured interview is that the researcher cannot know what questions are appropriate in advance, and because questions do not have the same meaning for all participants, the interviewer must develop questions and adapt probes that are specific to the present interview situation (Berg, 1989; Fontana & Frey, 1994).

The third interview type, the semi-structured, in-depth interview, is commonly used in qualitative research (May, 1991). Semi-structured interviews, as defined by May (1991), "are defined as those organized around areas of particular interest, while still allowing considerable flexibility in scope and depth" (May, 1991; p. 191). In the semi-structured interview, the interviewer maintains the freedom to digress and probe as novel categories emerge (Berg, 1989; McCracken, 1988). The semi-structured interview allows the researcher to obtain data from all respondents on key subjects while allowing the respondents the flexibility to define those subjects within their own contextual understanding.

The interview for this project centers around general themes and topics from previous social science research on HIV/AIDS, including issues related to AIDS stigma, familial social support to the PWA, the social support available to the family of origin, maternal reactions to the diagnosis, maternal roles in caregiving, maternal knowledge of HIV/AIDS, and maternal feelings and perceptions around the issue of AIDS. The interview schedule is viewed as an evolving and emergent tool, congruent with the grounded theory method of data analysis (Charmaz, 1988). As initial categories are identified in the coding of the data, the interview schedule for subsequent interviews is refined to reflect those categories (May, 1991).

Demographics

The 13 mothers interviewed for this project ranged from 47 to 82 years of age (median age 64.9 years), and the ages of their adult children with AIDS ranged from 27 to 45 years of age (median age 37.5 years). All of the mothers interviewed identified themselves as Caucasian. Four of the mothers were currently married; five were widowed; one was divorced; and three were divorced and remarried, not to the biological father of the PWA. Two of the mothers inter-

viewed shared a home with their son/daughter with AIDS, 10 of the
PWAs lived in their own homes, and one lived in a nursing home.
Two of the families had multiple members who had faced or were
facing AIDS. One of the mothers interviewed, in addition to her gay
son who is currently living with AIDS, had previously lost a son, also
to AIDS. Another mother was currently dealing with a daughter and
son-in-law who are both infected.

Of the 13 adult children with HIV/AIDS, 11 were male, and two were
female. The majority of the PWAs are identified as gay males, one is
heterosexual and married with a child, one is heterosexual and married with no children, one is bisexual with a history of intravenous
drug use, one is bisexual and married, and the final PWA is a former
intravenous drug user who is divorced with a child. Medically, at the
time of the interviews, one of the adult children was classified as HIV
positive, and the rest (n = 12) were defined as having progressed to
AIDS.

Conceptualizing Resiliency

McCubbin and colleagues (1998) have defined resiliency as "the positive behavioral patterns and functional competence individuals and
families demonstrate under stressful or adverse circumstances" as
well as the families' development of coping strategies and the meaning given to stressful life events (p. xvi). In terms of research on
families with a member facing AIDS, much of the existing social
science research has cited abandonment by the family of origin as a
common experience for PWAs, and the research has not focused on
the families who have remained actively involved in the social support and care of the PWA. Therefore, all of the mothers interviewed
for this project are identified as actively involved with their adult
child facing AIDS.

This chapter focuses on the creation of maternal coping strategies
and the creation of personal meaning around an HIV/AIDS diagnosis
and progression for mothers of adult sons and daughters with AIDS.

Maternal Concepts of Coping

A major category emerging in the data is the mother's concept of
coping by "taking one day at a time" without allowing herself to dwell
on the future. This is best illustrated by one mother who asserts that

> what we do is we take each day as it comes, and if that day gets
> good, then we'll go on to the next one. And that day, if that's good,
> then hey, we just go on to the next one. That's the only way to

handle it. I can't, I can't plan ahead, 'cause I don't know what's gonna happen.

Although participants acknowledge the progression of their children's illness, many expressed a need to resist allowing themselves to think too far into the future. As one mother expressed,

> Sometimes I think to myself, well, you know, you see him to this point now where it is getting harder for him to keep up. . . you think . . . how much longer is it gonna be until he can't—you know it goes through your mind, and then I think, you can't worry about what hasn't happened, you know, you have to take it as it goes.

As these mothers acknowledge, the progression of AIDS is not predictable, and the use of a day-to-day coping strategy helps to manage the experience of uncertainty. The social science literature has pointed to the uncertainty surrounding the progression of AIDS as a major factor in an individual's formulation of a framework for coping (Brown & Powell-Cope, 1991; Weitz, 1991). In a study of PWAs, Weitz (1991) found that individuals facing AIDS manage the uncertainty of their own illness by developing frameworks that help to normalize AIDS. Likewise, the mothers interviewed for this project recognized the uncertainty related to AIDS, and they have developed coping strategies that take the uncertainty into account.

Emotional Management

A dimension related to the uncertainty of the progression of HIV/ AIDS addresses how mothers of PWAs manage their emotions and feelings. For these mothers, the management of emotions can be both a personal and a relational concept. The expression of emotions serves as a personal stress release for mothers, but it is also important for the maintenance of connections to their son or daughter with AIDS and to other members of the family. Mothers tended to stress strategies that helped them to emotionally put their house in order, expressing a need to participate in daily emotional housekeeping. In addition to expressing their own feelings, mothers stressed the importance of discussing and settling problems with the PWA as they arose, and mothers took a proactive role in facilitating those discussions. This is illustrated by one mother in describing the resolution of a conflict with her son facing AIDS:

> He told his sister that he thought that sometimes we weren't as understanding as he thought we should be. So, when my husband was watching t.v. and my daughter had left on Sunday. . . I went downstairs and I said, "Do you want to talk," you know, and I said, "You know, if it seems like sometimes we don't listen and we're not

as understanding as we should be," I said, "we apologize, and maybe we are, but we're preoccupied, and I'm sorry, you know.". . . So, we talked. And he says sometimes he feels very frustrated, he gets clumsy, he drops things, and he doesn't feel good, and he just doesn't feel that he has anybody to talk to. And I said, "Well, you know, when you feel that way, just say 'hey, I'm having a bad day, I feel bad, I want to talk or I don't want to talk.' Just let us know how you feel." And, so, it was good, we talked for a long time and I think he felt better.

The majority of mothers interviewed cited the experience of AIDS as a catalyst to improved communication with their son or daughter. The desire for emotionally putting one's house in order is related to the unpredictable progression of the PWA's illness in that it is difficult for mothers to know what tomorrow will bring. By striving to achieve a sense of closure at the end of each day and in resolving conflicts as they arise, mothers seemed able to alleviate their own stress as well as attain a sense of closure with their son or daughter. As one mother set forth, her son's experience with AIDS has made her recognize the need for daily expression of emotions. She asserted, "You never know when you say goodbye to someone in the morning if you're gonna see them that night, and so tell 'em you love 'em and give 'em a kiss."

Determining Maternal Roles in Caregiving

Defining the maternal role in caregiving for the PWA emerged as a major issue in coping for mothers. Each of the mothers had formulated or implemented a general framework for her role in providing care to her adult child with AIDS. In creating the framework for care or future care, the mother often called upon preexisting paradigms of family illness in outlining her own responsibilities for care. Participants compared their roles in caring for their son or daughter with AIDS with examples of their roles in other serious illnesses in the family. In describing her son's recent hospitalization, one mother remarked, "I took his dirty clothing home and had it washed. You know, did all the things you do when a member of your family is in the hospital. So that's what I did." For other mothers, their role definition in caring for the PWA was compared to or emerged from their previous roles in caring for elderly mothers or other terminally ill family members.

Although all of the mothers interviewed saw themselves as a major source of support and care for the PWA, in general, they saw themselves as supervisors for the professional care needed by the PWA or as auxiliary care in support of primary or professional caregivers. Most of the mothers did not provide or anticipate providing hands-on caregiving for their son or daughter with AIDS. One parent, whose daughter is living in a nursing home, provided occasional assistance with her daughter's personal grooming needs, but she did not see those roles as her primary responsibility.   Mothers' definitions of their own roles reflected their own caregiving abilities and their definitions of a sense of boundaries around the issue of care. As one mother described this supervisory role:

> I advocate to make sure he gets the services he needs, and I coordinate them. If they don't get done, I do them, and try to get them back on track to get them done. Early on, I was doing everything, you know, I was cleaning his apartment, doing the laundry, doing all the grocery shopping, which I still do, um, cleaning the litter box for his cat, and I was going crazy. And then [his significant other] came into his life, and he's been there since August, and um, he's doing the cleaning and the cooking and emptying the litter box, and then they bring the laundry over here and do the laundry, and they stay here on the weekends. . . basically what I try to do is let them be as independent as possible, but we work together as a team. And [his significant other] will tell me when he needs my help—he'll call me. . . . We have real good communication, so I guess, basically, I see myself as coordinator of services, you know, and Mom.

In adopting a secondary or supervisory role, the mother plays an active role in caring for the the PWA while recognizing her own limitations in providing care. The older mothers in the study expressed concern about their abilities to provide care due to age-related limitations. One mother recognized the uncertainty of her future caregiving abilities: "I can't be much help to him that way. You know, I'm 68, how much longer am I gonna be able to drive myself up there?" Another mother suggested that the long-term nature of the AIDS progression added to the uncertainty of her abilities to be a caregiver for her son. "I think about if he should get bedridden that I would be able to help some. But each year I get older, I can't do as much as I used to, and I just figure I would help out where I could." For the older mothers, the use of professional caregivers was seen as a replacement for care they were unable to provide or might not be able to provide in the future due to age-related limitations.

The participants' frameworks for caregiving often reflected an assessment of both the physical and emotional needs of the PWAs. The son's or daughter's wishes were taken into consideration by the mothers in assessing their own caregiving role. As one mother expressed:

> What's gonna happen if he needs the care? I don't know. I don't know if I'll be able to do it, I don't know. He wants to stay at home,

> he wants to die at home. So, I don't know, but I, I know you can get special beds, I know the nurses society will come in, uh, there are. . . aids for them.

Other mothers pointed to the need to maintain the PWAs' personal dignity and independence by allowing them to determine when they needed assistance from the mother. One mother explained, "I let her more or less decide what she needs, but I kinda look after her here." Another mother, describing a similar strategy of respecting her son's independence, set forth that respecting those boundaries was sometimes difficult:

> It's kind of like when he was 9 years old and took off on his bicycle, you know, and. . . you know that you have to let him go, and you don't really want to, but you know, it's kind of like that. . . you got to let him go and you got to let him try to do what he's going to do within reason, taking the dementia into consideration, and then let it go.

Other mothers recognized the need for professional care as a buffer for their own stress and as a way by which to maintain their own sense of normalcy. For one mother, the decision to place her daughter in a nursing home reflected the care needs of the PWA as well as the personal needs of the mother. She remarked,

> No, I'm not gonna do that. I'm not gonna devote my whole time to [her] I have a life, and it is not totally taking care of [her]. . . it is totally not being, uh, with [her] 24 hours a day. I could not handle it.

The use of professional caregivers, such as visiting nurses or volunteer caregivers from the local AIDS project, gave mothers a respite from their caregiving roles while allowing the PWA to maintain a sense of autonomy and dignity in managing his or her own illness.

Making Future Plans

Although the uncertainty related to AIDS makes it difficult for mothers to plan ahead on a daily basis, the mothers are involved in making future plans for inevitable events. Mothers were actively involved in planning for funerals and burials and in making contingency plans, such as preparing to take leaves of absence from work when the PWA's condition deteriorated. Additionally, mothers were actively involved in helping the PWA to settle financial affairs, encouraging the PWA to write a will or to make plans for the dispersal of property; and encouraging the PWA to make decisions about his or her medical care in the end stage of the AIDS progression, including writing a living will or contracting for care with a hospice.

Some mothers expressed frustration when their son or daughter was resistant to completing future plans. One mother illustrated her frustration with her son's lack of planning: "Sometimes, I just want to say 'Damn it all. . . you gotta do this!'" Similarly, another mother related her experience of encouraging her son to make plans for medical care.

> I had to back off from sending stuff, information to him. . . . I'm highlighting and sending much less stuff to him. I think he would have been as—standoffish is not quite the right word, but he doesn't want to be enfolded to my motherly bosom . . . Maybe there will be a time, but he wants to be independent and, uh, doesn't want me to interfere too much.

For most mothers, their frustration with incomplete plans was tempered by an understanding of how difficult it was for their son or daughter to make those plans. Mothers expressed understanding for their son's or daughter's struggle over creating future care plans, in that those plans might suggest that the son's or daughter's health status had deteriorated. Mothers also came to the realization that they needed to respect their son or daughter as an adult who is able to make his or her own decisions. This boundary issue is best expressed by one mother who explained: "I think it's something like admitting that he hit the point where he's gonna need that help, and he doesn't want to admit it? He doesn't want to admit it yet, to himself, I think. . . you can't push him, you can *suggest*, but if you try to push him into something, he just gets stubborn."

When future plans were created, several positive aspects came out of planning for mothers, including the ability to give the PWA input into the settlement of his or her own affairs, as well as a sense of security for the mother that the PWA's wishes were respected. In some cases, the PWA's wishes were respected even if those wishes were in conflict with the mother's ideas. For example, one mother spoke of her son's desire to be cremated and of her plans to carry out his wishes despite the fact that cremation was against the family's religious faith. Additionally, there is a sense of relief for mothers when those necessary and unavoidable plans are finalized.

Participants discussed making plans for things they know that they will have to take care of without dwelling on the emotional meaning of those plans. Planning for the future is separated from a sense of emotionally living in the future. As one mother explained:

> Well, I think about it, but I don't dwell, I don't dwell on those, you kind of, in your mind prepare for things that you might have to take care of but you don't think emotionally how you're gonna feel because . . . I don't think it would be fair to either [my son] or my husband, if I did this, because you have today, and yes, we're all going to die, some know that they're gonna die earlier, but if you dwell on that, you miss today.

Similarly, another mother who had already created care plans for her son with a hospice asserted:

> I try to stay in today. . . . When I think about, you know, what is inevitable, my mind immediately shuts down and switches back to today. . . . I'm not in denial, I know what's coming, I can see it . . . but I'm just really trying to enjoy what we have today.

The focus on living in the moment is an important dimension of the general category of taking one day at a time. The focus on the present leads to a sense of reactive coping, or coping focused on day-to-day crisis management. As one mother explained,

> I just think about getting through the day rather than, you know, what's gonna happen. . . . As the problems occur, then I react to it. Not, you know, dwell on "Oh, what if this happened or what if that happened?" I just don't think about it.

Similarly, another mother asserted, "I guess, whatever stress comes along with it we just cope with as we go along." Reactive coping allows the mother to deal with the problems at hand without dwelling on hypothetical scenarios of the future.

When mothers do make plans for the future, both personal plans and plans that involve the PWA, they tend to employ flexibility as a strategy to cope with unavoidable changes in plans related to the PWA's illness. One mother gave an example of this strategy, saying,

> I'm planning to go to Florida in January, and, uh, of course, maybe it would be different if . . . he wasn't as good as he is. But, uh, you know, I just feel, well, I can get on a plane and come home in a day if I have to, and like I say, he is so good right now that—if he was, if he was really sick, I wouldn't even think of going.

Another mother recounted the use of flexibility during a recent weekend visit with her son, saying,

> We had some things planned that we were going to do, but he had chemo on Friday and was real sick, wasn't keeping food down, and,

uh, and so we didn't go out and do anything, we just rented some videos and stayed home, but I was there.

In a study of individuals facing chronic illness, Charmaz (1991) found that coping strategies based on living day to day allowed chronically ill people to focus on the present without the stress of unfulfilled future goals. Similarly, the ability of these mothers to use a strategy of flexibility in planning allows advanced planning to occur without placing unnecessary stress on themselves or the PWA.

For these mothers, the focus on living in the present moment and the appreciation and enjoyment of each day with their son or daughter with AIDS is accompanied by a changed sense of progress and success. The participants measure success for the son or daughter in smaller, daily events such as throwing a party for friends, planting a garden, attending a local parade or cooking a meal, rather than the fulfillment of long-term goals.

Although these reactive coping styles might be defined in the general stress and coping literature as Passive or Avoidant Coping, in the face of an illness progression that is as unique as the individual who faces it, the focus on day-to-day life, the emphasis on living in the moment, and the ability to be flexible seems to help to maintain a sense of normalcy for both the mother and the son or daughter with AIDS. The focus on living one day at a time suggests an acknowledgment of the uncertainty of AIDS and can be defined as an active coping strategy designed to manage that uncertainty.

Reframing the Experience of AIDS

The concept of resiliency can be further discussed in terms of the participants' abilities to reframe their understanding of AIDS and to identify positive aspects of the experience. Although the majority of the participants expressed sadness or a sense of inevitability about the anticipated loss of their son or daughter, as well as a sense of uncertainty or dread about their lives after their son's or daughter's death, many of the mothers could also identify positive aspects of their experiences. These positive reframings of the experience of AIDS centered around the issues of connectedness, reconnectedness, and personal growth, as well as the ability to connect a spiritual or political significance to the experience.

Connectedness

Many participants suggested that the experience of AIDS had made them feel more connected to their son or daughter. Examples of this connectedness can be seen in the value that mothers place on spending time with the PWA and the use of this time to gain a new appreciation of or to learn new things about the PWA. One mother, whose son has been an active AIDS educator, spoke of gaining a new appreciation of her son during his illness.

> Since he's been home now, and we've gotten close . . . I don't believe there is anything that you can ask [him] to do but what he can't do it! He's just one of those people . . . I just didn't know this . . . and I had that opportunity to learn it.

The majority of mothers also shared some activities or interests with their son or daughter, and they gained a sense of enjoyment and connectedness from pursuing these shared interests. Examples of shared activities include cooking, crafts, shopping, music, art, gardening, talking about politics, or even attending AA meetings together. In many cases, the shared activities allowed a mother to learn from the expertise of her adult son or daughter and added to her knowledge and appreciation of her son or daughter as a person.

Renewing Strained Relationships

For some mothers, an AIDS diagnosis served as a catalyst to renewing a strained relationship with their son or daughter. For example, two mothers whose children had been intravenous drug users were able to establish a closer relationship after the AIDS diagnosis because their children were no longer using drugs. As the mother of a former IV drug user explained,

> This has been really kind of a blessing and kind of a tragedy, because I have my son back—temporarily. You know, he put down the needle last February, so, he has been free of the needle for almost a year now, he's also . . . he quit drinking . . . he's been sober since August, so he's got four and a half months sober as well, so, he doesn't have the chemicals other than what they prescribed to him for pain management. So, I have my son back, but he's dying. But at least, we're having the opportunity to make all these memories and to say all the things that we needed to say. For the first time in his life since he left home he's got his own apartment, he's got his own furniture, he's got nice things, for the first time—and he is so happy.

For other mothers, the diagnosis of HIV brought an adult child back into the family who had previously been emotionally distant. One mother of a gay son saw his AIDS diagnosis as a catalyst to renewing a previously strained relationship;

> I think we are closer, in that respect it has brought us back—We were always close before when he was younger, and when he was a teen we did a lot of things as a family, we went camping, and out to dinner, and we traveled and it was just that when he became a young adult and he was, I think, trying to hide the fact that he was gay and he didn't face the issue at that time.

Similarly, another mother of a gay son with AIDS saw her son's illness as a motivation to become more accepting of her son's significant other. In discussing working with her son's significant other to manage her son's care, she said, "I think it will probably be a growing experience for me. . . . I'll have to be more accepting. I'm trying to be now, but I have to say, it is hard."

For six of the families, the HIV/AIDS diagnosis had brought the son or daughter home after a geographic separation. For most of these families, the concept of "coming home" did not involve the PWA residing in the parent's house but reflected a sense of renewed involvement between the son or daughter and the family of origin. The concept of coming home consisted of both the geographic or residential relocation of the son or daughter as well as a component of emotionally redefining the relationship between the son or daughter and the family of origin. Coming home was viewed as a positive adaptation to HIV/AIDS for these mothers. As one mother set forth, having her son nearby during his illness was less stressful for her: "I'm more comfortable about it, um hmm. Not that I'm trying to take control of it or anything, but mothers do have that tendency to wanna be sure they're safe, and I feel like he's safer here." Other mothers suggested that having their son or daughter geographically close to the family of origin strengthened the relationship, which had been less active due to geographic separation.

For some mothers, the terminal nature of AIDS led to a reassessment of their relationship with their son or daughter. Their previous objections to their son's or daughter's lifestyle choices became secondary to the present reality of the illness. In the literature on parents of PWAs, some maintain that a focus on illness allows a parent to be actively involved with the son or daughter without addressing preexisting conflicts over lifestyle issues (Levine, 1990; Weitz, 1991). Others have suggested that the illness of the PWA may separate them from those lifestyle issues that had been problematic for the family of origin—for example, a homosexual son may not be actively dating because of AIDS-related illness, or an IV drug user may be forced to give up drugs in order to seek AIDS-related medical treatment (Weitz, 1991). For several of these mothers, however, involvement in their son's or daughter's illness meant a needed acceptance or tolerance of those lifestyle issues that they had previously found objectionable.

Although participants felt that their son's or daughter's illness had brought their adult child more closely into the family, they also asserted that the family had a shared sense of obligation or responsibility to care for a sick member. For the majority of the participants interviewed, a sense of responsibility to care for the PWA was shared by multiple family members, including the other parent, siblings, extended family, and, in some cases, close family friends, and for most of these mothers, the responsibility for caregiving and social support involved multiple family members. This sense of group cooperation or cohesiveness in support of the PWA served as a respite for the primary caregiver, whether that primary caregiver is the mother or another significant person, and the support between family members is an effective coping strategy in dealing with the AIDS diagnosis in the family. Other family members provide emotional support for the mother, as well as emotionally and practically supporting the PWA. One mother, who fulfills a primary support role for her daughter who has AIDS, spoke of the emotional support she received from one of her sons: "He worries about me. He says, 'Mom, I worry about what's happening to you. 'Cause we want *you* around for a long time,' you know." Another mother spoke of the important role that her other son plays in emotionally supporting both her and the son with AIDS. When she feels stress about her son's illness, she describes the positive aspects of her other son's support of her: As she explains, her son reassures her, saying, "'I feel the same way. What can I do? Can I come down? Can I help you?' and then I don't feel so alone."

The experience of having a family member with AIDS can also be defined as a shared growth experience for the family that affects the communication and interaction patterns in the family. As illustrated by one mother, "I think it's been a real growth process, I think we are probably more accepting of one another's differences." Other mothers define the experience as unifying for the family:

> I hate to say this, but I think it has been a real blessing. I think our family is closer than it's ever been, I really do. . . . My husband and I are closer, I mean, he and [my son] were estranged and he didn't want me to bring [him] home. And they're just like this now. . . and I'm just surprised.

Facing Family Conflicts

Not all of these families share a unified understanding of the meaning of the AIDS diagnosis. In some families, the AIDS diagnosis has
caused divisions between the two parents or between the parent and
the PWA's siblings. Some mothers spoke of sibling anger or even
jealousy over the attention given to the PWA. When the family does
not have a shared commitment to the care of the PWA, the mothers
describe the need to restructure the family boundaries and roles in
order for them to remain actively involved in the care of the PWA.
For example, in several families, the nonsupportive members were
not expected or called upon to offer caregiving or support. One mother
described a confrontation she was planning with an unsupportive
sibling of the PWA. She intended to tell her unsupportive son, "Look,
you're either behind us in this, and you're gonna be part of the process, or you're out of it, and we'll see you when it's over." The redefinition of family boundaries or the development of factions within the
family, for this parent, reflected the need to minimize the conflicts
surrounding her son with AIDS. Her son was a person who faced
serious dementia related to AIDS and did not handle excessive conflict well. In explaining the willingness to exclude her other son, she
said, "The stress is too much for all of us." Congruent with other
coping strategies, the parent's willingness to redefine the family boundaries gives central focus to the needs and support of the PWA.

For other families, the redefinition of family boundaries is more positive, allowing a broader definition of family to emerge. In so doing,
close friends or significant others of the PWA were granted "familylike"
status in providing caregiving and support, and families of origin and
significant others in these cases could function as a more unified
group in facing the AIDS progression. For several mothers who are
members of community AIDS support groups, the other group members were defined as providing familylike support or were granted
familylike status in their importance to the mothers. One mother
described her support group as providing support that was not available from her own relatives: "I mean, I really don't have, I don't have
the—like people have families, I got my support group. That's my
family. I don't have a family like people have to go to." Comparably,
another mother defined her support group as filling a support need
that was not available from her family or friends:

> There's no one else for me to really talk about it . . . my two friends
> have now gone, passed away. And, uh, there isn't anyone else except
> my husband, and as I say, he won't say probably two sentences . . . so
> I go to them because they're like my relatives, they're like my family.

Experiencing Personal Growth

In addition to reframing the AIDS diagnosis in terms of interpersonal growth, many participants identified this experience in terms of their personal growth as well. The experience of parenting a PWA served as a challenge to their personal beliefs, priorities, definitions of roles, and definitions of personal abilities. Many participants cited this experience as expanding their abilities to be compassionate and understanding of others: "I think it made me much more tolerant, much more accepting of people with differences. I hope so." Another mother echoed this perspective:

> I feel like I am becoming a better person . . . becoming more tolerant and compassionate. It's like, the little trivial things are not that important . . . it's showing me what is really important in this life and it's not things, you know, it's people and love . . . it's not what you get in this life, it's what you give, and that is becoming more and more of a need for me to do.

Other participants acknowledged the difficult paradox they felt between the personal growth they were experiencing and the pain experienced by their son or daughter. This paradox was acknowledged by one mother, who explained:

> On the positive side, it has been a real growth experience. . . . I don't know that I would have learned the things I've learned about me, about my family . . . if it hadn't been for that. On the other hand, if it hadn't been for that, maybe I would have been perfectly happy not knowing, not learning those lessons, I don't know. It *has* been a growth experience for me. Uh, but again, those negatives are, well, I still don't know that [my son's] gonna die before I do, you know, I mean, he may be around a long time yet. And if he's not going to be sick, or very sick or sick for very long, um, you know, right now, it's not bad. He's doing well. But to see him, and especially with that meningitis, *that* was *awful*. He was *so* sick. He couldn't eat, he was throwing up all the time. To see him with the IV bags, um, you know, and they had the permanent line in his arm and, you know, he was walking around with that. That was, that was really hard. I think if I had to trade the growth for [his] health, I'd trade it in a minute.

Understanding the Spiritual Significance of AIDS

For some mothers, the construction of meaning of their experiences with AIDS included an exploration of the spiritual or religious significance of AIDS. Mothers cited prayer, faith, involvement in church activities, and spiritual support groups as important in coping with their son's or daughter's illness. For example, one mother saw prayer as a way to deal with specific difficult emotions:

> I do a lot of praying . . . particularly with anger, 'cause I don't like dealing with anger, and I don't like how it makes me feel and the things that I say and do when I'm angry, and so I ask for my anger to be removed so I can deal with things constructively.

Another mother saw religious faith as a more general support, saying, "I ask God to go before me and with me and after me."   One mother saw AIDS as directly related to her understanding of religious faith:

> Well, I don't want to say it's a privilege, but probably it is considered a privilege, probably that's what God made it to be. For us to see what we can, how we can handle it. Probably we were given this thing to happen so we can show how we can, um, how we handle it, how we have faith in God—and to be a family, and help our members that are ill. I think it's . . . something happens to a family, I just think it's like a test that God gives you, to see how you can handle it. That's how I believe in my faith, uh, that everybody somehow has something in their families that they have to handle, and I think that's to show if you have the strength, the courage, and, um, to show that you love them [crying].

Other mothers cited examples of this experience having prompted a change or expansion of their spiritual or religious life.   For some participants, this experience prompted them to become more involved in their churches, to join a spiritual support group, or to create spiritual rituals to address the significance of AIDS in their lives. One mother described her family's annual participation in a memorial service for families who had already lost members to AIDS. Another mother described her family's use of ritual as spiritual support and as acknowledgment of the importance of AIDS in their family:

> [My son] practices Native American kinds of religion. . . . We do like a circle with incense and everything, so we do lots of very interesting kinds of things—we look for little ideas . . . to make a time, maybe more meaningful, to draw attention to our egos, ourselves inside— that this is important . . . and you know, we need help here.

Additionally, a few mothers felt that their experiences with AIDS have encouraged them to rethink or challenge their spiritual beliefs. This is illustrated by one mother who is very involved in the Catholic Church:

I've really had to work on, on my spiritual life, and I really feel that that has been my saving grace. Is, uh, uh, coming to terms with, with where God is in all this. Uh, you know all of those old sayings like "God doesn't give you more than you can handle" and then you think, you know, he must have me mixed up with somebody else, I'm not really all that strong. I guess I've really come to terms with God doesn't really give us *anything*. God doesn't *do* anything. Uh, we play the hand we're dealt, and, uh, God lets us work our way out of it by *ourselves*. And we do the best we can—Now, um, I can take all this and say "Screw it, who needs God!" I don't feel that way, say. I don't feel that. I feel that somewhere in there is a learning experience, a growth experience, something that I can use to make the world a better place. And that sounds real big and flowery, but making the world a better place may be making my house a better place. Or my neighborhood, or my relationship with one other person. If that improves because of this, then, then it's positive. Then it, it *becomes* a positive experience. . . . If we're building, uh, building friendships and getting to know people and being supportive of one another, that's making the world a better place . . . maybe that's what I'm called to do in this particular situation. It certainly has made it a livable thing for me.

Understanding the Political Significance of AIDS

As the previous interview excerpt indicates, in addition to defining a spiritual understanding of this experience, it may also become for the mother, on some level, a political understanding of AIDS. This was articulated by many participants, who, in addition to defining the internal family growth and the personal and spiritual growth aspects of their experiences, acknowledged the emergence of a public or political significance as well. Some mothers saw AIDS as a formal political issue and felt anger or frustration with the government's reaction to the AIDS crisis. As one mother described it, her anger about AIDS focused on the government's role: "Angry at the government now, not doing more for research than ever. I mean, we have a horrible epidemic, sweeping the world, and what are we doing? Nothing, nothing in comparison."

Similarly, other mothers felt frustration and anger about their interactions with the bureaucratic system on behalf of their son or daughter. One mother, in assessing her personal growth through this experience, focused her frustration and anger on the system:

I feel that my boundaries are being stretched by dealing with this, and I guess none of us feel really angry that AIDS is here, we feel angry about what we have to deal with because of it and the roadblocks we run into from the system.

For some mothers, their experiences as mothers of PWAs led to an expanded understanding of the government benefits and services, and, by necessity, the mothers became actively involved in challenging limitations in those services. In advocating on behalf of the PWA, some participants waged an active challenge against the government bureaucracy. Their efforts included writing letters to politicians or newspapers in protest of inadequate benefits and services, as well as serving on community boards and committees that influence the availability and organization of services.

More commonly, the public or political significance of AIDS for mothers can be seen on a local or interpersonal level. Parallel to the feminist principle that the "personal is political," these mothers began to identify themselves as members of a larger societal group: a group of people affected by AIDS. Although few of the mothers had anticipated that they would ever be affected by AIDS, their personal experiences led them to express their sense of group identity with other families facing AIDS, evidenced by their participation in AIDS-related activities; they participated in local AIDS benefits, walked with other parents in the statewide AIDS walk, volunteered to coordinate an AIDS support group for parents, joined an AIDS-related advocacy group, and offered to share with other families their expertise in negotiating the bureaucracy of services. Several of the mothers cited a desire to help other parents and families as their motivation for participating in this study.

In addition to their public connections to other families facing AIDS, most of the mothers interviewed saw themselves fulfilling a public role in educating others in their communities about AIDS. This was done in both formal and informal settings. Participants found themselves educating others in informal settings, including family members, extended family, friends, and co-workers, about AIDS transmission, risk factors, and AIDS testing. The informal educational role helped mothers to combat the fear of AIDS and the misperceptions held by members of their own social support networks and by people with whom they interacted on a regular basis. Other families saw open disclosure and education about AIDS as a more overt political role. This is illustrated by one mother, who explained:

> We don't keep it a secret, and one of the reasons is, and this came up very early on, we decided that AIDS needed a face. Everybody talks about AIDS, and nobody really knows anybody or anything about it. And we decided that we wanted people to know, that we're intelligent, educated people and we have AIDS in our life and we're dealing with it. And, I don't know, that's the philosophy behind all the telling is that, we want to educate people, we want people to know, we don't want to keep secrets.

This emphasis on politicizing the experience is important in that it points to the participants' acknowledgment of the social and personal effects of AIDS on them as mothers, and furthermore, it suggests their willingness to identify themselves in terms of their role as parents of PWAs, and in terms of their group identity with other families facing AIDS.

Families Facing AIDS: Using Qualitative Methods

From this project, we can begin to identify the strength of qualitative methods in the study of families facing an HIV or AIDS diagnosis. First, the emergence of AIDS-related social science research on families has reflected a pathological model of family functioning, and the question of active family involvement by the family of origin has been largely understudied. Influenced by the social stigma related to AIDS, the assumption that the family of origin is an unreliable source of support to the PWA has been widely referenced in the literature, and an understanding of the experience of AIDS from the perspective of the family of origin has not been addressed. From the literature, we know little about the family of origin's lived experiences with AIDS. Second, the complexity of social support networks for PWAs and the meaning of the often complex relationships within the PWA's social network to the members of that network could be well explored through the use of qualitative techniques.

From these interviews, we can begin to see the active roles that mothers play in coping, social support, caregiving, and the creation of personal meaning around an AIDS diagnosis in the family. These families, however, are not without their internal and external conflicts. Whereas some families are able to create a shared definition of this experience and employ a cohesive paradigm for caregiving and support, others cannot. The complexity of developing a shared definition of AIDS within the family unit could be explored further through qualitative inquiry.

Many of these mothers employ a complex collection of resilient coping and social support techniques, including flexibility, focusing on interpersonal connectedness, concentrating on day-to-day coping techniques, recognizing and managing their own stress, and reframing the experience in a way that addresses the need to define the personal and often growth-producing significance of this experience. By focusing on the positive and adaptive strategies employed by these mothers, researchers and social service providers can begin to address the positive aspects of the family of origin's involvement in the caregiving and support of PWAs. Qualitative research allows us to acknowledge and begin to uncover the resilient strategies of these mothers without denying or oversimplifying the complexity of their experiences.

References

Anderson, V. N. (1992). For whom is this world just? Sexual orientation and AIDS. *Journal of Applied Social Psychology, 22,* 248–259.

Aranda-Naranjo, B. (1992). The effect of HIV on the family: Implications for care. *AIDS Patient Care, 7,* 27–29.

Atkins, R., & Amenta, M. O. (1991). Family adaptation to AIDS: A comparative study. *The Hospice Journal, 7,* 213–215.

Bennett, M. J. (1990). Stigmatization: Experiences of persons with Acquired Immune Deficiency Syndrome. *Issues in Mental Health Nursing, 11,* 141–154.

Berg, B. L. (1989). *Qualitative research methods for the social sciences.* Boston: Allyn & Bacon.

Berger, P. L., & Luckmann, T. (1966). *The social construction of reality.* Garden City, NY: Doubleday.

Bonuck, K. A. (1993). AIDS and families: Cultural, psychosocial and functional impacts. *Social Work in Health Care, 18,* 75–87.

Brander, P., & Norton, V. (1993) *Women living with HIV/AIDS.* Discussion paper No. 18. Wellington, New Zealand: Ministry of Health, Health Research Services.

Brown, M. A., & Powell-Cope, G. M. (1991). AIDS family caregiving: Transitions through uncertainty. *Nursing Research, 40,* 338–345.

Caplan, G. (1974). *Support systems and community mental health: Lectures on concept development.* New York: Behavioral Publications.

Charmaz, K. (1988). The grounded theory method: An explication and interpretation. In R. M. Emerson (Ed.), *Contemporary field research* (pp. 109–126). Boston: Little Brown.

Charmaz, K. (1991). *Good days, bad days: The self in chronic illness and time.* New Brunswick, NJ: Rutgers University Press.

Christ, G. H., Siegel, K. L. S. & Moynihan, R. T. (1988). AIDS: Psychosocial issues, prevention and treatment. In V. T. DeVita, Jr., S. Hellman, & S. A. Rosenberg (Eds.), *AIDS: Etiology, diagnosis, treatment and prevention* (2nd ed., pp. 321–337). Philadelphia: Lippincott.

Crandall, C. S., & Coleman, R. (1992). AIDS-related stigmatization and the disruption of social relationships. *Journal of Social and Personal Relationships, 9,* 163–177.

Duffy, V. J. (1994). Crisis points in HIV disease. *AIDS Patient Care, 8,* 28–32.

Fontana, A., & Frey, J. H. (1994). Interviewing: The art of science. In N. K. Denzin & Y. S. Lincoln (Eds.), *Handbook of qualitative research* (pp. 361–376). Thousand Oaks, CA: Sage.

Frierson, R. L., Lippman, S. B. & Johnson, J. (1987). AIDS: Psychological stresses on the family. *Psychosomatics, 28,* 65–68.

Geis, S. B., & Fuller, R. L. (1986). Lovers of AIDS victims: Psychosocial stresses and counseling needs. *Death Studies, 10,* 43–53.

Guba, E. G., & Lincoln, Y. S. (1994). Competing paradigms in qualitative research. In N. K. Denzin & Y. S. Lincoln (Eds.), *Handbook of qualitative research* (pp. 105–117). Thousand Oaks, CA: Sage.

Kelly, J., & Sykes, P. (1989). Helping the helpers: A support group for family members of persons with AIDS. *Social Work, 34,* 239–242.

Kubler-Ross, E. (1987). *AIDS: The ultimate challenge.* New York: Collier.

Laryea, M., & Gien, L. (1993). The impact of HIV-positive diagnosis on the individual, Part 1: Stigma rejection and loneliness. *Clinical Nursing Research, 2,* 245–267.

Levine, C. (1990). AIDS and changing concepts of family. *The Milbank Quarterly, 68,* 33–58.

May, K. A. (1991). Interviewing techniques in qualitative research: Concerns and challenges. In J. Morse (Ed.), *Qualitative nursing research: A contemporary dialogue* (rev. ed. pp. 171–182). Newbury Park, CA: Sage.

McCracken, G. (1988). *The long interview.* Newbury Park, CA: Sage.

McCubbin, H. I., Thompson, E. A., Thompson, A. I., & Fromer, J. E. (1998). Preface. In H. I. McCubbin, E. A. Thompson, A. I. Thompson, J. E. Fromer (Eds) *Resiliency in Native American and Immigrant American families.* (pp. xvi-xvii). Thousand Oaks, CA: Sage.

McDonnell, J. R., Abell, N., & Miller, J. (1991). Family members' willingness to care for people with AIDS: A psychosocial assessment model. *Social Work, 36,* 43–53.

Nicholson, W. D., & Long, B. C. (1990). Self-esteem, social support, internalized homophobia and coping strategies of HIV+ gay men. *Journal of Consulting and Clinical Psychology, 6,* 873–876.

O'Donnell, T. G., & Bernier, S. L. (1990). Parents as caregivers: When a son has AIDS. *Journal of Psychosocial Nursing, 28,* 14–17.

Raveis, V. H., & Siegel, K. (1991). The impact of care giving on informal or familial care givers. *AIDS Patient Care, 5,* 39–43.

Reinharz, S. (1992). *Feminist methods in social research.* New York: Oxford.

Rinella, V. J., Jr., & Dubin, W. R. (1988). The hidden victims of AIDS: Healthcare workers and families. *The Psychiatric Hospital, 19,* 115–120.

Roberts, C. S., Severinsen, C., Kuehn, C., Straker, D., & Fritz, C. J. (1992). Obstacles to effective case management with AIDS patients: The clinician's perspective. *Social Work in Health Care, 17*, 27–40.

Robinson, C. S. (1994). Counseling gay males with AIDS: Psychosocial perspectives. *Journal of Gay and Lesbian Social Services, 1*, 15–32.

Rowe, W., Plum, G. E., & Crossman, C. (1988). Issues and problems confronting the lovers, families and communities associated with persons with AIDS. *Journal of Social Work & Human Sexuality, 6*, 71–88.

Schwandt, T. A. (1994). Constructivist, interpretivist approaches to human inquiry. In N. K. Denzin & Y. S. Lincoln (Eds.), *Handbook of qualitative research* (pp. 118–137). Thousand Oaks, CA: Sage.

Stuhlberg, I., & Buckingham, S. (1988). Parallel issues for AIDS patients, families and others. *Social Casework, 69*, 355–359.

Takigaku, S. K., Brubaker, T. H., & Hennon, C. B. (1993). A contextual model of stress among parent caregivers of gay sons with AIDS. *AIDS Education and Prevention, 5*, 25–42.

Tiblier, K. B., Walker, G., & Rolland, J. S. (1989). Therapeutic issues when dealing with families of persons with AIDS. In E. Macklin (Ed.), *AIDS and families* (pp. 81–128). New York: Harrington Park Press.

Weitz, R. (1990). Living with the stigma of AIDS. *Qualitative Sociology, 13,* 23–38.

Weitz, R. (1991). *Life with AIDS.* New Brunswick, N. J: Rutgers University Press.

Zich, J., & Temoshok, L. (1987). Perceptions of social support in men with AIDS and ARC: Relationships with distress and hardiness. *Journal of Applied Social Psychology, 17*, 193–215.

6

Variations in Families' Explanations of Childhood Chronic Conditions:

A Cross-Cultural Perspective[1]

Ann W. Garwick, Claire H. Kohrman, Janet C. Titus, Clara Wolman, and Robert Wm. Blum

How do caregiving families make sense of the occurrence of chronic illness or disability during childhood? To what extent do they focus on biomedical versus other types of explanations for the cause of childhood chronic conditions[2]? Our aim is to discover how Hispanic, African-American, and European American families explain the cause of childhood chronic conditions and the extent to which indicators of resilience are evident in these explanations. The data for this study were drawn from the *Cross-Cultural Meanings of Chronic Illness and Disability* project.[3]

Although the etiology of the condition is a core component of the description of chronic conditions in the medical literature, little is known about how caregiving families explain the cause of childhood chronic conditions. Given that families play such a major role in caring for these children, understanding the meaning of chronic conditions from the family's standpoint is imperative. A number of family stress researchers have found that the meanings that families attribute to childhood chronic conditions influence how they manage and adapt to these conditions (Garwick, Patterson, Bennett, & Blum, 1995; McCubbin & McCubbin, 1993; Patterson & Leonard, 1994;

Patterson, McCubbin, & Warwick, 1990). Information on how families from diverse cultural backgrounds view chronic conditions is needed so that providers can inform and support families more effectively in ways that promote their healthy adjustment.

Because children with chronic conditions typically require medical intervention, families are exposed to a medical culture that is based on a scientific, biologically based framework (Lupton, 1994). This framework is evident in Western medical literature, which explains the etiology of childhood chronic illness and disability in objective, biomedical terms. Health care providers, in turn, tend to inform families about chronic conditions using biomedical terminology. Although family caregivers learn about chronic conditions from health care providers whose professional socialization focuses on a biomedical model, our clinical work suggests that family caregivers have additional explanations about chronic conditions that stem from their own experiences, beliefs, and ethnocultural background.

Because of the dearth of research on caregiving families from different ethnocultural backgrounds, this study focuses on identifying the situational meanings (or explanations[4]) that families from three ethnocultural groups attribute to one aspect of the chronic condition—the cause of the condition. This study builds on Patterson and Garwick's (1994b; 1994c) theoretical work on family-level meanings in family stress theory, in which they propose that families as a whole construct and share meanings on three levels that affect how they adapt to stressful circumstances. As they interact with each other, family members collectively construct meanings about (a) specific stressful situations, such as caring for a child with a chronic condition; (b) their identity as a family—how family members view themselves as a unit; and (c) their view of the world—how they interpret reality, what their core assumptions are about their environment, and their existential beliefs. Although this study focuses on identifying the situational meanings that families attribute to the cause of the condition, the family's identity and view of the world can influence how the family explains the cause of the condition. Conversely, how the family defines a stressful situation can alter how they view themselves as a family and their view of the world.

Building on Kleinman's (1978) work on patients' and physicians' explanatory models of illness, this study examines how families who care for school-aged children with chronic conditions describe the first element of the explanatory model. Components of the explanatory model include beliefs about (a) the cause, (b) the reason for symptoms, (c) pathophysiology, (d) care, and (e) treatment. According to Kleinman, patients' explanatory models of the illness are usually less fully articulated than physicians' explanatory models, because physicians are trained to articulate features of illness within a scientific framework based on evidence. In contrast, patients and families have a broader range of experiences on which to draw because of their exposure to a variety of cultural contexts.

Culture influences how illness is defined and treated by patients, families, and providers (Harwood, 1981). Their respective ethnocultural beliefs about chronic conditions can complement, compete, or conflict with each other. The degree of convergence between family and provider orientations can influence health-seeking behavior, doctor-patient communication, treatment choices, adherence, and outcomes. The explanatory model of illness provides a tool that researchers and providers can use to better understand the relationship of culture to patient care (Kleinman, Eisenberg, & Good, 1978).

There is a growing awareness of the importance and value of providing care that is family centered and culturally sensitive (Davis & Voegtle, 1994; Garwick & Miller, 1996; Patterson & Blum, 1992). However, less is known about how to implement such care. Our premise is that providers need to understand how families view chronic conditions so that they can design interventions to fit the families' needs and preferences. Furthermore, the experience of childhood chronic illness and disability needs to be understood within a family and cultural context. Numerous authors have emphasized the importance of understanding the health and illness beliefs of people from different cultural backgrounds. Yet little research has been done within ethnically diverse populations on family caregivers' perceptions of the cause of childhood chronic illness (McCubbin, Thompson, Thompson, McCubbin, & Kaston, 1992). However, anecdotal reports from health care providers suggest that conflicting beliefs between families and providers can disrupt the provider-family relationship and interfere with treatment adherence (Anderson, Elfert, & Lai, 1989; Kalyanpur & Rao, 1991). In addition, family caregivers' perceptions of the cause of the child's condition can influence the types of services they choose for their child as well as how they manage the child's condition (Brookins, 1992; Groce & Zola, 1992).

Literature Review

A growing body of literature on children with various chronic illnesses and disabilities suggests that the meanings that families attribute to these chronic conditions are critical factors that influence their adaptation (Patterson & Garwick, 1994a). An important group of factors that has significant repercussions on the process of adaptation for families and children with chronic conditions belongs to the cognitive domain (Affleck & Tennen, 1993; Thompson & Bennett, 1991). These factors include personal interpretations, beliefs, and meanings attributed to stressful situations or events such as chronic illness and disability. The threatening nature of chronic conditions, both socially and personally, challenges individuals to develop belief systems with meanings and interpretations that allow them to make sense of and cope with the illness experience (Blumhagen, 1980; Garro, 1988). Scholars from many disciplines have emphasized that the way in which individuals and families think about what is happening to them is a critical factor influencing the processes and outcomes of adaptation to life events (Antonovsky, 1979, 1987; Berger & Luckmann, 1966; Lazarus & Folkman, 1984; Reiss, 1981; Taylor, 1983). For families who must cope with chronic conditions, their beliefs shape their definition of the condition and help them develop coping strategies that are associated with positive psychological outcomes (Patterson & Garwick, 1994b). Furthermore, family members' interpretations, meanings, and beliefs about chronic conditions have an impact on a variety of health behavioral outcomes, such as the decision to seek medical care (Berkanovic & Telesky, 1985; Berkanovic, Telesky, & Reeder, 1981), cooperation with treatment regimens, and relationships with health providers (Patterson & Garwick, 1994a).

Beliefs and meanings attributed to life events are shaped by cultural values, the family's worldview, and experiences. Although each person's explanatory model of illness is unique, many of its components are based on a shared cultural model (Garro, 1988). Blumhagen (1980) defines three major sources that influence personal illness beliefs and explanatory models: idiosyncratic, popular, and expert. The idiosyncratic source is derived from a person's own experiences; the popular or lay health source is the folk health system that derives information from the social network and close cultural group; and the expert source of information is derived from expert explanatory models. Blumhagen maintains that the popular health system is probably the most important source of personal illness beliefs.

Lupton (1994) maintains that most people develop health beliefs derived from folk models of illness, alternative models of medical care, the media, and commonsense understandings of illness based on their personal experience and consultation with friends and family. Although health care providers enter professional training with popular health beliefs, they soon become socialized into a system that focuses on a scientific, biomedical model of illness. Conflict and misunderstanding can occur between family caregivers and providers when their respective beliefs knowingly or unknowingly collide. Thus, health care providers must be aware of their own cultural beliefs as well as those of the family in order to provide culturally sensitive care (Krefting, 1991).

Recent studies provide support for the proposition that ethnocultural beliefs about the cause of childhood chronic conditions influence how these conditions are defined and managed. In their review of cross-cultural studies, Groce and Zola (1993) found that the culturally perceived *cause* of a chronic illness or disability was a significant issue in all cultures studied. Cultural beliefs played a major role in determining family and community attitudes toward the person with the chronic condition.

A few studies have illustrated how family members' ethnocultural beliefs about childhood chronic conditions influence family adaptation. Weisner, Beizer, and Stolze (1991) investigated the influence of religious beliefs, affiliation, and practices on family adjustment and found that more religious parents reported a clearer sense of meaning about why they had a child with a developmental delay. Weisner, Matheson, and Bernheimer (1996) also found that ecocultural circumstances, the parents' beliefs about the child's delay, and the nature of the delay were stronger influences on family adaptation than was the age at which the child was identified as delayed. In a study of Mexican American parents of children with severe disabilities, Mardiros (1989) found that parents provided a variety of biomedical and sociocultural explanations for the cause of the disability. Although most parents reported positive attributions about the condition, a few beliefs about causation, such as personal feelings or past transgressions, were associated with negative affect and less active parental involvement in the child's care. McCubbin et al. (1992) compared Native American Indian, Native Hawaiian, and Anglo American perceptions of the source of chronic illness and found that different ethnocultural standpoints influenced treatment choices and family roles. These findings indicate that family caregivers' beliefs about causation can influence how they manage that condition. Additional cross-cultural studies of ethnic groups in the United States are needed to determine how families from different ethnocultural backgrounds view the cause of childhood chronic conditions and whether indicators of family resilience differ by ethnicity.

Method

Given the lack of research on the ethnocultural meanings of childhood chronic conditions, a qualitative research design was selected because it focuses on the discovery of important variables and concepts. Because our primary goal was to identify how families view the cause of chronic conditions, a grounded theory approach was selected to guide the analysis (Glaser & Strauss, 1967). Instead of testing hypotheses, grounded theory methods and content analytic strategies were used to identify concepts about causation and indicators of resilience that emerged during family conversations. The following research questions were addressed in this study:

1. What types of explanations do families provide for the cause of childhood chronic conditions?

2. What are the indicators of resilience evident in family explanations about the cause of the condition?

The present study is based on the assumption that meanings are constructed and shared with others through language (Berger & Luckmann, 1966). Situational meanings about causation will be identified by analyzing the content of families' conversations about the reasons for various childhood chronic conditions. Indicators of family resilience will be identified by investigating *how* families construct and process these meanings. The operational definition for indicators of family resilience is based on McCubbin and McCubbin's (1988, 1996) definition of family resiliency that includes "characteristics, dimensions, and properties which help families to be resistant to disruption in the face of change and adaptive in the face of crisis situations."

Participatory Action Research Framework

The development of this project was based on a participatory action research (PAR) model (Whyte, 1989) that was developed to foster active, collaborative working relationships between researchers and community members. In participatory action research, one or more members of the organization or community are invited to play active roles in the research process. This community-based research project on childhood chronic illness was developed in partnership with families, community leaders, and providers. Figure 6.1 illustrates the collaborative nature of these relationships.

The investigators encouraged the active participation of community members during all phases of the research project. Leaders from community organizations that serve children and families were involved in the design, recruitment, and implementation of this project. For example, community leaders helped identify and invite families to participate in the project. Because the literature indicates that families from minority backgrounds often have difficulty accessing medical services (Newacheck, Stoddard, & McManus, 1992) and that families from different ethnocultural backgrounds frequently use both traditional medical and alternative health care services (Lupton, 1994), we recruited families through informal community networks rather

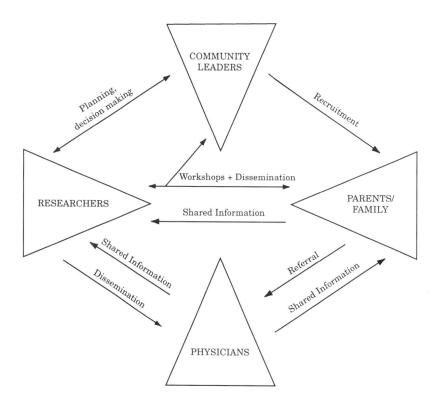

Figure 6.1. Relationships Among Researchers and Participants

than the conventional method of recruiting through medical institutions. Our goal was to include families with varying degrees of access to services as well as families with different preferences for traditional or alternative forms of medical care.

Recruitment of Participants

The same recruitment procedures were used to recruit families from two large metropolitan areas in the Midwest—Minneapolis-St. Paul, Minnesota and Chicago, Illinois. Investigators updated each other on a weekly basis to discuss recruitment efforts and findings in order to ensure that similar methods were used in recruiting this diverse sample.

Families were recruited from a variety of community organizations, including (a) organizations that serve school-aged children, such as the YMCA, YWCA, and Boys' and Girls' Clubs; (b) community park and recreation centers; (c) community programs that serve ethnic groups; (d) religious organizations; and (e) parent advocacy or support groups.

A snowball sampling technique was used to identify families who might be interested in participating in the study. Our goal was to include a broad range of families from different ethnocultural and socioeconomic backgrounds and children with a variety of chronic conditions. These characteristics were tracked as families were enrolled, and continuing recruitment efforts were focused to ensure diversity in the sample. The number of children with a particular type of diagnosis was limited to four per ethnicity.

The recruitment process began with the advisory boards in both cities, whose members represented the three ethnocultural groups in this study. Advisory board members suggested strategies for recruitment and identified additional community leaders to contact. At each site, about 100 community leaders were informed about the study and invited to tell families about the project. Interested community leaders received packets of information about the project that they could then distribute to families. Family caregivers then contacted one of the project coordinators, who informed them about the project in more detail and conducted a telephone screening interview. A weakness of this recruitment strategy is that the actual number of families who were informed about the project is unknown. Although the vast majority of community leaders were interested in the project, relatively few knew families who had school-aged children with chronic conditions. They often suggested that we contact hospitals and clinics. Of the 67 family caregivers who contacted the project coordinators, 63 met the following inclusion criteria: (a) the child had a chronic illness or disability with a physical health impairment, (b) the child was between 5 and 12 years of age, and (c) the child was living at home at the time of the family interview. Two of the families were excluded because their children were too young, and two others because their children had cognitive impairments without any physical health impairments.

Institutional review board approvals of the study were obtained before its initiation. Informed written consent was obtained from all family caregivers who were present prior to their participation in the interview. Subjects were informed that their participation was voluntary and that they could withdraw from the study at any time.

Participants' Characteristics

This community-based sample included 63 families who have school-aged children (ages 5–12) with a variety of chronic physical health impairments. Thirty families were recruited from Minneapolis-St. Paul, Minnesota and 33 from Chicago, Illinois. There were participants from the three ethnic groups represented in the study; approximately one third of the families at each site were from each ethnic background. Twenty-one of the families identified themselves as African-American, 20 as Hispanic, and 22 as European American. Total family incomes ranged from less than $10,000 to greater than $100,000 per year, with a median family income of $25,380. Approximately one fourth of the families also received need-based assistance, such as AFDC and/or food stamps, and one third of the families received Medicaid benefits. More than one third of the children (n = 22) received SSI. (See Table 6.1 for further background information.) Because of the community-based nature of the recruitment, education and income were not equally distributed across the ethnic groups in this sample. However, the lower median income and educational attainment of the Hispanic and African-American groups reflect patterns reported by the U.S. Bureau of the Census.

Table 6.1
Family Demographics

Family Composition			Household Size	
	_N_	_%_		
1-parent families	24	38	Range 2 – 9	
2-parent families	38	60	Median 5	
Grandparents	1	2		
Primary Language			**Total Annual Income**	
	_N_	_%_		
English	44	70	Median $25,380	
Spanish	17	27	Range <$10,000 – >$100,000	
English & Spanish	2	3		

Additional Benefits		
Source of Benefit	_N_ of Families	_%_ of Families
AFDC	15	24
Medicaid	21	33
Food stamps	17	27
SSI	22	35
Child Support	8	13
Other income	7	11

A noncategorical approach was used to recruit children with a variety of chronic physical health impairments. The noncategorical approach identifies and classifies children with chronic health conditions by common features of the condition (e.g., type of impairment, degree of visibility, prognosis) rather than by the particular medical diagnosis (Pless & Pinkerton, 1975; Jessop & Stein, 1983). This method is based on the premise that most children with chronic conditions and their families have similar experiences and encounter similar problems, regardless of the specific diagnosis.

A chronic condition was defined as an ongoing physical health condition that has a biological, anatomical, or physiological basis with long-term sequelae (Stein, Bauman, Coupey, Ireys, & Westbrook, 1990). Because this study focused on children with physical health impairments, children with cognitive impairments who did not have physical health impairments (e.g., autism, learning disability) were excluded from the study.

A wide variety of chronic conditions were represented in this sample. Table 6.2 lists the primary medical diagnoses for the children in this sample. Most of the children (60%) had more than one chronic condition (e.g., asthma and diabetes, seizure disorder and Down syndrome). In addition to physical health impairments, parents reported that 13 of these children also had some type of cognitive impairment (e.g., developmental delay or mild mental retardation).

The children ranged in age from 5 to 12 years (median age = 6 years, 5 months; mean age = 7 years, 6 months). The children in the sample had been living with their chronic conditions for at least 1 year (range = 1 to 12 years). Approximately half of these children were males (n = 31) and half females (n = 32). Fifty-six of the children were born in the United States, three in Mexico, two in Puerto Rico, one in Honduras, and one in Bolivia. Several families stated that they immigrated to the United States to obtain medical care and services for their children with special health care needs.

The age range of family caregivers was 19 to 52 years (mean = 35 years; SD = 6.4 years). The educational level of family caregivers ranged from less than 7th grade to graduate or professional degrees. Twenty-one percent of the male caregivers (n = 8) and 16% (n = 10) of the female caregivers had less than a high school degree; all except two of these caregivers had been educated outside the United States. A higher proportion of Hispanic-American family caregivers had less than a high school education; however, Hispanic-American caregivers were also represented in each of the other educational groups. Ten percent of the male caregivers (n = 4) and 25% of the female caregivers

Table 6.2
Types of Chronic Conditions by Primary Diagnosis

Primary Diagnosis	Frequency
Arthritis	1
Asthma	8
Asthma with Allergies	2
Biliary Atresia	1
Blood Dyscrasia	1
Cerebral Palsy	7
Cerebral Palsy with Mental Retardation	1
Congenital Heart Disease	1
Congenital Hypothyroidism	1
Deafness	3
Diabetes Insipidus	1
Diabetes Mellitus	7
Genetic Disorder	1
Hydrocephalus	2
Kidney Problems	3
Neuromuscular Problems	1
Seizure Disorder	7
Seizure Disorder with Mental Retardation	1
Short Bowel Syndrome	1
Spastic Quadriplegia	3
Spina Bifida	6
Stroke	1
Tuberous Sclerosis	1
Turner's Syndrome	2
Total	**63**

(n = 15) had a high school diploma, and 25% of the male caregivers (n = 10) and 37% of the female caregivers (n = 23) had some vocational/ technical education or college education. Forty-four percent of the male caregivers (n = 17) and 21% of the female caregivers (n = 13) had completed a college education. Approximately half of the female caregivers (n = 33) were employed outside the home.

Procedure

The family interview protocol for the *Cross-Cultural Meanings of Chronic Illness and Disability* project includes a semi-structured family interview and three brief questionnaires: (a) a family demographic form; (b) a child status form that includes information about the child's background, diagnosis, and special education services; and (c) the Impact-on-Family scale (Stein & Jessop, 1980). Spanish and English versions of the protocol were developed, reviewed by the advisory boards, and then piloted with two families. Revisions in wording were made to clarify ambiguous terminology and ensure the cultural relevance of items for families. This chapter focuses on the analysis of collective family responses to the following open-ended question in the interview guide:

> After people find out that their child has a chronic condition, people often wonder about what caused it to happen. People sometimes ask why this happened. When you wonder, how do you explain how this happened?

Two teams of interviewers representing the three ethnocultural groups were recruited and trained by one of the investigators, who used the same training methods at both sites. Interviewers had ethnocultural backgrounds similar to the families they interviewed. Families had a choice of English- or Spanish-speaking interviewers, and 17 interviews were conducted in Spanish.

Interviews were conducted in home settings with the child's family caregivers. The composition of the family included all individuals who fit the family's definition of their own family. During the telephone intake, the project coordinator asked the family contact person to describe who was in the child's family and then identify which family members over the age of 16 were involved in providing care for the child with the chronic condition. All of the family caregivers over the age of 16 were invited to participate in the interview. The majority of interviews included two parents (n = 38). Eighteen of the interviews were conducted with mothers alone (16 of these mothers were from single-parent households, and two were from dual-parent households). Six of the interviews were conducted with mothers and other family members (e.g., the child's grandmother, aunt, uncle, the child's adult sibling, or a mother's friend who was defined as a family member). One of the interviews was conducted with the child's grandparents, who had custody of the child with the chronic condition and two of the child's aunts. The number of family caregivers at the family interviews ranged from one to four. Family interviews were audiotaped and then transcribed verbatim. Interviews conducted in Spanish were translated into English.

Analysis

The family is the unit of analysis in this project. Open-ended interview questions were posed to the family as a group. The subsequent analysis focused on the collective response of family caregivers to the question rather than on individual family members' particular viewpoints.

Content analytic techniques (Weber, 1985) were used to code the family interview data. First, two of the investigators (A.G. and C.K.) reviewed the verbatim transcripts of family interviews on a line-by-line basis. After extensive review and discussion of the findings, a theoretical model was developed to guide the analysis. Next, coding categories based on the theoretical constructs were generated, tested, and revised. The coding scheme was pilot tested on randomly selected transcripts by several coders. Revisions in the coding scheme were made until a high degree of agreement was achieved between raters. In addition, the conceptual clarity of the coding scheme was validated by two independent raters who had not been involved in the development of the coding categories. Once the trustworthiness of the coding scheme was established, raters at both sites were trained on how to use the coding scheme. The accuracy of coding was evaluated by the investigators at periodic intervals.

The investigators organized the coding scheme into a computer-based coding template based on the theoretical model, so raters could enter codes into data files on the computer. This approach to coding was based on Crabtree and Miller's (1992) template approach to text analysis in which a template or codebook is constructed after a preliminary scanning of the text. Then an in-depth analysis of the data is undertaken. Coding instructions, operational definitions for codes, and flow sheets for coding different aspects of the family interview by topic were included in the coding template. An advantage of this template approach to coding is that data can be organized for specific analytic purposes, such as the investigation of how families explain chronic conditions. One of the flow sheets was designed specifically for coding the types of explanations that families provided regarding the cause of the condition, and this analysis focuses on these data.

An independent rater verified the accuracy of the coding done by other members of the research team. If a disagreement occurred between two raters, a third rater independently coded the explanation, and the final coding was based on the consensus of two of the three raters. Next, a matrix was developed for displaying all of the participant families' types of explanations by case number, ethnicity, and type of condition. Themes were then identified by comparing the types of explanations by these variables.

Findings

There was considerable variability in the ways in which families explained the cause of the chronic condition. However, a sense of coherence characterized the majority of the families' stories about causation. Although each family had a unique way of explaining the condition, common themes were evident in the types of explanations that families provided, and indicators of resilience emerged as family caregivers constructed meanings and shared their understanding of the cause.

Because our aim was to identify the range and types of meanings that families expressed, findings are presented in terms of common themes that families emphasized. Twenty-two different types of explanations about the cause of the chronic condition were identified in the 63 family interviews. These explanations were then organized into six larger categories: biomedical explanations, environmental explanations, traditional beliefs, fatalistic beliefs, absence of known causes, and personal attributions (see Table 6.3). The total number of types of explanations per interview ranged from zero to eight, with a mode of two. Two of the families did not provide explanations in response to the question. Instead, one family talked about how they coped by *not* asking why the condition happened and focused on living in the present. The other family stated that they never considered the question.

Approximately 30% of the families focused on one type of explanation for their child's condition, and the rest of the families talked about a combination of reasons for the child's condition. The two families who reported the most explanations had children with more than one chronic condition (e.g., cerebral palsy and asthma; spina bifida and asthma). There were no substantive differences in the explanations by site and few differences in explanations by type of condition.

Biomedical Explanations

Forty-five percent of the families' explanations (n = 68) were categorized as biomedical, and nine types of explanations were included in this category. The majority of the biomedical explanations were associated with the perinatal period (e.g., prenatal factors, premature birth, birth trauma, and genetic factors). Families also described physiological explanations and attributed some chronic conditions to a child's illness (e.g., meningitis) or an accident. A few chronic conditions (e.g., cerebral palsy and deafness) were associated with complications of medical treatment, and most of these children were born prematurely.

Genetic explanations and prenatal factors were the two most common biomedical reasons identified by families from all three ethnocultural backgrounds as sources of a variety of chronic conditions. Families described genetic predisposition, chromosomal explanations, and positive family history as the genetic factors that helped explain the occurrence of conditions such as asthma, biliary atresia, diabetes,

Table 6.3
Families' Explanations for the
Causes of Childhood Chronic Conditions

Type of Explanation	African-American	Hispanic American	Euro-American	Total
Biomedical Explanations				
Genetic factors	8	5	8	**21**
Prenatal factors	4	6	5	**15**
Physiological explanations	2	2	2	**6**
Premature birth	2	2	2	**6**
Result of child's illness	1	2	2	**5**
Birth trauma	0	3	1	**4**
Poor medical care	0	2	3	**5**
Complications of medical treatment	2	1	0	**3**
Diet/Food intake	1	1	0	**2**
Accident or trauma	0	1	0	**1**
Environmental Explanations				
Environmental factors	4	4	4	**12**
Traditional Beliefs				
Spiritual/religious beliefs	1	6	2	**9**
Folk beliefs	0	4	0	**4**
Superstitious beliefs (e.g., "bad luck," "family curse")	1	1	0	**2**
Fatalistic Beliefs				
Schicksal, "This is the way life is."	1	2	6	**9**
Condition is random event	1	1	3	**5**
Condition is predetermined	2	0	0	**2**
Cause Unknown				
Biomedical cause unknown	1	3	7	**11**
Family does not know why condition happened	3	1	4	**8**
"There is no reason."	1	3	4	**8**
Personal Attributions				
Caregiver questions personal responsibility	3	1	4	**8**
Caregiver blames self or others	1	4	0	**5**
Total Explanations	**39**	**55**	**57**	**151**

epilepsy, spina bifida, tuberous sclerosis, Turner's syndrome, and stroke.

In addition to identifying genetic factors, several families described how they did not blame family members for genetic conditions. For example, one mother of a child with Turner's syndrome stated,

> I do not really feel a need to blame either of us for what happened. I mean, it is so irrelevant to life. . . . I just explain that it is a chromosome problem and that is how it is.

In contrast, both parents of a child with diabetes identified genetic family history as an explanation for the child's diabetes, but, the father went on to say: "I just always blamed it, you know, on her [the mother]," to which the mother replied, "That's not fair." Acknowledging a genetic explanation without assigning blame to the carrier was an indicator of healthy family functioning noted in several family discussions about causation.

A wide range of prenatal factors was identified by families as explanations for the child's chronic condition. These factors included (a) age of the mother; (b) exposure to smoke, alcohol, or foods treated with chemicals; (c) lack of prenatal care; (d) poor health of the mother during pregnancy; (e) physiologic factors (e.g., prenatal anoxia, lack of intra-uterine room to grow); and (f) physical abuse of the mother during pregnancy. Some families clearly identified prenatal factors as causal factors, whereas others questioned whether particular prenatal factors caused the condition.

Except for the identification of partner abuse, the prenatal factors cited are consistent with those typically reported in the literature. In one case, the stepfather pointed out that the mother had been mistreated by her first husband while she was pregnant and suggested that the baby was born with cerebral palsy because of this maltreatment. The mother also pointed out that she had a number of asthma attacks during her pregnancy that could have caused the baby's "brain to be damaged." In another case, the mother stated that she did not know what caused her son's deafness. She reported a healthy pregnancy except for the fact that the child's father was abusive and violent toward her during that time. In both of these cases, family members questioned whether the physical abuse was associated with the development of the chronic condition.

The significance of biomedical explanations is evident in the relative emphasis that families placed on biomedical explanations compared to other explanations for the cause of the condition. The importance of biomedical explanations is further underscored by the 11 families who emphasized that health care providers could provide no biomedical explanations for the cause of the condition. Implicit in this finding is the family's expectation that health care providers will be able to provide information about the etiology of the child's chronic condition.

Environmental Explanations

The environmental factors category was another common type of explanation that families from all three ethnocultural backgrounds emphasized. Environmental factors were associated with chronic conditions such as asthma, diabetes, cerebral palsy, juvenile rheumatoid arthritis, and spina bifida. Factors such as cold air, dust, and exposure to secondhand smoke triggered asthma attacks. Living in a cold, damp basement was the sole reason that one mother attributed to the development of her daughter's arthritis.

Three families who had no clear biomedical explanations for the cause of their children's conditions identified exposure to toxic substances as a possible explanation. One family identified pollutants as a possible reason for spina bifida. Another family identified contaminants in heating ducts as a potential source for a rare seizure disorder. In the third case, a father questioned whether his exposure to Agent Orange during the Vietnam War caused his son's hydrocephalus.

> I know other veterans who had trouble with their children, so I thought, you know, maybe it was something . . . so I took the screening test, but I doubt seriously if anything will come out of it . . . there is not conclusive evidence that is directly linked . . . so we really don't know.

Traditional Explanations

Folk beliefs, religious/spiritual beliefs, and superstitious beliefs were the three types of explanations that most directly reflected the family's particular ethnocultural background. The folk belief category was the one type of explanation in which the ethnic identity of the family made a distinct difference in how families interpreted particular chronic conditions. For example, two Hispanic families described specific traditional folk beliefs that are documented in literature on Hispanic beliefs about health and illness (Harwood, 1981; Maduro, 1983; National Coalition of Hispanic and Human Services Organizations [COSSMHO], 1990). Although both families expressed the belief that strong emotions, such as fear ("susto") and anger ("coraje"), can cause illness, they also discussed additional alternative explanations for the child's condition.

One family who described themselves as Catholic and Latino provided a number of possible explanations for their child's diabetes, including the child's frightening experience, parental behaviors, spiritual beliefs, and fatalistic beliefs. However, the onset of the child's diabetes was primarily associated with the fear she experienced at Halloween. The account of this experience is similar to reports in the literature about "susto," in which a frightening experience is believed to cause the illness (COSSMHO, 1990; Maduro, 1983).

> And Maria went trick or treating with my sister. And the little girl
> got really scared when a vampire came out of a house and scared the
> girl. My sister says that the girl, I was not there, could not move her
> feet. . . . And it does not matter to me what doctor, what person tells
> me that it cannot be that my girl got scared by this, that she got
> scared and became ill. . . . And I say that this girl got so frightened,
> that this changed her.

Although she focused on the child's fright as causing the diabetes,
this mother also described additional explanations that the family
explored as they tried to make sense of why the condition occurred.

> I think every parent has this thought, why did this occur? Was it
> something I did because I am a bad mother, or because I did not give
> her the right food to eat. . . . My husband also says, "Things do not
> work out well for us because you are always cursing." I believe in
> that. You have to stop cursing, because we are unlucky. Everything
> turns out bad for us . . . . Sometimes I think, well, perhaps Maria
> had the potential of being fat, to be fat like me. And so that she may
> not be fat, God gave her diabetes so that she remains in control of
> her body. . . . This could be it, because nobody knows what God does
> in this world, because I believe in God. I believe in the saints. I
> believe there is a spiritual thing that commands one's life. I am not a
> person who says, I am in control of my life. I do not believe that life
> is like this, that one can control the way. I think that the way of the
> life of a person is a road in which one never knows what will be
> behind the door. One has to have the power inside oneself, the strength
> not to be afraid of this, because in life there are going to be a lot of
> doors and one has to make a decision regarding what to do. Like, for
> example, in "The Price Is Right," you have Door Number 1, Door
> Number 2, Door Number 3; you are going to go for the big deal or
> what? That is it. We are in control. When I was a little girl, in
> religion class, the first thing that I remember them teaching us is
> that God gave us a gift. The gift was free will—the free will to choose
> good or bad. Each person has it within them. Do I choose the good or
> do I choose the bad? And the only one who has control over that is
> yourself. But there are many different opportunities out there. And
> you are the one who is in control of which one you are going to
> choose. So if bad luck happens upon you, who is to say why that
> happened, or what is the reason for that? I am not. . . . I cannot put
> my energy into that. I could, if I wanted to, easily, very easily, very
> easily. And I think that everybody has to search the best way for
> them.

Biomedical explanations were noticeably absent from this family's
explanations about the cause of the diabetes. The other six families
who had children with diabetes included biomedical explanations for
the child's condition. Although this family did not describe traditional biomedical explanations of diabetes, this child was receiving
traditional medical care for her diabetes and adapting well to the

treatment regimen. Her parents described her as having a "good attitude."

Another family who emigrated from Mexico discussed several different types of possible explanations for the child's spina bifida and asthma. These explanations included descriptions of traditional folk beliefs such as "coraje" anger as a possible cause of the spina bifida and an imbalance of hot and cold as a possible cause of the asthma. Unlike other families, this family was not able to come to an agreement about the cause of the child's chronic conditions and tended to blame family members for the child's health problems. The mother, who is separated from her husband, included an adult son in the family interview. Mother and son had different explanations for both conditions. Whereas the mother attributed the cause of the asthma to the child's being born in winter and "breathing in cold air," the son openly disagreed. "I think that any normal person can get it, that doesn't know how to take care of him/herself. And, the temperature doesn't have anything to do with it, is what I think." In addition, he tended to blame the spina bifida on his parents' behavior.

> Well, the problem with the spinal column, um, it could be a lot of things. It could be a coraje anger on the mother's part. Uh, something, lifted something heavy that she carried. Perhaps she pulled something, a fall, an emotional problem, a family conflict, perhaps the age, it could be, could be that, a vice that the father had, or something taken by the mother. No, no, I, the only way I know of that, that occur, that children are born with those types of illness is that way.

Although both mother and son described a variety of possible explanations for the chronic conditions, a lack of coherence and resolution marked their discussion about the causes of the condition. Unresolved conflict about the cause of the condition distinguished this family interview from others. The mother maintained that "we never discovered the reason why that type of disability exists" and "to date nobody has explained to us the truth." It is difficult to determine how much information this family actually received from health care providers, or whether language was a barrier that hindered this Spanish-speaking family's understanding and access to information.

Although the mother's explanation about "breathing cold air" sounds like an environmental reason for the asthma, she also refers to "hot" and "cold" in other parts of the interview. For instance, she does not give her child anything cold, like cold water, because she does not want to "affect him more in the chest." She finds it strange that hospital workers do not think anything about giving him cold water. Her belief that the imbalance between hot and cold causes illness is consistent with literature on humoral (hot/cold) theory in which diseases are believed to be caused by a humoral imbalance, and particular foods and medications are thought to cure disease by restoring balance (Harwood, 1981). Hot/cold theory is a common explanation for illness in Hispanic cultural groups (Harwood, 1981). Asthma is considered a cold illness, and treatments often center around restoring balance by dressing warmly, preventing colds, and controlling the temperature of the home (Pachter, Cloutier, & Bernstein, 1995).

It is interesting to note that family members espoused different traditional beliefs. Whereas the adult son listed "coraje" anger as a potential cause of the spina bifida, he dismissed his mother's theory about exposure to cold causing asthma. Despite a lengthy discussion and description of a number of different types of explanations, none of the possible explanations for the asthma or spina bifida was viewed as satisfactory by the whole family. Also, family conflict was not limited to the discussion of causation because family members also disagreed about the child's care. Unresolved conflict seemed to interfere with this family's ability to function effectively. The lack of resolution and conflict that characterized this family's discussion about causes suggests that the process in which the family engages during the discussion of explanations provides important clues about the family's functioning that need to be considered in conjunction with the content of explanations.

The folk belief category itself was neither a protective nor a risk factor. Although both families included folk beliefs in their explanations, the first family included positive attributions about the condition, whereas the second family focused on negative attributions. Indicators of resilience were evident in how these families talked about the cause of the condition, rather than the labels they assigned to the cause.

Religious/Spiritual Explanations

Religious or spiritual affiliation is another important element of culture that influenced families' explanations. In the first section of the interview, families were asked to describe their ethnocultural background and the groups with whom they identified. Seventy-one percent of the families ($n = 44$) volunteered information about their faith and religious backgrounds. Families described belonging to a variety of religious groups (e.g., Baptist, Catholic, Jehovah's Witness, Jewish, Presbyterian) and having a variety of spiritual beliefs (e.g., universalist, multireligious).

In addition to describing their religious affiliations, nine of these families specifically attributed spiritual or religious explanations to their child's chronic condition. Each of these families had a child with a different type of chronic condition. Most of these families also talked about how their religious and spiritual beliefs helped them cope. For example, one single parent stated, "I do not feel that I am raising him alone, I feel like I have good support just from praying." In addition to religious beliefs, families talked about church members and communities as sources of support.

Spiritual beliefs influenced families' interpretations of chronic illness and disability, and families emphasized that God had a purpose or reason for the child's condition. Only one family talked about the illness as a punishment from God. When her son was first diagnosed, the mother asked why God was going to punish her and her child, but now she believes that her child's condition was caused by a virus. The other families described positive attributions that helped them cope with a difficult situation. One father whose child has epilepsy stated,

> It's just a way of being tested. I have a tendency to rationalize everything according to the way I was brought up, and I have always been brought up in a Catholic school and have always been pretty close, you know, with my beliefs, and I just think that it is something that has been given us to make something out of. So I have always tried to do that.

His wife went on to say,

> I do not think we have really questioned why a whole lot. Occasionally we do, but most of the time we really try to bypass that. We have never really felt guilty or anything.

In another case, a family of a child who has tuberous sclerosis stated,

> I do not spend a lot of time wondering how or why. I do not ask why. I figure, why not? Why would I ever think that I should be spared what so many mothers have to go through. My faith carries me through, and I remember saying when she was sick, when she was first diagnosed, that if the Blessed Mother had lost her son, why did I think I shouldn't if it was God's will? If it was the way it was supposed to go. Why I just gave it all to God. It was the easiest thing for me to turn it over to Him. . . . I did not ask "why me" or I just figured, just give me the strength to handle what I have to. I remember, even that night, praying, "Thy will be done."

Spiritual beliefs helped these families make sense of difficult situations.

Fatalistic Beliefs

Fatalistic explanations were divided into the following three categories to reflect the nuances of meanings in family discussions: (a) random accidents or events; (b) predestined events not attributed to a higher power; and (c) *Schicksal*, a German term that means "this is the way life is." Schicksal refers to a belief system that involves the acceptance of situations and events not because of a law or predetermination by a higher power, but because they are part of life (Boss, 1988). Fatalistic statements that mentioned a higher power were categorized in the spiritual/religious explanation category.

Random events were defined as chance events. Family caregivers frequently used metaphors that referred to games of chance to explain the occurrence of the child's condition. One father of a child with cerebral palsy said, "It was the roll of the dice and we came up short on this one." Another father whose child was diagnosed with spina bifida stated, "It's just the luck of the draw."

A distinction was made between families who believed that the condition was predetermined and unavoidable and those who believed that chronic conditions just happened because "that's the way life is." Two families emphasized that the condition was meant to be, whereas nine others pointed out that situations like chronic conditions "just happen" in life. Fatalistic beliefs were expressed by families from all three ethnic groups, and no particular patterns were found by type of condition.

After describing fatalistic types of beliefs, families often went on to describe how they coped with their situations. As one family of a child with congenital heart disease stated,

> Saying "why me" is such a useless exercise. I hate deals where the people like to say, "Well, these special kids are special people." Well, maybe that is true, but that is not necessarily. I mean, no, I think life is a crap shoot. You get what you take and you deal with it, you just deal with it.

The belief that chronic conditions are a part of life helped many families put closure to questions about why the condition happened so that they could move on to deal with the management of the condition within the context of family life. Families talked about fatalistic beliefs in a way that implied an acceptance of the chronic condition.

For example, one European American family of Germanic/Scandinavian descent emphasized both fatalistic and biomedical explanations in their discussion about their child's hypothyroidism and developmental disabilities. However, fatalistic beliefs, rather than biomedical explanations, were reflected in how the family managed the condition. Although this family believed that these conditions happened "when he was developing," they concluded, "These things happen." This schicksal type of explanation is also evident in their coping strategies: "We never talked about it, but both our attitudes have been, this is what it is and you just take it for what it is."

Cause Unknown

Approximately one third of the families (*n* = 20) talked about the lack of known reasons for the child's condition. Seven of these families emphasized more than one of the following explanations. Eleven families noted that doctors had not been able to provide them with definitive biomedical explanations for their children's conditions. Eight families stated that they themselves did not know why the condition happened, and eight families concluded that there was no known reason for the child's condition.

Absence of known causes was the only category in which a pattern was noted by type of condition. Most of these children (*n* = 15) had conditions that involved some type of neurologic impairment, such as cerebral palsy or epilepsy. Families found it difficult to deal with the uncertainty surrounding the etiology and course of these conditions. For example, one family of a child with cerebral palsy stated,

> It was real difficult because we have no idea how it happened. It was something happened when the egg split. I think it is something that happened right away when we conceived. The doctors really did not have much of an explanation for it other than something just did not go right with the splitting of the eggs.

Although this family found it difficult to deal with the absence of clear explanations for the condition, they went on to discuss how they coped with the ambiguity. They pointed out that they "try not to dwell too much on why it happened, rather to deal with it" and focus on the "now and the future instead of the past." When the interviewer asked how these coping strategies were helpful, the family concluded, "Well, you are not going to be able to get on with your life if you continually try to answer why it happened, because there really is not an answer."

Another family of a child with epilepsy described a fatalistic, schicksal type of explanation and repeatedly stated that there was no reason for the child's condition.

> Mother: Shit happens. And there is no reason.
>
> Father: Yes, there is no reason.
>
> Mother: There's no reason. That is, what is. And I am fortunate to have had the opportunity to reflect on it theologically for at least the last six years. There is no reason. It just is one of the things that happens. Why does my kid have epilepsy and somebody else's does not? No reason. Why does my kid have epilepsy and somebody else's kid has leukemia? No reason. It just happens.

This family conveyed a sense of acceptance about the lack of known reasons for their child's condition. Furthermore, they concluded, "We have adjusted to it pretty well."

Conditions for which there is no known cause or treatment add an uncertainty factor that makes it more difficult for families to find closure in their search for why the condition happened. Instead of dwelling on the absence of biomedical explanations, many families put an end to the why question by clearly identifying that there was no known cause for the condition. Other families used fatalistic or traditional beliefs to explain the condition.

Only two families were still struggling to find answers for their child's condition. One family, whose child was diagnosed with spina bifida 12 years ago, commented that they were still going to different medical providers looking for answers. Another family talked about their search to find what caused their child's rare seizure disorder, which was diagnosed 5 years ago: "There is no explanation. I think that is why it hurts. That's why we are going all over looking to find the answer." Even though a number of years had passed, neither of these families had found a way to explain the chronic condition to their satisfaction.

Personal Attributions

A number of family caregivers attributed the chronic condition either to themselves or to another family caregiver. Some caregivers raised the issue of possible personal responsibility for the child's condition; others blamed themselves or other family members for the condition.

Several families ($n = 8$) recalled questioning whether they had done something to cause their child's condition and posed a number of hypothetical explanations for the child's condition. Half of these families also reported that health care providers did not have a biomedical explanation for the child's condition. The absence of a clear-cut reason appeared to fuel the questioning process for these caregivers.

Four mothers recalled that they asked why the condition happened and searched for answers when their child was first diagnosed. They retraced the time period before the diagnosis to determine if any of their own behaviors could have caused the condition. After finding out more information and identifying their own explanations for the condition, three of the mothers stated that they no longer asked why the condition occurred. However, another mother stated that she still questions whether she could have done something differently but does not blame herself for the child's condition.

Five families in this study suggested that a family caregiver was in some way responsible for the child's condition. Although each of these families had additional explanations for the cause of the child's condition, a sense of blame and personal responsibility dominated these conversations. In two cases, the child's cerebral palsy was associated with the father's history of alcohol use. An older brother of a child with cerebral palsy stated, "I always blame my father, because many say that children who come with that illness have a father who drinks and a father who doesn't give love." In another case, the father blamed himself for the child's condition. "Sometimes, I think that I am guilty . . . sometimes, I realize that it isn't my fault and I try to be optimistic. Other times, I blame it on myself, you know, I used to drink a lot, and I asked myself if it was because of that."

Family caregivers who talked about blaming themselves or someone else in the family for the child's condition also seemed to have more difficulty coming to terms with the child's condition. For example, one grandmother reported that she still blames herself for not being more involved in her grandchild's care and preventing his meningitis even though doctors told her that there was nothing she could have done. Meanwhile, the child's aunt blames the biological mother for not taking care of the child and not seeking medical treatment sooner. The child had been living with his mother, who had a chemical dependency problem, when he first became ill. At 5 months of age, he developed meningitis and is now totally dependent on others for his care. The grandparents currently have custody and provide total care for the child.

Blame was also evident in the two cases discussed earlier in the traditional beliefs section of this chapter. In one case, the mother questioned whether she had done anything wrong to cause her child's diabetes and pointed out that her husband believed that their problems are due in part to her cursing. In the other case, the adult son blames his brother's spina bifida primarily on his parents. He suggests a variety of possible explanations for the condition, including the possibility that his mother had lifted something heavy or that emotional problems, anger, or family conflict led to the spina bifida.

Combined Explanations

The majority of families (70%) provided more than one type of explanation for their children's chronic conditions. The combination of explanations often included a mixture of beliefs that reflected the family's worldview and their exposure to biomedical culture. Families did not separate their explanations into particular categories. Instead, explanations were woven together within the family's account of how they made sense of the condition.

In the following illustration, a mother who described herself as an African-American, divorced single parent of two school-aged children named several different types of explanations for her son's asthma and subsequent stroke. At the time of the interview, she was working on a college degree in sociology.

> Why did it happen to my child? I guess I look at, you know, all these other little kids that do not have anything. My other son has nothing. He is fine. But it is real curious, because in my family it seems like out of one child in each family there is something. My son had the chronic asthma and then now the episode with the thrombosis. My sister's son has attention deficit disorder and has had chronic ear problems. One of my brother's daughters has sickle cell and so she is ill. She gets ill quite often. Then I have my other brother and his little girl has bronchial problems and we were not sure for awhile if she was going to have the asthma or not, but she seems to be doing pretty good now. So, it seems like out of each family there has been something, you know, that at least one child has had something so, you know, in a way it is kind of like, okay, well this must be my child that is going to. . . I hate to even get into that mind-set of thinking that way—kind of like a family curse or something, but it is just why, you know, why does he have to go through all of this, you know. I just feel like it is a lot, you know. It is a lot for me, but it is even more for him, you know, because he is the one going, actually going through it.

In addition, she described biomedical explanations for the child's stroke, including "the predisposition on his father's side of the family to clotting" and a medication that the child was taking for asthma that the doctors think could have contributed to the blood clot. Instead of dwelling on the "why" question and the negative consequences of the asthma and stroke, this mother goes on to emphasize the importance of coping with these conditions in a positive way, which is clearly an indicator of resilience.

> I want to see him completely healed from all of that, but I guess the main thing is that he has the coping skills, you know. And that is something no matter what life brings or what happens to you that you develop these coping skills that, you know, you can deal with it. And that is the thing I am trying to get him to deal with now. And his teacher said that he does a wonderful job, you know, because they look at all the things that he has had to go wrong and that he is still having to deal with on a daily basis and that they said that his disposition, his self esteem—it is like it does not change, and that is real important to me. . . . I told him life is going to have all kinds of things for you, but the thing is that you stay stabilized, you know, and really have a God in your life that is going to be your stabilizer, because there is going to be so much that is going to happen.

Changing Explanations Over Time

Families often talked about how their explanations for the condition changed over time. At the time of the diagnosis, several families found themselves asking a number of questions about the cause of the condition. After living with the condition for several years, these families typically reported that they no longer asked "why" the condition happened. Instead, they focused on a particular explanation that made sense to them or decided that there was no reason for the condition. As one mother whose child was diagnosed with diabetes stated, "I used to say why, now I just say, it just happened."

Some families also found that their beliefs sometimes changed with new experiences. For example, one father attributed the biliary atresia to "bad luck" and blamed God when he first found out about the condition. Eight years later, he recounted how his spiritual beliefs had changed.

> Now, sometimes, I just say, "Thank you, Lord, for giving me this problem. . . I have learned a lot of things." I have learned to respect people more and to have faith that things can be worked out. . . my daughter is my inspiration. . . and the problem with my daughter has brought us together.

Like this father, other family caregivers reported that negative attributions at the time of diagnosis often shifted to positive attributions as they learned more about the chronic condition and focused more on the child than the condition. The ability to reframe negative attributions as positive attributions is another characteristic of resilient families. The meanings that families attribute to the cause of the chronic condition are not necessarily static but can change in response to new experiences and exposure to different viewpoints.

Discussion

Families provided a variety of explanations for their children's chronic conditions that reflected their beliefs and exposure to different cultural viewpoints and contexts. Because all of the children in this project required medical treatment, families were exposed to a medical culture and providers who used biomedical terminology. The influence of this exposure is evident in the biomedical language that families used to describe genetic, physiological, and medical treatment explanations related to chronic conditions. The importance of biomedical explanations to families is reflected in the presence as well as the absence of biomedical explanations they reported.

The impact of traditional ethnocultural beliefs on families' explanations is most evident in descriptions of folk beliefs about illness and religious/spiritual interpretations of the chronic condition. The influence of culture is also apparent in expressions of fatalistic and superstitious beliefs that reflect the family's worldview. Collectively, Hispanic-American families shared proportionately more traditional types of explanations for the child's condition and offered more fatalistic types of explanations for the condition. Recency of immigration and the heavy reliance in mainstream American culture on scientific explanations of disease are possible explanations for these group differences. Approximately one third ($n = 7$) of the families who identified themselves as Hispanic had immigrated to the United States within the past decade, whereas none of the European-American or African-American families were first-generation immigrants. Religious affiliation is another potential explanatory factor. African-American and European-American female caregivers endorsed a broader range of religious affiliations than did the majority of Hispanic female caregivers (79%) who identified themselves as Catholic. Whereas all of the Hispanic caregivers identified with some religious group, a few family caregivers in the African-American and European-American groups did not identify with any religious group. Expressions of spiritual beliefs reflect the family's worldview and cultural context.

Relatively few traditional folk beliefs were discussed in the family interviews. This may be due to the fact that families were talking about chronic conditions that require medical intervention. In her study of hospitalized patients, Mardiros (1984) found that Mexican American patients did not readily volunteer evidence of folk beliefs, and when they did, folk beliefs had little influence on how they viewed illness that required hospitalization compared to more common illnesses. Likewise, Lupton (1994) asserts that people are more likely to draw on traditional folk models of illness when the illness is common and not serious. The complex and serious nature of childhood chronic conditions calls for explanations that extend beyond the experiences of most lay people in the community. Because of the complex nature of chronic conditions and the fact that families hear biomedical explanations during their encounters with the health care providers, families are more likely to emphasize biomedical explanations for the cause of the condition than other explanations. Another possible explanation for the low number of folk beliefs expressed is that families may not have felt comfortable sharing this information even though interviewers and families were from similar cultural backgrounds.

Families differed in the ways in which they talked about the cause of childhood chronic conditions. Some had clear-cut explanations about the condition, whereas others raised a variety of hypotheses about the source of the condition. Families who posed a number of possible reasons for the condition tended to have children with conditions characterized by uncertainty. In the absence of clear biomedical explanations for the condition, most families identified alternative explanations (e.g, traditional, fatalistic, or religious/spiritual beliefs) that helped them make sense of their situations. Other families resolved ambiguity about the cause of the disease by no longer asking "why" questions and deciding that there was no reason for the condition or that knowing the reason did not matter. For example, one family's immediate and only response to the interview question about cause was, "We don't ask why." After much questioning, another family decided that "only God knows why He sent her that way."

Families' explanations provide important clues about how families view and manage childhood chronic illness and disability. Indicators of resilience were found within families' descriptions of all of the different types of explanations, except for the caregiver blame category. Once they identified their understanding of the cause, families often went on to describe how particular explanations helped them cope. For example, a number of families emphasized that religious and spiritual beliefs helped them cope by providing a sense of meaning and purpose. One mother of a child with cerebral palsy stated,

> Well, I just look at it as saying that it was meant to happen. You know, that's the way God planned it for some reason. At one time, I wondered what I did. You think about what you did to make it happen and there really is no answer. . . . When I feel bad, I figured out that, you know, it's just some powerful being that said this is

how it is. That is the way God said it. So, it must be for a reason, and she'll show us what the reason is and I don't dwell on it so much, you know, because if I dwell on it, I'll start getting upset and feeling sorry for myself. . . and that's not helping her or our family, you know. And so we just try to deal with it in a positive way.

Other family researchers have also found that particular religious and spiritual beliefs influence how families respond to childhood chronic illness and disability (McCubbin et al., 1992; Patterson & Leonard, 1994). The relationship between a family's traditional beliefs and coping behaviors warrants further investigation.

A follow-up study is needed to determine whether the meanings that families attribute to the cause of the child's condition change over time (e.g., as the child grows or the condition improves or deteriorates). Also, further research is needed to identify the relationship between situational meanings about causation, family identity, and family worldview. The findings suggest that the family's worldview and family identity may change as families find new ways to make sense of the chronic condition and its impact on the family. Future studies should compare how families and their physicians explain the etiology of the chronic condition and assess whether the degree of congruence in perceptions influences child, family, and/or treatment outcomes.

The coherent ways in which the majority of families made sense of childhood chronic illness reflected their ability to cope with difficult and complex situations. The family's ability to integrate various types of explanations about chronic illness and disability from health care providers and community members into their own positive attributions about the condition is a hallmark of resilient family functioning. Like other investigators (Austin & McDermott, 1988; Bristol, 1987; Patterson, 1991), we found that resilient families tend to ascribe positive rather than negative attributions to the child's condition, and that these attributions help them manage stressors related to the condition more effectively.

Although particular explanations for chronic conditions varied from family to family, common patterns of family resilience were found in family caregivers' discussions about causation. The following characteristics were emphasized by African-American, Hispanic, and European-American families of children with different types of chronic conditions:

- Emphasis on positive versus negative reasons for the condition

- Lack of preoccupation about why the condition happened

- The ability to move beyond focusing on why the condition happened to managing the demands of the condition within the context of family life

- The family's ability to decide on a coherent explanation about the cause of the condition consistent with their beliefs

Our findings suggest that families search for suitable explanations for the cause of the chronic condition soon after the diagnosis. Although there is considerable variation in the types of explanations that families described, the majority of families discovered meanings that helped them cope with their situations. Families drew on a variety of family, health care, and community resources for their explanations. The emphasis that families placed on particular explanations reflected their particular worldview and the nature of the chronic condition. Resilience was evident in families who were able to decide on coherent explanations congruent with their beliefs.

Only a few families were still struggling to make sense of their child's condition several years after the diagnosis. A lack of resolution about the cause of the condition and unresolved family conflict characterized these interviews. No explanations were viewed as satisfactory by these families. Lack of closure on the issue of causation also seemed to affect how the family managed the child's condition. For example, in one case, a family went from provider to provider in search of answers several years after the diagnosis. In contrast, those families who were able to make sense of the condition were able to redirect their energies toward coping with other illness and family demands.

Coming to terms with why the condition happened helps families move on to deal with other issues. A number of families talked about the importance of not dwelling on the "why" question and living in the present. A key feature of resilient families was their ability to find an explanation about the cause of the condition that made sense to them.

Implications for Providers

Understanding how the patient, family, and provider view the chronic condition is a prerequisite to providing family-centered care that is culturally sensitive. Providers can avoid providing biased care by understanding their own explanatory models of illness and listening to how families define chronic conditions. Knowledge of both congruent and divergent beliefs helps the clinician provide information and plan treatment strategies that support healthy family functioning.

Providers need to listen for negative attributions that family caregivers give to the child's condition, such as blaming oneself or others for the condition. The key in assessing family explanations is to consider whether they are harmful to the child or family. If so, further assessment and possible intervention is warranted. For example, health care providers need to be aware of family caregivers who assign unnecessary personal responsibility or guilt to themselves or other family members for the child's condition. Additional information about the child's condition, alternative explanations, and opportunities to talk with each other (with or without a professional present) can help families find new ways of thinking about the condition that are less destructive. Providers can foster the development of positive attributions by focusing on the child's strengths and abilities rather than his or her deficits (Garwick & Millar, 1996).

Only a few types of explanations were related to particular chronic conditions. Not surprisingly, genetic explanations were attributed to conditions that are well known in the literature for having genetic linkages, such as Turner's syndrome and Down syndrome. In addition, the presence of some type of neurologic impairment was associated with the absence of known reasons for the condition. The ambiguous nature of these conditions was particularly stressful for families. When the biomedical etiology of the condition was unknown, families often struggled to understand what caused the condition. Providers can help reduce the stress by naming the uncertainty, keeping the family informed about the child's status, and updating them as new knowledge about the condition is acquired.

Most of the participants asked a lot of why questions at the time of diagnosis but came to some kind of resolution within a couple of years. Only two families in this study were still focusing on why the condition happened 5 to 12 years after the diagnosis. Health care providers need to listen for families who are dwelling on questions about the cause of the condition a number of years after the diagnosis. These families might benefit from meeting together with their health care provider or counselor to address the issue and explore alternative explanations.

Coming to terms with the cause of the chronic condition is an important step for families to accomplish soon after the diagnosis. Coming to terms does not mean that a family must find a biomedical explanation for the child's condition. Instead, coming to terms means that the family finds an explanation that makes sense to them in a way that fits their belief system so that they can move on to deal with other issues. For some families in this study, naming the absence of known causes was the explanation that helped them cope with the condition. Others found biomedical, traditional, and/or fatalistic explanations helpful. In contrast, lack of information from health care providers, language barriers between families and providers, a history of unresolved family conflict, and conditions with unknown biomedical causes and uncertain courses were a few of the factors that made it difficult for families to make sense of the condition.

Most of the family conversations about causation reflected the family's strengths and ability to make sense of difficult situations. Some families focused on single explanations, whereas others drew on a variety of explanations from different sources. Only a couple of families were still struggling to make sense of how and why the condition happened several years after the diagnosis.

The "caregiver blame" category was the only type of explanation in which indicators of resilience were not evident as family caregivers discussed the cause of the condition. Our findings suggest that blaming oneself or other family members for the condition is a risk factor that can interfere with the family's healthy adaptation to the chronic condition. The blaming process keeps families from developing positive attributions and working together in a constructive manner.

Health care providers can support healthy family functioning by acknowledging and supporting beliefs that promote resilience. Providers need to be aware of how families view and explain chronic illness and disability so that they can communicate with families in ways that support, and do not undermine, the family's belief system. By listening respectfully to how a family explains the child's condition, the provider gains an understanding of what the condition means to the family and acknowledges the importance of the family's viewpoints. Providers can build on the family's understanding as they provide follow-up instructions and plan interventions that fit the family's particular needs.

Notes

1.   Preparation of this manuscript was supported by the National Institute on Disability and Rehabilitation Research Grant #H133G30005.

2.   The term "chronic condition" refers to chronic illness and disability.

3.   The *Cross-Cultural Meanings of Chronic Illness and Disability* project is a multisite, field-initiated research study funded by the National Institute on Disability and Rehabilitation (#H133G30005).

4.   The terms "situational meanings" and "family explanations" are used synonymously and interchangeably in the text.

References

Affleck, G., & Tennen, H. (1993). Cognitive adaptation to adversity: Insights from parents of medically fragile infants. In A. P. Turnbull, J. M. Patterson, S. K. Behr, D. L. Murphy, J. G. Marquis, M. J. Blue-Banning (Eds.), *Cognitive coping, families, and disability* (pp. 135–150). Baltimore, MD: Paul H. Brookes.

Anderson, J. M., Elfert, H., & Lai, M. (1989). Ideology in the clinical context: Chronic illness, ethnicity and the discourse of normalization. *Sociology of Health and Illness, 11,* 253–278.

Antonovsky, A. (1979). *Health, stress and coping.* San Francisco: Jossey-Bass.

Antonovsky, A. (1987). *Unraveling the mystery of health.* San Francisco: Jossey-Bass.

Austin, J. K., & McDermott, N. (1988). Parental attitude and coping behavior in families of children with epilepsy. *Journal of Neuroscience, 20,* 174–179.

Berger, P., & Luckmann, T. (1966). *The social construction of reality.* New York: Doubleday.

Berkanovic, E., & Telesky, C. (1985). Mexican-American, Black-American and White-American differences in reporting illnesses, disability and physician visits for illnesses. *Social Science Medicine, 20,* 567–577.

Berkanovic, E., Telesky, C., & Reeder, S. (1981). Structural and social psychological factors in the decision to seek medical care for symptoms. *Medical Care, 19,* 693–709.

Blumhagen, D. (1980). Hyper-tension: A folk illness with a medical name. *Culture, Medicine and Psychiatry, 4,* 197–227.

Boss, P. (1988). *Family stress management.* Newbury Park, CA: Sage.

Bristol, M. M. (1987). Mothers of children with autism or communication disorders: Successful adaptation and the Double ABCX model. *Journal of Autism and Developmental Disorders, 17,* 469–486.

Brookins, G. K. (1992). Culture, ethnicity, and bicultural competence: Implications for children with chronic illness and disability. *Pediatrics, 91* (5 Suppl.), 1056–1062.

Crabtree, B., & Miller, W. (1992). A template approach to text analysis: Developing and using codebooks. In B. Crabtree & W. Miller (Eds.), *Doing qualitative research* (pp. 93–109). Newbury Park, CA: Sage.

Davis, B. J., & Voegtle, K. H. (1994). *Culturally competent health care for adolescents.* Chicago: American Medical Association.

Garro, L. C. (1988). Culture and high blood pressure: Understandings of a chronic illness in an Ojibwa community. *Arctic Medical Research, 47* (1 Suppl.), 70–73.

Garwick, A., & Miller, H. (1996, April). *Promoting resilience in youth with chronic conditions and their families.* Washington, DC: Maternal and Child Health Bureau, Health Resources & Services Administration, U.S. Public Health Service.

Garwick, A., Patterson, J., Bennett, C. F., & Blum, R. W. (1995). Breaking the news: How families first learn about their child's chronic condition. *Archives of General Pediatrics and Adolescent Health, 149,* 991–997.

Glaser, B., & Strauss, A. (1967). *The discovery of grounded theory.* Chicago: Aldine.

Groce, N. E., & Zola, I. K. (1992). Multiculturalism, chronic illness, and disability. *Pediatrics, 91* (5 Suppl), 1048–1055.

Harwood, A. (1981). *Ethnicity and medical care.* Cambridge, MA: Harvard University Press.

Jessop, D. J., & Stein, R. E. (1983). A noncategorical approach to psychosocial research. *Journal of Psychosocial Oncology, 1(4),* 61-64.

Kalyanpur, M., & Rao, S. S. (1991). Empowering low income black families of handicapped children. *American Journal of Orthopsychiatry, 61,* 523–532.

Kleinman, A. (1978). Clinical relevance of anthropological and cross-cultural research: Concepts and strategies. *American Journal of Psychiatry, 135,* 427–431.

Kleinman, A., Eisenberg, L., & Good, B. (1978). Culture, illness and care. *Annals of Internal Medicine, 88,* 251–258.

Krefting, L. (1991). The culture concept in the everyday practice of occupational and physical therapy. In S. K. Campbell & I. J. Wilhelm (Eds.), *Meaning of culture in pediatric rehabilitation and health care* (pp. 1–16). New York: Haworth.

Lazarus, R. S., & Folkman, S. (1984). *Stress, appraisal, and coping.* New York: Springer.

Lupton, D. (1994). *Medicine and culture.* Thousand Oaks, CA: Sage.

Maduro, R. (1983). Curanderismo and Latino views of disease and curing. *The Western Journal of Medicine, 139,* 868–874.

Mardiros, M. (1984). A view toward hospitalization: The Mexican American experience. *Journal of Advanced Nursing, 9,* 469–478.

Mardiros, M. (1989). Conception of childhood disability among Mexican-American parents. *Medical Anthropology, 12,* 55–68.

McCubbin, H. I., & McCubbin, M. (1993). Family coping with health crises: The resiliency model of family stress, adjustment, and adaptation. In C. Danielson, B. Hamel-Bissell, & P. Winstead-Fry (Eds.), *Families, health, and illness* (pp. 21–63). New York: Mosby.

McCubbin, H., & McCubbin, M. (1988). Typologies of resilient families: Emerging roles of social class and ethnicity. *Family Relations, 37,* 247–254.

McCubbin, H., Thompson, E., Thompson, A., McCubbin, M., & Kaston, A. (1992). Culture, ethnicity, and the family: Critical factors in childhood chronic illnesses and disabilities. *Pediatrics, 91* (5 Suppl.), 1063–1070).

National Coalition of Hispanic and Human Services Organizations. (1990). *Delivering preventive health care to Hispanics.* Washington, DC: COSSMHO.

Newacheck, P. W., Stoddard, J. J., & McManus, M. (1992). Ethnocultural variations in the prevalence and impact of childhood chronic conditions. *Pediatrics, 91* (5 Suppl.), 1031–1039.

Pachter, L., Cloutier, M., & Bernstein, B. (1995). Ethnomedical (folk) remedies for childhood asthma in a mainland Puerto Rican community. *Archives of General Pediatrics and Adolescent Health, 149,* 982–988.

Patterson, J. M. (1991). Family resilience to the challenge of a child's disability. *Pediatric Annals, 20,* 491–499.

Patterson, J. M., & Blum, R. W. (1992). A conference on culture and chronic illness in childhood: Conference summary. *Pediatrics, 91* (5 Suppl.), 1025–1030.

Patterson, J. M., & Garwick, A. (1994a). The impact of chronic illness on families: A family systems perspective. *Annals of Behavioral Medicine, 16,* 131–142.

Patterson, J. M., & Garwick, A. (1994b). Levels of family meaning in family stress theory. *Family Process, 33,* 287–304.

Patterson, J. M., & Garwick, A. (1994c). Theoretical linkages: Family meanings and sense of coherence. In H. McCubbin, E. Thompson, A. Thompson, & J. Fromer (Eds.), *Sense of coherence and resiliency: Stress, coping, and health* (pp. 71–89). Madison: University of Wisconsin.

Patterson, J. M., & Leonard, B. J. (1994). Caregiving and children. In E. Kahana, D. E. Biegel, & M. Wykle (Eds.), *Family caregiving across the lifespan* (pp. 133–158). Thousand Oaks, CA: Sage.

Patterson, J. M., McCubbin, H. I., & Warwick, W. (1990). The impact of family functioning on health changes in children with cystic fibrosis. *Social Science and Medicine, 31,* 159–164.

Pless, I. B., & Pinkerton, P. (1975). *Chronic childhood disorder: Promoting patterns of adjustment.* London: Henry Kimpton.

Reiss, D. (1981). *The family's construction of reality.* Cambridge, MA: Harvard University Press.

Stein, R. E., Bauman, L. J., Coupey, S. M., Ireys, H. T., & Westbrook, L. E. (1990). *An operational definition of chronic conditions in childhood* (Working Paper No. 90-08). New York: Preventive Intervention Research Center.

Taylor, S. B. (1983). Adjustment to threatening events: A theory of cognitive adaptation. *American Psychologist, 38,* 1161–1173.

Thompson, S., & Bennett, L. (1991). Life schemes: A framework for understanding the search for meaning. *Journal of Social and Clinical Psychology, 7,* 260–280.

Weber, R. P. (1985). *Basic content analysis.* Beverly Hills, CA: Sage.

Weisner, T. S., Beizer, L., & Stolze, L. (1991). Religions and the families of developmentally delayed children. *American Journal of Mental Retardation, 95,* 647–662.

Weisner, T. S., Matheson, C., & Bernheimer, L. (1996). American cultural models of early influence and parent recognition of developmental delays: Is earlier always better than later? In S. Harkness & C. M. Super (Eds.), *Parents' cultural belief systems* (pp. 497–531). New York: Guilford.

Whyte, W.F. (1989). Advancing scientific knowledge through participatory action research. *Sociological Forum, 4,* 367–385.

7

Surviving the Demise of a Way of Life

Stress and Resilience in Northeastern Commercial Fishing Families[1]

Helen J. Mederer

The world's oceans cover approximately 70% of the earth. For most of history, the bounties of the oceans seemed endless, but unrestrained harvesting of seafood has begun to define its limits. It is generally agreed now that many world fisheries are in crisis, with the majority of world fish stocks overexploited, fully exploited, or rebuilding from an overexploited status. What the causes of the crisis are, how serious the situation is, and how the problem should be resolved are points of vigorous, often hostile debates between environmentalists, marine scientists, governmental regulators, and fishermen. The Northeast commercial fishing industry has been especially hard hit. Once the source of abundant life, the rich fishing grounds in the North Atlantic have experienced overexploitation and alarming declines of cod, haddock, yellowtail flounder, and other commercially significant groundfish species.

This problem is not only ecological and biological in nature, but social as well, because commercial fishing constitutes a "way of life" for New England fishermen, their families, and communities. This chapter describes the first several years of a longitudinal qualitative study of the effects of changes in the conditions of commercial fishing on family life. Resilient characteristics of families who make their living from commercial fishing are uncovered and discussed. This type of study could be done on any number of industries as economies continue to restructure and jobs are downsized out of existence. Although the effects of unemployment on individuals and families are well documented, less is known about the familial effects of job insecurity (Larson, Wilson, & Beley, 1994). The major focus of this chapter is to locate within the stress and resiliency theoretical literature these qualitative data about families' responses to the external stressor of job regulation; however, there are important implications for policy in this theoretical examination.

The impact of job transformation upon families is underrecognized in economic and political decision making. In this regard, qualitative research may be less easily dismissed than the statistics and "faceless" numbers generated by more traditional quantitative research. What happens to these fishermen and their families, how they adjust their lives and their jobs, and how fishing communities will be changed are important questions. Equally important is information about the conditions under which the changes will be more or less stressful for those who stay and for those who leave the fishing industry. For both family scientists and government policymakers, the stories of crisis and coping that fishing families tell through repeated interviews over several years of dealing with change can be used to further both theory and policy.

What Happened to the Fishing Industry?

Domestic overexploitation of groundfish began in earnest in 1976, when, under pressure from New England fishermen, Congress passed the Magnuson Fishery and Conservation Act. The Magnuson Act was set up to protect American waters from overfishing by foreign vessels by enacting a 200-mile fishery conservation zone (now called Exclusive Economic Zone, or EEZ) off the coast of the United States and leaving control of fishing rights within the EEZ open to American fishing. The legislation also created eight regional management councils throughout the coastal areas of the United States. The Magnuson Act, however, created a "gold rush" for U.S. fishermen, particularly those in the northeastern United States. Despite the existence of the management councils, the industry became hugely overcapitalized (Collins, 1994), and "the Magnuson Act fueled a rat race many fishermen were unable to retire from" (O'Neill, Aug. 18, 1991, p. A-01). Between 1977 and 1984, backed by low-interest government loans, the number of groundfishing vessels (those fishing for bottom-feeding species) nearly doubled, from 650 to approximately 1,021 (Duffy, 1994). In Gloucester, Massachusetts, for instance, the number of small vessels decreased, whereas the number of large vessels increased five-fold. In all New England ports, the number of fishing trips per year, as well as the length of each trip, increased (Collins, 1994). At the same time, technology significantly increased the efficiency in landing fish. With the addition of the Loran C., a computerized navigational device that allows fishermen to pinpoint the exact location of a rich fishery, and video fish finders that can spot even a few fish from a great distance, the "fish don't have an even chance of getting away" (interview with a Point Judith fisherman, July 1994). During the boon years of the 1980s in New England, deckhands on groundfish boats were earning between $40,000 and $60,000 a year, and scallopers were making up to $3,000 a trip, or nearly $100,000 a year (Duffy, 1994). The harder one fished, the more one could earn. The most successful fishers were those who had bigger boats and made more trips. Fishermen fished hard during the 1980s, many with short-term financial (rather than with long-term sustainability) interests. This "tragedy of the commons" (Hall-Arber, 1992) allowed commercial fishermen, especially boat owners, to live a comfortable, middle-class life style: "They had nice cars, they bought big houses, and their wives didn't have to work" (Duffy, 1994, p. 103).

Under these conditions, the number of fish declined steadily. In 1993, groundfish landings were reportedly down by 30% (NMFS, 1995). Landings of cod, haddock, and winter flounder reached their lowest levels in history (Collins, 1994). The environmental community began to focus on the plight of marine fisheries in the late 1980s and demanded a response from the regional fishery management councils.

In 1994, the Northeast Regional Fishery Management Council (NEFMC) finally passed Amendment 5 of the Groundfish plan of the Magnuson Act (NEFMC, 1992). The primary objective of Amendment 5 was to eliminate overfishing within 5 years by reducing fishing mortality by 10% each year until 1999. Even before these provisions were implemented, fisheries scientists realized that these measures were too little, too late for stock rebuilding. Emergency measures went into effect immediately, while a more stringent plan, known as Amendment 7, was drafted. The emergency measures closed 6,000 square miles of George's Bank, historically the richest fishing grounds in the Northeast. It is now agreed by all parties that the days of hands-off management are gone (cf. NMFS, 1995).

Amendment 7 went into effect in the spring of 1996 and dictated more severe measures. Large areas of George's Bank remain closed for the foreseeable future. Net mesh sizes increased, and quotas (limits on how many pounds of fish one can bring in per season) were enacted for more species and became more restrictive. The New

England commercial fishing industry is being irreversibly changed, and with it, a way of life central to New England cultural identity might be lost.

The Study

Sample

The data presented here are part of a qualitative study of a sample of commercial fishing families in two ports in southern New England: Point Judith, Rhode Island (also known as the Port of Galilee), and Gloucester, Massachusetts. These two samples (Point Judith, n = 20 families; Gloucester, n = 10 families) are being followed for a total period of 4 years (1994–1997)[2] during a time of increasing governmental management of the fishing industry. New families are added on an ongoing basis in both ports to ensure representation of those who leave and stay in fishing. All families represent groundfish draggers. These ports were chosen for comparison because of several key differences: the Gloucester fishing industry is more dependent on the regulated groundfish than is Point Judith (Gloucester landings are 85% regulated species; Point Judith's are 20%, according to NMFS, 1991); Gloucester is more ethnically identified than Point Judith, with Point Judith fishermen less dependent on traditional fishing and family practices. Gloucester boats generally take longer trips than do Point Judith boats, and finally, the Gloucester fishing community is more defined geographically than is Point Judith. Thus, the two ports are facing a similar fishery crisis, but with some important differences for comparison.

Within the two samples are two subgroups, boat owners (n = 20) and crew members (n = 10). These subgroups were chosen for representation because the impacts of the fishery crisis are very different for these two groups, with owners typically better off in terms of resources and social service interventions. Among the owners, the sample includes equal representation of levels of business success, what are referred to in the industry as "highliners," "midliners," and "lowliners." Specific comparisons between owners and crew, however, are not made in the present analysis. All of the families interviewed are either married or living in a long-term (i.e., more than 5 years) marriage-like relationship, and all have been fishing for at least 5 years.

In general, Gloucester families exhibit more stress than do Point Judith families because large portions of their fishery are now closed. Point Judith fishermen want the government to buy back the Gloucester and other Massachusetts port boats so that these fishermen will not intrude in "their" fisheries for underutilized species such as squid and butterfish. That is, Point Judith is worried about more competition for underutilized species because displaced efforts will force more George's Bank boats to diversify.

Sample Characteristics. Analysis of the first-year questionnaire data yielded the following information: The respondents in the sample have a mean age of 41 years, with females 4 years younger than their husbands, on average. They have an average of 2.4 children, 1.6 living with them. Their average income in 1994 was in the $40,000–$49,000 range, with 53% reporting a decline in income since 1993. Sixty-three percent are Catholic, 29% Protestant, and 8% are not affiliated with any particular religion. Forty percent describe themselves as having strong religious beliefs, 37% as having moderately strong beliefs, and 23% as having weak religious beliefs.

Research Design

Two methods of data collection are used: qualitative data, collected through face-to-face, semi-structured interviews of fishermen and their wives, and quantitative data, collected through written questionnaires. Fishermen and their wives were interviewed separately, and each filled out a questionnaire. The qualitative interviews elicited information about the following topics: a wide variety of family interaction, family stress, job stress, coping, attitudes about fishery management, perceptions of the future, emotive commitment to fishing, perceptions of breadwinning, and the need for social services. The questionnaire contains more structured questions, including demographic information, family events, four dimensions of the SCL-90-R distress symptom inventory (Derogatis, 1992), as well as measures of boundary ambiguity, health behaviors, and social support. The qualitative interviews, the data from which are presented here, are tape-recorded, transcribed, and analyzed for relevant themes using a qualitative data analysis program, NUDIST.

Commercial Fishing as a "Way of Life"

Research on commercial fishing has described the uniqueness of fishing family structure and interaction. In traditional fishing families and communities, fishing was not a job but a way of life (Ellis, 1984; Palsson, 1989). Indeed, almost every fisherman and his wife in the present study described fishing as "in my blood" or "in their blood." It is this identity and lifestyle that fishermen seem to value above all. In her interviews of New England fishermen, Madeleine Hall-Arber (1993) found that this way of life seems to keep people fishing despite the long hours of hard work and the uncertain financial reward. Hall-

Arber's work describes some of the content of the lifestyle, such as the myriad types of independence of wide open, solitary space; freedom from the rhythms and routines of regular society that fishermen experience; the strong egalitarian ethic between all types of fishermen; and the sense of community. Mederer (1993) similarly found that commercial families' structure involves at least six elements: segregated household labor, physical and psychic independence, acceptance or denial of the physical danger of commercial fishing, social support, acceptance of unpredictability, and the definition of "normal" family life as the period when the husband was gone to sea.

Most of the research on families in commercial fishing has examined the effects of father absence on family interaction and power (Anderson & Wadel, 1972; Binkley & Thiessen, 1988; Danowski, 1980; Davis & Nadel-Klein, 1992; Dixon, Lowery, Sabella, & Hepburn, 1984; Forsyth & Gramling, 1987; Gerstel & Gross, 1984; Gersuny & Poggie, 1973; Orbach, 1978; Sabella, Dixon, & Hepburn, 1979; Solheim, & Bauer, 1983; Thompson, 1985). Traditionally, these studies show that, fishing families relied on a gender-defined division of labor, with husbands as main breadwinners and wives as full-time homemakers, but with men having limited power and roles when on land. Fishing success typically depended upon family cooperation and coordination, with women actively involved as financial managers, administrators, onshore information agents, and purchasers of gear and supplies (Davis, 1986; Dixon et al., 1984; Green, 1985; McCay, 1988; Nadel-Klein & Davis, 1988; Smith & Jepson, 1993; Thompson, 1985). Today, wives generally have become less involved in the financial end of fishing (the extensive record-keeping tends to require the services of a professional accountant) and more involved in political activism on behalf of commercial fishermen (Pollack, 1992). However, the particular family organization that fishing families develop to deal with the regular absences of the husband from daily life involves clearly delineated roles, with women dominating family life and men dominating work life. This arrangement creates independent lives for men, on one hand, and for women and children on the other hand. As one wife put it, "We like him being gone." Part of the family organizational strategy is that labor force participation of wives tends to be lower than that of wives in general. Wives report feeling strongly that they need to "be there" for children, and that breadwinning is not their responsibility. This lifestyle has been possible until now because of the relatively high income of fishermen over the past 15 years.

Men have highly circumscribed roles in families and are often treated as "periodic guests" (Forsyth & Gramling, 1987), with their main family role defined as that of breadwinner. When they are at home between trips, they interrupt, for better or for worse, the "normal" flow of family life (Forsyth & Gramling, 1987; Mederer, 1993). The periodic guest strategy is similar to the organization of single-parent households except that the head of the household is not the breadwinner, and the family is visited periodically by a guest, the husband/father (Forsyth & Gramling, 1987).

In the interviews, families speak of regular adjustments to the fishermen's presence and absence. This approach to family roles constitutes an intricate and effective coping strategy for periodic absences. For instance, one wife commented:

> To tell you the truth, if he worked 9 to 5, I would probably kill him! I hate when he is home. . . . If he takes regular time off, that's fine, anything beyond that . . . everyone just drives each other crazy. The kids will say, "It's time to leave.". . . You find yourself sitting, not being occupied, and every little thing is fidgety. My husband's family, they say, "I don't know how you do it," and I say, "I love it." There are some nights I can do whatever I want. . . . If I want to sew, I don't have to stop at 3 o'clock and pick it up, make supper . . . I do my thing, the kids do their thing, and he fishes. (34-year-old wife of a captain)

Another 40-year-old wife of a former owner described fishing family organization:

> Everything is left up to the wife at home. They come home for their one day, and everything is supposed to be fun and games when they come home, and all the work's supposed to be put aside, and then they leave. For him, it's like having a girlfriend, and then he has kids to come home and visit and you leave, and you don't have a care in the world, and you're out on the water. . . . We lived here for three years, and he didn't know where anything was. I mean, he had to ask. And he got me a cordless screwdriver for Christmas.

Her husband continued:

> I usually spend only one night at home, . . . the boat is what your life revolves around. Most of us, our lives revolve around the home; my life revolves around the boat, you never get away from it, you just come home to visit. . . . I really don't fit in here. I don't enjoy being here. I don't enjoy living on land. (40-year-old former owner)

Another fisherman described his role in family life:

> I've always been the family head, and I've always supported my family, and they always look to me for important decisions, but the

actual interaction—I've had more of an interaction with my crew than I did with my family. (49-year-old owner).

This wife described the independence and separateness:

I don't need somebody else here to make everything all right. . . . One of my first questions when he comes in is, when are you going fishing again, because he has come in and invaded my territory. And he will say, "oh, a couple of days," and that's O.K. (50-year-old wife of a dragger/lobsterer)

The issue of male intrusion and invasion was evident in the wives' interviews. Although they were able to articulate the theme of adjustments in family roles, they clearly had defined what was "normal" family life. For instance,

We used to laugh about it, another woman and I. It's like an interference, an intrusion, you get so used to making your own decisions, coming, going as you please, really being your own boss. When they are in . . . there is extra supper and more laundry. It's like leading a dual life. You have to almost flip, you're independent, and then you play a game. When they come home, now it's time to flip the hat just to pacify them for 2 or 3 days when they are around. . . .When he comes home and says, "Did the kids have supper yet?" it's insulting, and yet you try and understand where they are coming from. They want to feel involved, but [yet] imply that when he's not there, the kids don't get dinner. All of a sudden, someone coming in and wants to have some involvement with the family. . . . He asks dumb questions in front of the kids, like if one of them is sick, he'll ask if he's got his medicine. He's trying in his own way to be involved. Then you start to feel resentment, because, gee, if you weren't here, do you suppose the kid wouldn't get his medicine? (46-year-old wife of a dragger)

Similarly, another wife commented:

I like to sit down for dinner, I don't like when he—and he does this a lot—he'll come in and I'll just be putting dinner on the table, and I'll go and get his dish, . . . and he'll say, "I'm not hungry." Then nobody wants to sit down because Daddy is home. So that is an intrusion. But I don't think it would be fair to say, "Well, look, if you cannot be here for dinner, do not come in and interrupt our dinner." He's only here for one day, and I would feel like a witch if I said [that]. (34-year-old wife of a dragger)

One wife spoke of two schedules:

When he is home, he wants a set schedule, because that's how he grew up and that's the way they do it on the boat. So you adjust again, sometimes it's a constant adjustment, and there are some days when you wonder if you are going to have any time to yourself. I think having a schedule bothers me more than anything, having to do things at a certain time. . . . I have two routines, when he is here, and when he is not. . . . When he's home, it's his routine. . . . When he is not around, I do what I like. (50-year-old wife of a dragger/lobsterer)

Theoretical Explanations of Family Adjustments to Routine Member Absences

These descriptions of family role adjustments to routine absences of a member echo findings from other research on alternative work schedules (Boss, McCubbin, & Lester, 1979; Clark, McCann, Morrive, & Taylor, 1985; Forsyth & Gramling, 1987; Gerstel & Gross, 1984; Gramling & Forsyth, 1987; McCubbin, Dahl, & Hunter, 1976; McCubbin, Dahl, Lester, Benson, & Robertson, 1976) and are informed by the vast research on military families' adjustment to members' POW status, a nonroutine absence (McCubbin & Dahl, 1974; McCubbin, Dahl, Lester, & Ross, 1975, McCubbin, Hunter, & Dahl, 1975; Metres, McCubbin, & Hunter, 1974). Research on work scheduling and family interaction finds that nontraditional work scheduling is generally defined as problematic (Gerstel & Gross, 1984; Gramling & Forsyth, 1987), and that wives tend to cope with work-related absences of the husbands by developing increased independence, supportive social networks, and role realignment that minimizes the need for continuous male presence (cf. Boss et al., 1979; Forsyth & Gramling, 1987). The research on families of POWs concerns the process of adaptation: of men to war and captivity, of the family unit to the prolonged and ambiguous absence of a husband/father, and of family members to reintegration into the family structure of the returned soldier (McCubbin & Dahl, 1974). Relevant to the present study is the finding that wives of POWs and MIAs develop the ability to live with ambiguity and to run the family household independently. The extensive analysis of reintegration problems points to variations in the ability of wives to share family power and roles, and in the ability of husbands to accept that their families had changed and to treat wives as more equal partners.

The conceptual frameworks through which these findings are interpreted tend to be in the family stress and family problem solving theoretical traditions; however, theoretical elaboration and integration of the process of role/boundary change remains underdeveloped. Theoretical examinations have tended to focus on the initial adjustment to the routine absences of husbands/fathers. These analyses assume that because this family type differs from mainstream family organization,[3] families initially define the periodic absences/visiting by the male as a stressor that renders family boundaries ambiguous (Boss, 1977). These studies have described family reorganization responses during absences (such as "independence") and the role boundary readjustment that takes place upon the absent member's return as coping strategies. As families become used to these predictable familial exits and entrances over time, they come to accept the coping strategies and perform them with more ease. Thus, Boss et al. (1979, p. 83) found corporate wives "fitting into the corporate lifestyle," Clark et al. (1985) found oil workers' wives defining the material rewards of oil workers as beneficial to family life, and Forsyth and Gramling (1987) found five different arrangements used by fishing families. These strategies can be thought of as the way of life that families develop. As Gerstel and Gross (1984) and Gramling and Forsyth (1987) have pointed out, the longer the process of defining themselves continues, the more real the definitions become and the more they guide and define the individuals involved and the situations within which they interact. Thus, through this definitional process, the routine absences and visits come to be redefined as normal. It is only deviations from this pattern that henceforth may be defined as stressors. This makes some sense of the present study's data: After the work-family schedule has been established, when husbands are home "too long," the family experiences stress.

Another research tradition can be brought to bear on the data. In the present study, fishing families' way of life can be considered to be their construction and definition of reality (Berger & Kellner, 1970; Gramling & Forsyth, 1987). This notion has been developed in a number of theoretical perspectives, among them the study of family paradigms, developed most fully by Reiss and Oliveri (1980) and by Reiss (1981). Elaborated from the family problem-solving tradition, family paradigms are defined as shared constructs and sets of fundamental assumptions about the social world. Families develop a shared paradigm about the nature and meaning of life, what is important, and how to cope with the world in which they live (Ransom, Fisher, & Terry, 1992). These paradigms serve as the enduring, central, and shared assumptions that a family uses as they choose and modify goals, use resources, make decisions, and evaluate how well they are functioning (Constantine, 1986). Similarly, Gubrium and Lynott (1985), applying a symbolic interactionist perspective, refer to family rhetoric as the social order of the family, or situated articulations of enduring family conduct. Family paradigms, reality construction, and/or rhetoric include attitudes and behavior: *conceptions* of what the family is like, how it fits into its social world, and the process of defining norms and rules of interaction, as well as the actual *behavioral manifestations* of the conceptions. Thus, the fishing family paradigm is their way of life–how they define themselves in regard to personal identity, family roles, work scheduling, and community involvement.

For most fishing families, then, the way of life becomes normal, comfortable, and predictable. However, as regulation of the fishing industry continues, the paradigm becomes more difficult to maintain. The regulations result in husbands/fathers being home more often, with either no paycheck or a paycheck that reflects a decreased ability to perform their primary (and often only) family role. Thus, men are losing their "ticket" into family life and are occupying a space in family interaction that is not normally available to them and in which they have, at best, limited roles. If families are to adjust to men's increased time at home, or a different work schedule in general, their hard-won and intricate family paradigm will have to change to accommodate the changed conditions of work. Moreover, for those who inevitably leave the industry, their changes will be profound. As the recently divorced wife of an unsuccessful fishermen, who has since left the industry, put it, "He couldn't adjust to not being the captain at home."

Industry Change and Family Stress

Imposed changes in the location, timing, methods, and rewards of fishing have affected the ability of families to maintain their customary family paradigm. Family stress theory can offer interpretations of how families respond to both economic/job insecurity as well as to demands for paradigm change. Traditional family stress theory is based on the idea of the family as a system. This approach describes the process by which families come to recognize and label events or circumstances as stressors, attribute their causes, and use various family resources to respond to or manage their impact (McCubbin & Patterson, 1983). Traditional stress theory posited factors that influence resistance to stress and factors that influence ability to recover from system disruption caused by a stressor event—the "B" factor (Burr, Leigh, Day, & Constantine, 1979). In their treatise on family stress theory, Hansen and Johnson (1979) departed from the system-based approach and asked a different, more interactionist question about family stress: How do families interact in stressed situations, and what are the relative probabilities that they will maintain established patterns and/or negotiate institutive, or newly created, patterns of interaction?

The emphasis on dynamic processes rather than just static characteristics of resilient families is a characteristic of more recent family stress theory and is useful in interpreting the role/boundary change process demanded of fishing families. The established patterns of interaction constitute a paradigm; the regulated changes in the nature of work call for changes in the family paradigm, where established strategies no longer work, and institutive or new strategies must emerge. Much of the redefinition revolves around redefining gender boundaries (Gerson & Peiss, 1984) or a need to "do gender" (West & Zimmerman, 1987) differently, especially with regard to breadwinning, but also in regard to the reallocation of other family roles. Much like the POW literature on family reintegration, the independence of fishermen's wives is problematic to creating "institutive" patterns. Letting the fisherman in and redefining breadwinning as a joint responsibility are difficult adjustments. The separate boundaries around work and family, men and women need to be negotiated. The stress involved in renegotiation is revealed by this wife, whose husband was home for a 9-month period after his boat burned:

> Now that we are together all the time, I'm not used to it . . . and I do need my space. I'm just a person who likes to just go in a room and close the door. . . . But now it's like I walk in the door and it's what do we want to eat . . . and he is right there, and I just want to eat when I finish doing what I want to do. . . . It's hard at night because I'm in bed by 8:45, and now he is watching t.v. and I have the pillow over my head. Now I'm dragging myself out of bed because he's a night owl. . . . When he was at sports practice, I would actually try to come home early to have some time to myself. . . . I liked it when he finally found balance, when he would go out on three trips and have one home. . . . For those two thirds [of the year when he was gone], I could handle it. I finally found a balance, and now it's PFFT . . . down to how we do the dishwasher. We never had these pica-yune things before because we didn't have time. It's almost hysteri-cal if it wasn't pathetic. . . . It's been very difficult.

A poignant view of the difficulty of reintegration is offered by this 37-year-old wife of an unsuccessful dragger:

> He was tied up at home all winter—fished off another boat, so he was only gone half the time. And that was a real difficult adjust-ment. It was funny, because the kids would look at him and say, that's not the way we do things around here, Dad. And it was more difficult for him than it was for us, because I think it really hit him how much of a life we had built without him. And we went about our routine, and he met friends of the children that he didn't know.

The difficulty of reintegration when the husband is unable to fulfill his role of breadwinner is illustrated by this 40-year-old wife, whose husband sustained a serious back injury and was unemployed for 7 months:

He was in the hospital in traction and home traction. We went for 7 months without a paycheck. We came this close to losing our house, because being self-employed, too, there's nothing you can collect. Out of the 14 years we've been married, the last 2 years were the worst 2 years of our whole marriage. And it's not like we haven't had hard times before, especially when we were first married. We literally went to bed hungry some nights. We didn't marry for money, that's for sure. But when he came home . . . it was a terrible strain with what was going on financially in the house. Prior to him even hurting himself, it was starting to become a strain . . . but when he came home, I accepted two food baskets. My girlfriend said, "I hope you're not going to be angry," and tears were just rolling down my face, because if it were just [husband] and I, we would have gone hungry. But this was Thanksgiving, and this was Christmas, and I had kids.

The husband recovered but stayed out of fishing for 2 years and worked at another job. He reported:

We had never lived as husband and wife. You've got to understand, when you run a fishing boat, you're Jesus Christ himself. And I had my boat, she had the house. When I gave up fishing, I gave my boat to somebody else, and she still had her house. So all I had was the Toyota. So I lost my identity coming back for all practical purposes. And I hated it, and it took us a long time to get used to being together with one another. We're happy now, a year and a half ago, we weren't so happy. I've only been up walking around again for a year. And it changed my whole attitude towards life. I can't do the things I used to do, and it was a real abrupt change for me. It hurt to do that. . . . It's very hard to live here on land. You're not socialized.[4]

Financial Stress

A recent application of family stress theory adapted by Elder and colleagues (1992) to focus specifically on economic instability of midwestern farm families during the agricultural crisis of the 1980s[5] focuses attention on the different types of stress produced by economic hardship: the chronic financial difficulties associated with stressful economic conditions, as well as stress stemming from psychosocial transitions, that is, changes affecting one's beliefs about the world and his or her place in it (Conger & Elder, 1994). Using this perspective, fishermen appear to be undergoing both types of stress as their incomes and resources decline, and also as their decreasing ability to perform their family breadwinner role changes their individual identities and their family paradigms.

Financial pressure. In general, research findings indicate that financial pressure in families contributes significantly to family tension and stress and has a lasting impact on their emotional well-being and interpersonal relationships (Conger & Elder, 1994; Elder et al., 1992; Voydanoff, 1990; Voydanoff & Majka, 1988). According to Conger and Elder (1994), four factors contribute to financial pressure: low family income, unstable work, a high debt-to-asset ratio, and income loss. These factors are present among commercial fishermen. First, fishing is unstable for both owners and crew members in the Northeast, and some suggest that the instability will increase the longer George's Bank remains closed. Second, for both owners and crew, decreased income is causing increased debt and deferred purchases. Instability and fear were common themes in the interviews. For instance, a 50-year-old dragger spoke to this point:

> [Do you think you'll be fishing a year from now?] I doubt it. I think things are winding down for us. You can only go backwards so long and then you run out of . . . well, there's nothing else to take from. I'd say we're down to the wire now. . . . How many mortgage payments are they going to let us get behind before they do something?

His 49-year-old wife similarly commented:

> I don't like going [to the boat] because it's stressful, because you have this envelope of bills and there's our little paycheck. It's scary. It's like, "How much longer can we hang on?"

Another 31-year-old boat owner said:

> If we didn't have financial problems, I don't think we'd have any stress.

Still another, a 35-year-old struggling boat owner, said:

> Money. Financial. Wondering where the rent is going to come from. Getting the bills paid. My bills are my biggest stress.

The 40-year-old wife of a successful dragger said:

> It's very scary. I like control. I like to know where we're going to be next year in terms of our income.

When asked what the biggest stresses in his life were right now, this successful boat owner said:

> Just the last mortgage payment. And the boat needs some more attention when that last payment is made, so I might take out a small loan and put it right into the boat . . . I worry about my crew as much as I worry about myself. It bothers me when I can't give them a good week's pay because the guys that work with me have two kids and houses they're trying to pay for. That's pretty important to me, (49-year-old successful dragger)

Finally, this 29-year-old crew member's wife described her marriage and stress:

> We were separated last month. We were going to be getting a divorce but decided to reconcile instead and try to give it a shot. But it's tough . . . and the way the money's been with fishing, it's just so much less than it used to be. And I'm working and he's working and we're trying. But it's not like it used to be. . . . Money is always a problem. . . . We probably wouldn't fight if it wasn't for money. Ninety-nine percent of our arguments are over money. One percent are the kids.

The reconciliation she refers to did not last, and this couple has since divorced.

Psychosocial Stress. The second type of stress resulting from economic hardship is that stemming from psychosocial transitions. Conger and Elder (1994, p. 7) note:

> Chronic and acute stresses or strains, including financial difficulties often have their greatest impact on individual well-being through the troubles they create in one's closest social ties, such as those found in the family. Indeed, the conflict and withdrawal in family relations that sometimes result from economic problems may become the most significant stressors in family life, continuing in time even when the original external precipitant, e.g., unemployment for the family breadwinner, no longer exists.

Other studies of families experiencing economic stress indicate that job insecurity and unemployment have significant negative impacts on family functioning. Research suggests that economic pressures will first affect the emotional lives and marital interactions of adults, and through this process, the caretaking environment and development of children. Children are placed at risk for adjustment problems (Conger & Elder, 1994; Liem & Liem, 1988, 1990).

Financial pressure affects family members differently. Research suggests that men may react more to the change in occupational identity, whereas women tend to be most distressed by the loss of economic resources (Conger & Elder, 1994). Children are affected through the need for them to increase their contributions to household work and/ or paid employment. Their educational plans and future goals may change. This change tends to affect older adolescents more directly than younger children.

In their study of midwestern farm families, Conger and Elder (1994) found that wives tend to exhibit more stress reactions and experience them as more severe than do their husbands. Both husbands and wives tend to report lower marital adjustment, less clarity about family roles and responsibilities, fewer affective responses between husbands and wives and between parents and children, and poorer overall family functioning. Additionally, wives tend to report poorer family communication, poorer family problem-solving success, and less effective control on family members' behavior. Repetti (1989) found that in a sample of air traffic controllers, work stress led to withdrawal— stressed-out men avoided social contact with family members in order to avoid a further increase in anger and aggression. Although this may be seen as a positive strategy, the men were less emotionally responsive to their wives and children, and less involved in homework and routine discipline in evenings following stressful days. With regard to fishermen, this strategy may make their regular reintegration into family life even more complicated and become a further source of stress.

Additionally, Conger and Elder (1994) found that the transition out of farming was more than occupational change–that farming was a way of life as well. In a similar vein, the particular commitment to fishing as a way of life, rather than as an activity that is traded for a paycheck, adds to the strain of occupational change. Fishermen and their families feel very strongly identified as fishers and find it difficult to imagine doing something different. Fishermen report being uncomfortable on land and extremely wary of the "9-to-5" routine. They value above all the independence of fishing, and like farmers, most fishermen (although not necessarily their wives) report being willing to undergo reductions in their incomes if they can remain fishing. As one fisherman who went bankrupt and left the industry in late 1994 put it prior to his transition:

> I started fishing when I was 13, now I'm 49. . . . My biggest fear is when I can't fish anymore, what will I be? Like what will be the repercussions of my self-worth, did I make a big mistake? . . . A lot of question marks . . . (50-year-old dragger)

He subsequently commented:

My biggest stress is what I'm going to do with myself for the remainder of my life here . . . I've just lost the industry. You can't even make it today. See, the thing of it is, is that there are no other alternatives to go to.

Another wife of a third-generation fisherman commented:

[The regulations] affect his ability to run his business, which affects his relationship to the family. It definitely has an impact. The more restrictions that come, he could be out of business, at some point with the regulations coming, which will definitely impact us [in terms of] making a living, and in terms of who he is as a person. Because he is a fisherman, that's who he is. So it can really be a mess. (54-year-old wife of a lowliner)

A particularly articulate example of wives' identity change is noted by the wife of the fisherman whose boat burned:

When he was away, I used to say, "Oh, I'd love to have more help." And when he did get these days in between or his week off, it was wonderful because he cooks and he cleans and he does all those things . . . and the kids would love it because he would drive them to school. Because of the drastic change, my whole identity and existence in this whole family just kind of went out the window. At first, he didn't feel good, and then when he felt better, I had to start letting go of responsibilities, which I was almost too happy to. But then, it was where do I fit in? . . . My routine was totally gone. . . . Even though I'm thrilled, it's like he is part of that too, and this used to be part of just me. . . . And to tell you the truth, that was the biggest mind-blower of all . . . I never realized that fishing was so much a part of my life until it was gone.

Attributing the Causes of Stress

The stress process includes fishing families' recognition of economic pressure as a stressor and their attribution of the cause(s) of the pressure, the "C" factor. In some research, examination of this "C" factor finds that families who define a problem as their fault experience more stress than families who locate the cause of stress in external events or circumstances (McCubbin & McCubbin, 1988, 1996). Conger and Elder (1994) found that families differ as to what they attribute the cause of stress: personal responsibility or larger social forces. The attribution process is interesting in fishing families because most fishermen recognize governmental entrapment, followed by regulation and pollution, rather than overfishing, as the root causes of economic strain. No blame is placed on the fishermen themselves, and although their attribution of pollution and government as causes may help them cope, it might also contribute to stress because of their perceived powerlessness. The independence these men value in their jobs is threatened by forces beyond their control. For instance,

> [Is overfishing the main cause of the decline in fish?] No, the thing is, that the egg sacs float and come to the surface. I worry about the ozone layer and pollution. Something else is disturbing the environment other than the fishermen. (45-year-old wife of an offshore dragger).

Another wife suggested:

> Because of the Magnuson Act and because the government and banks said to go buy these huge boats with a lot of horse power and go out and catch all the fish and make lots of money . . . (35-year-old wife of a dragger)

And a successful fisherman asserted:

> Probably a good deal of it is overfishing, but it gets back to the government creating the problem with investment tax credits. They created the problem and now they are working very aggressively to try and get rid of it by closing areas and raising the . . . fish size instead of buying the boats back and taking them out of the fishery. . . . I've been told up in Canada a lot of the fish decline is blamed on the seals. It's probably a combination of pollution, fishing vessels, and seals, all of the above. (38-year-old dragger)

Coping and Resilience

Recent stress theory has focused on identifying personal and social resources that operate as *protective factors* in the process of negotiating stressful life events or conditions (Rutter, 1987). Three broad sets of variables are generally identified as key elements of resiliency: personality features, such as self-esteem; family cohesion and an absence of discord; and the availability of external support systems that encourage and reinforce coping efforts. Resilience is not only the possession of these resources but the investigation of life experience that promotes the development of such resources (Conger & Elder, 1994). Additionally, resilience is not seen as a fixed attribute of individuals and families, but rather as an interaction between external circumstances and individual and familial attributes; that is, individuals, families, and circumstances interact in any given situation (cf. Luthar & Zigler, 1991; Rutter, 1987, for descriptions of individual attributes). For instance, much research has found that the quality of family life prior to the stress situation predicts strongly the degree of interpersonal distress that families experience during crisis. Families most at risk for difficulties are those who had problems regarding finances, health, family, and marital relationships before a crisis occurred (Crouter & Manke, 1994).

In their search for factors that enable some families to negotiate their way through transitions and cope with hardships, McCubbin and McCubbin (1988, 1996) elaborate the construct of family cohesion. They identify critical family strengths such as accord, celebrations, communication, financial management, hardiness, health, leisure activities, personality, support networks, time and routines, and traditions. Each of these strengths was more germane to different points in the family career. This research implies that resilience includes both interactional and structural qualities of families.

Individual Features of Resilience

Research suggests that a feeling that one has control over his or her life situation is a vital psychological resource in successfully dealing with stress. "Evidence indicates that it is the psychological characteristics that are the more helpful in sustaining people facing strains arising out of conditions over which they may have little direct control—finances and job" (Pearlin, Lieberman, Menaghan, & Mullan, 1981; Pearlin & Schooler, 1978, p. 13). Perceptions of lack of control over management decisions characterize most fishermen in this study. One 35-year-old fisherman put it eloquently:

> [What are the biggest stresses in your life?] . . . Not [only] economic, just the uncertainty that the government is affording us with their ever evolving theory of fisheries conservation management. It really . . . it's like you don't even know how to do battle with it. You don't know how to combat it. You don't know where they're going. They might shut me down in 5 years. They might get to the end of this formula and say, "That didn't work. Plan B! Give me your boat. Here's a five-cents-on-the-dollar buyout scheme that's going to be financed by the sports fishermen. See you later. You're out of business. You're out of work. You don't have a lifestyle anymore."

However, an important strategy for fishermen and fishing families is to participate in the development of fishing policies through participation on the management councils, attendance at public hearings, and generally developing political skills to articulate their needs and observations to regulatory agencies (Smith & Jepson, 1993). Fisherman's wives' clubs have played important roles in making known the needs of families and by acting as watchdogs of and counterbalances to the data that are used in the creation of policy (Acheson & Lello, 1981; Pollack, 1992). Thus, this role can aid fishermen in keeping current with changes, helping them to be proactive rather than reactive. It is not a desirable role to take on, but its importance is recognized. As one wife of a struggling fisherman put it:

> The last thing he wants to do on his 2 days home is sit and read through management plans. He tries to attend the meetings—he doesn't want to go out to a meeting when he hasn't been home in a week. . . . So they say, "Have your wife go." . . . Now wait a minute. Now, the wife is working two jobs and raising the family, and I don't want to go either, but our lives depend on it. (37-year-old wife of an unsuccessful dragger)

There is some evidence, however, that attending meetings does not increase feelings of efficacy:

> Well, we are definitely informed of [the public hearings about fishery regulation] . . . they are scheduled for more the management than for us. The meetings that I've gone to, I don't think everything is explained so we can get it. It is a waste of time to attend. The feeling and perception is that it is lip service when you voice your opinion. I think that the hearings are a requirement that they have to go through, they don't really listen to us. They are getting paid to be there, and if you don't have someone to man your boat you might miss a trip worth thousands of dollars, just to attend a meeting. (48-year-old wife of a struggling dragger)

Structural resources also play a part in resilience. Education has a positive effect on mastery and self-esteem. The more education one has, the more positive comparisons one has for dealing with money and job problems (Pearlin & Schooler, 1978). In this study, a broad-based knowledge of the fishing industry, including economics of the industry, political developments, fishing technology, and fish biology, is also an important set of resources in adapting to occupational changes. In contrast, a reluctance to participate in and understand these changes leaves more traditional fishermen vulnerable to changes. In this regard, Gloucester is more vulnerable than Point Judith, because in the latter port, fishermen are generally less tied to tradition and, years ago, refitted their boats to fish underutilized species before fishery regulations began to affect them. This foresight has protected them more than fishermen in other New England ports to this point, and it is generally agreed that Point Judith will feel the effects of occupational change later than most. The strategy of social service intervention has been to increase education and training to allow those fishermen who stay in the industry to be more successful and to provide transferable skills to those who want to leave.

Family Interactional and Structural Features of Resilience

With regard to interactional qualities that predict resilience, Conger and Elder (1994) found that families create specific strategies for managing economic pressure that include both concrete behavior as well as redefinitional processes. Thus, the ability of families to cut back financially and redefine wives' labor force participation in terms of family breadwinning are important resources in adapting to economic pressure (see also Liem & Liem, 1990; McCubbin & Thompson, 1989; Voydanoff, 1990). Both types of strategies, behavioral and redefinitional, are part of an interactional process of changing family paradigms.

For fishing families, an important family resilience strategy is boundary flexibility. The connections between economic hardship, financial pressure, and stress are very much affected by flexibility in family roles. Families whose paradigm includes the ability to share roles, as well as less traditional attitudes toward gender and family, are better equipped to adapt their lives to the new economic and interactional circumstances, such as instituting new definitions of breadwinning and parenting. Flexibility in roles leads to less marital tension under conditions of economic uncertainty.

In the present study, boundary flexibility is emerging as an important resilience strategy during occupational uncertainty. For instance, the comments of this wife, whose husband has gone from a boat owner (third generation) to a hired captain through a process of bankruptcy, make clear that their paradigm has always included flexible boundaries:

> When he was home, it is a little bit different, because we would try and have time with him, where if we had plans, . . . we would change our plans to do something with Dad. We would make sure we made room for him in the family when he came back. . . . We would get caught up in our goings and comings. So we worked at it . . . very flexible. We set out saying we will still have our family, because his father was gone so much that he remembers saying to his mother, "Does Dad live here anymore?" So he remembers that, he has been determined to be more a part of the family. . . . It's important to him that his family is here when he gets home. (54-year-old wife of a lowliner)

Over a 3-year period of interviews, this family withstood severe economic crisis and identity change. Their outlook during the most recent interview spoke to their resiliency:

> I can't complain about my standard of living. Look at this house, my family, my grandchildren. I have problems, sure, all families do, but I'm also lucky. (55-year-old lowliner)

Another way that families include the absent member as part of the family strategy is illustrated by the comments of the wife of the dragger who is temporarily out of work due to a fire that destroyed his boat:

> I used to keep a log when the kids were little of what they did, and when he was on the boat years ago, he didn't even have t.v. or hear the news or anything, so I'd write down big things that happened, whatever. That was just a way of me trying to keep him abreast of things that were going on, but he's very involved. . . . We talk about everything when he comes in and I talk about things that are coming up. And I've always tried to involved him because like I said, when I was younger seeing many, many families bite the dust, and we saw a lot of them.

But another wife, now divorced from her fisherman husband, illustrates a paradigm where boundaries were not flexible:

> He doesn't know where he fits. I mean, on the boat, he's the captain, he's in charge, he orders people around. When he comes here, I'm the captain. I'm in charge, I order people around. And we function real well [when he's not here] . . . and I've gotten so I don't ask him. (37-year-old wife)

The ability to share roles and to create flexible boundaries is somewhat rare in fishing families' worldview because a typical way to cope effectively with the periodic absences is to create independent lives. As Gerson and Peiss (1984) point out, boundaries are complex physical, social, ideological, and psychological structures. One practical way to function normally during regular absences is to rigidify the boundaries so that the absent member is not missed. Families in this situation may not possess the flexibility needed to regularly negotiate the complexity of boundaries. When boundaries are rigid, families do not possess the flexibility needed to regularly negotiate boundary changes, much like the semi-permanent alternative family organization developed by families coping with a member's unexpected, crisis-induced absence of ambiguous duration. The two strategies may require different coping skills.

Under conditions of occupational change, the physical, social, ideological, and psychological structures that create family life have to change. All of these structures are affected when decreased control by males over breadwinning changes established definitions of the husband/father role. If husbands are no longer the sole or dominant breadwinners, then to be resilient, families need to negotiate work/ family boundaries, gender boundaries, and other role boundaries. From the perspective of family stress theory, they need to try out institutive patterns, and from the perspective of family paradigms, families need to alter their ideology. By redefining the meaning and significance of wives' employment, families are changing their conceptions of gender and identity. Most families in the study, however, report a reluctance to think differently about roles. For instance, a 50-year-old dragger, who subsequently left fishing, said during his first interview:

> We've had 25 years of a successful marriage. . . . My wife has done a wonderful job at raising our children and maintaining our home and our family. It's up to me to earn the money for necessities. . . . You gotta do what you gotta do to make what you gotta have.

His 45-year-old wife, when asked about her employment, offered a compatible view:

> No, I don't [work outside the home]. I tried it for a while. I found it very hard. I hated leaving [my child] at the day care, and when I got a chance to quit, I did. To tell you the truth, I'd rather be poor. I haven't worked in 22 years.

This couple had grown children at the time of the first interview.

Another wife gave the following account of stressful aspects of her life:

> Well, the only issues that bother me right now is the fishing thing. I told him not to talk to me about it. I have enough to worry about, the kids, the house. He says we are going to starve to death, I don't want to hear that "You go out and get a second job." (30-year-old wife of Gloucester dragger)

Finally, this wife put it bluntly:

> Nope, that's his job, not mine. I like my life the way it is. (41-year-old wife of crew member)

Resilient families, however, did adapt. The wife of the fisherman whose boat burned commented:

> Nothing is a pattern. It's just different. Major decision making really comes from me when I'm here. Some of it he goes along with, some of it he says well, let's change it. And I say fine, that's fine.

> We try to compromise when he's around. It's really hard because
> . . . you're going from always doing and then you have to learn to
> step back. And I'm a very dominant personality, so it took me a long
> time to just take that giant step back and let somebody else do
> something or make a choice, you know? That's from being together
> for so long. But it wasn't always like that. [You learn things over
> the years?] Yeah.

This family had two important strategies: flexible boundaries and
good financial planning. The former skill provided practice in boundary negotiation, and the latter skill enabled the family to cope with
the husband's unemployment without any change in lifestyle. Similarly, another wife commented:

> I don't think we could make it on his salary. When I first went back
> to work, it was just because I was tired of staying home, but now I
> need to work. Sometimes, mine is the only paycheck we see for a
> couple of weeks. (44-year-old wife of a Point Judith offshore dragger)

Social Support as a Resiliency Strategy

The availability of social support, especially for women, consistently
has been found in research to reduce the detrimental impact of economic pressure on psychological well-being. However, as research
becomes more refined, social support has been found to have differing
effects, depending on the sources of support. In Conger and Elder's
(1994) study, they expected that traditions of self-reliance and the
maintenance of appearances should lead to decreased social support
as farmers withdrew from social networks to conceal their economic
problems and feelings of failure (see also Newman, 1988). Commercial fishing shares many of the same traditions of self-reliance and
independence. Therefore, it may make sense to expect that the fishermen who remain successful will distance themselves from those
who are becoming less successful as part of a strategy to convince
themselves that they are, indeed, different and therefore will not
suffer the same fate. Limited data directly support this idea. For
instance, one wife said:

> How do those families . . . everyone now is blaming all commercial
> fishermen. . . . I don't think people realize that the small fishermen,
> the little family fishermen, people like him, their lives and the way
> they fish are very, very different. . . . He's still responsible and he's
> never taken more than he's needed. . . . And he's very different from
> a lot of those big fishing families that I've seen in the Point. And I
> truly believe that's why he'll survive and maybe this is good. Maybe
> this is what needs to happen. Survival of the fittest. And we're
> pretty fit. (49-year-old wife of an offshore dragger)

Indirect evidence of this idea is that most of the fishermen and their wives in the study report that their closest friends are not fishermen. This was especially likely to be the case among successful, longer term fishermen and their wives. This finding was surprising, and we interpreted it to mean that the sense of community was breaking down. However, this tendency may reflect the distancing phenomenon of the successful from the less successful. It also may indicate that as competition increases among fishermen, they are less likely to be able to provide social support for one another, indeed, a breakdown of "community."

Other data indicate that social support coming from outside the fishing community is essential to coping for most families. Women, especially, report relying on friends for discussion of marriage and family problems. When asked directly who they go to to discuss marriage and family problems, husbands overwhelmingly denied talking to anyone, and wives were likely to mention "girlfriends."

Structural family features associated with resilience also need to be considered. Age and family career stage are relevant resources. In general, older fishing families are better able to withstand the impacts of decreased income because they tend to have lower debt loads and lower expenses (if children are grown) and may be able to stay fishing at reduced income until retiring. Families with adolescents in the home may be more severely affected because the economic needs of children are high at this time. Changes in fathers' occupational identity may affect children's future occupational choices and the father-child relationship as well. Younger fishermen are harder hit as well because their debt loads tend to be higher, they have more of a future occupational identity to protect, and they have longer term economic survival issues as well.

Economic Strategies

Planning and effective management of the household economy are also important resources for families trying to stay in their occupation under economic stress (Conger & Elder, 1994). Families under economic strain can reduce their needs by cutting back on consumption (minimizing or postponing purchases); they can attempt to increase family income through multiple earners or a change in jobs; or they can "minimize any major decline in living standards by mortgaging future income through the use of loans, credit, and savings" (Conger & Elder, 1994, p. 80).

One wife commented:

> When I first met [my husband], I didn't know a lot of financial [information]. . . . Things got tight. But now that we've mortgaged and refinanced and put everything into budget perspective instead of just going with the flow, we've definitely been more flowing and smoother. (30-year-old wife of a midliner)

The 41-year-old schoolteacher wife of a formerly successful dragger, whose boat burned during a prosperous year, exhibited the best example of economic strategies. She spoke of the lack of economic difficulty they have experienced since the accident:

> We had gotten ahead a lot, more than ahead. The boat was insured, so we got to pay off everything and have a down payment for another one if he decides to do that. And we put some money away for a rainy day. We can run the household with what I earn, with no extra, but that at least makes me feel secure because we wouldn't lose anything major because someone was out of work. We always did it like that, because that was the nature of the business.

Another wife of a successful dragger commented:

> Well, my job is secure, and I think that for us that's been really good because we never had to worry about medical coverage and things like that. But a lot of the families that I'm seeing through my job, medical is a huge [thing]. . . . I've always had my paycheck when he's had lean weeks. You know, if he goes 8 weeks without a paycheck, [we're OK]. (48-year-old wife)

Macrosocial Context of Resilience

Finally, Kessler and colleagues (1989) found that psychological effects of job loss can be minimized if opportunities exist in the wider economy for stable reemployment. The macrosocial context within which occupational change and economic strain occur is a level seldom considered by traditional developmental research, which assumes a benign, constant social environment (Gore & Colten, 1991). Deindustrialization and a prolonged recession have been a continuing basis for economic uncertainty throughout New England. Thus, opportunities for stable reemployment are scarce. Other recent research suggests that job insecurity and the ambiguity it produces may, by itself, affect marital adjustment and problem solving in families (Larson et al., 1994; Voydanoff & Donnelly, 1988). Zvonkovic and colleagues (1994) found, for instance, that decision-making power tends to be based on a spouse's ability to provide rewards to the family system.

* * *

Resiliency in the face of occupational changes is fragile, and even the most resilient families are feeling their coping resources strained. It is useful to analyze these data using notions of family paradigms and family stress. Fishing families face a difficult task: The occupational requirements create a unique family paradigm, one that, somewhat paradoxically, demands ongoing flexible boundaries and independent lives. This strategy works while the occupational structure remains intact. But governmental management of commercial fishing makes it difficult to maintain this paradigm and, at the same time, points to its internal contradictions.

Stress theory has been most useful in identifying structural factors of resilient families, but the interactional process of paradigm change has been left underexplored. The data presented in this chapter point to the need to think more about the Hansen and Johnson (1979) treatment of family stress theory. We need to understand more about the process of replacing established patterns of family interaction with institutive patterns and need to identify the skills necessary to enhance this resiliency process. The notion of paradigm change has to incorporate change on different analytical levels: individual, family, community, and political-economic.

Economic resiliency is a necessary but insufficient ingredient to family resiliency and individual adaptation. Stress theory, especially as it is applied to occupational stress, recognizes the importance of the external context within which stress occurs; however, work remains to be done to incorporate theoretically the larger political context in which stress and resilience occur. In the present study, a continuing unstable economy in New England, continuing deindustrialization, and constant changes in fishery management produce a unique ambiguity in job conditions, and this context interacts with individual resources and family interaction to produce stress (Luthar & Zigler, 1991; Rutter, 1987). Additionally, unexpected stressors occur, such as the January 19, 1996 oil spill directly on the Narragansett coast that spilled more than 800,000 gallons of home heating oil into prime fishing grounds. This not only added to the pileup of stressors, but for some, it was the last straw. It is especially this larger economic-political context within which families cope with stress that needs to be added to theoretical ideas about resiliency.

Notes

1. The research reported here was supported by grant NA36RG0503 of Rhode Island Sea Grant and NOAA.

2. In 1996, a third subsample was added to the study. The new port is New Bedford, Massachusetts, which has an active and very affected groundfishing community. Most of the groundfishermen in New Bedford are Portuguese, many first generation. Most of the New Bedford interviews were conducted in Portuguese. No data are reported here from New Bedford.

3. Perhaps these families differ from mainstream families in degree only; as Clark et al. (1985) ask: "Are not all husbands periodically absent?"

4. As a footnote to this family, who are no longer in the study: He went back to fishing about a year after the first interview. During the second interview, he was very hostile about fishing regulations, and his wife was generally less communicative about their life. He refused a third interview and was unwilling to let us speak to his wife.

5. See also Marotz-Baden, Hennon, and Brubaker (1988) for a similar study.

References

Acheson, J., & Lello, J. (1981). The fishermen's wives association. In J. Acheson (Ed.), *Social and cultural aspects of New England fisheries: Implications for management*, *Vol. 2*, (pp. 375–400) Final report to the National Science Foundation, University of Rhode Island, University of Maine.

Anderson, R., & Wadel, C. (Eds.). (1972). *North Atlantic fishermen: Anthropological essays on modern fishing*. Newfoundland Social and Economic Papers No. 5. St. John's, Newfoundland: Institute of Social Economic Research.

Berger, P., & Kellner, H. (1970). Marriage and the construction of reality. In H. P. Dreitzel (Ed.), *Recent sociology Vol. 2*. New York: Macmillan.

Binkley, M., & Thiessen, V. (1988). Ten days a "grass widow"—forty-eight hours a wife: Sexual division of labour in trawlermen's households. *Culture, 8*, 39–50.

Boss, P. (1977). A clarification of the concept of psychological father presence in families experiencing ambiguity of boundary. *Journal of Marriage and the Family, 39*, 141–151.

Boss, P., McCubbin, H., & Lester, G. (1979). The corporate executive wife's coping patterns in response to routine husband-father absence. *Family Process, 18*, 79–86.

Burr, W., Leigh, G., Day, R., & Constantine, J. (1979). Symbolic interaction and the family. In W. Burr, R. Hill, F. I. Nye, & I. Reiss (Eds.), *Contemporary theories about the family, Vol. 2*, (pp. 42–111) New York: Free Press.

Clark, D., McCann, K., Morrive, K., & Taylor, R. (1985). Work and marriage in the offshore oil industry. *International Journal of Social Economics, 12*, 36–47.

Collins, C. H. (1994). *Beyond denial: The Northeast fisheries crisis.* Unpublished report prepared with funding from Kendal Foundation, Surdna Foundation, Inc., Rockerfeller Brothers Fund, and National Fish and Wildlife Foundation.

Conger, R., & Elder, G., Jr. (1994). *Families in troubled times.* Hawthorne, NY: Aldine De Gruyter.

Constantine, L. (1986). *Family paradigms: The practice of theory in family therapy.* New York: Guilford.

Crouter, A., & Manke, B. (1994). The changing American workplace: Implications for individuals and families. *Family Relations, 43*(2), 117–124.

Danowski, F. (1980). *Fishermen's wives: Coping with an extraordinary occupation.* Sociology and Anthropology, NOAA/Sea Grant. University of Rhode Island, Marine Bulletin 37.

Davis, D. L. (1986). Occupational community and fishermen's wives in a Newfoundland fishing village. *Anthropological Quarterly, 59*, 129–142.

Davis, D. L., & Nadel-Klein, J. (1992). Gender, culture and the sea: Contemporary theoretical approaches. *Society and Natural Resources, 5*, 135–147.

Derogatis, L. (1992). *SCL-90-R: Administration, scoring and procedures manual-II.* Towson, MD: Clinical Psychometric Research, Inc.

Dixon, R. D., Lowery, R., Sabella, J., & Hepburn, M. (1984). Fishermen's wives: A case study of a Middle Atlantic coastal community. *Sex Roles, 10*, 33–52.

Duffy, T. (1994, June). The end of the line. *Boston Magazine,* pp. 50–53, 102–104.

Elder, G., Conger, R., Foster, E. M., & Ardelt, M. (1992). Families under economic pressure. *Journal of Family Issues, 13*, 5–37.

Ellis, C. (1984). Community organization and family structure in two fishing communities. *Journal of Marriage and the Family, 46*, 515–526.

Forsyth, C., & Gramling, R. (1987). Feast or famine: Alternative management techniques among periodic-father absence single career families. *International Journal of Sociology of the Family, 17*, 183–196.

Gerson, J., & Peiss, K. (1984). Boundaries, negotiation, consciousness: Reconceptualizing gender relations. *Social Problems, 32*, 317–330.

Gerstel, N., & Gross, H. (1984). *Commuter marriage: A study of work and family.* New York: Guilford.

Gersuny, C., & Poggie, J. (1973, April). The uncertain future of fishing families. *The Family Coordinator,* pp. 241–244.

Gore, S., & Colten, M. E. (1991). Adolescent stress, social relationships, and mental health. In M. E. Colten & S. Gore (Eds.), *Adolescent stress: Causes and consequences,* (pp. 1–14) Hawthorne, NY: Aldine de Gruyter.

Gramling, R., & Forsyth, C. (1987). Work scheduling and family interaction: A theoretical perspective. *Journal of Family Issues, 8*, 163–175.

Green, B. (1985). *The finest kind.* Macon, GA: Mercer University Press.

Gubrium, J., & Lynott, R. (1985). Family rhetoric as social order. *Journal of Family Issues 6*, 129–151.

Hall-Arber, M. (1992, November). Solution to the "tragedy of the commons" or tragedy for the common man? *Commercial Fisheries News*, 3.

Hall-Arber, M. (1993). "They" are the problem: Assessing fisheries management in New England. *Nor'easter: Magazine of the Northeast Sea Grant Programs, 5(2)*, 16–21.

Hansen, D., & Johnson, V. (1979). Rethinking family stress theory: Definitional aspects. In W. Burr, R. Hill, F. I. Nye, & I. Reiss (Eds.), *Contemporary theories about the family, Vol. 1,* (pp. 582–603) New York: Free Press.

Kessler, R., Turner, J. B., & House, J. S. (1989). Unemployment, reemployment, and emotional functioning in a community sample. *American Sociological Review, 54*, 648–657.

Larson, J., Wilson, S., & Beley, R. (1994). The impact of job insecurity on marital and family relationships. *Family Relations, 43*, 138–143.

Liem, G. R., & Liem, J. (1988). The psychological effects of unemployment on workers and their families. *Journal of Social Issues, 44*(4), 69–86.

Liem, J., & Liem, G. R. (1990). Understanding the individual and family effects of unemployment. In J. Eckenrode & S. Gore (Eds.), *Stress between work and family* (pp. 175–204). New York: Plenum.

Luthar, S., & Zigler, E. (1991). Vulnerability and competence: A review of research on resilience in childhood. *American Journal of Orthopsychiatry, 61*(1), 6–22.

Marotz-Baden, R., Hennon, C., & Brubaker, T. (Eds.). (1988). *Families in rural America: Stress, adaptation and revitalization.* St. Paul, MN: National Council on Family Relations.

McCubbin, H., & Dahl, B. (1974). Social and mental health services to families of missing in action or returned prisoners of war. In H. McCubbin, B. Dahl, P. Metres, Jr., E. Hunter, & J. Plag (Eds.), *Family separation and reunion: Families of prisoners of war and servicemen missing in action,* (pp. 191–199) Washington, DC: U.S. Government Printing Office, Superintendent of Documents.

McCubbin, H., Dahl, B., & Hunter, E. J. (1976). *Families in the military system.* Beverly Hills, CA: Sage.

McCubbin, H., Dahl, B., Lester, G., Benson, D., & Robertson, M. (1976). Coping repertoires of families adapting to prolonged war-induced separations. *Journal of Marriage and the Family, 38*, 461–471.

McCubbin, H., Dahl, B., Lester, G., & Ross, B. (1975). The returned prisoner of war: Factors in family reintegration. *Journal of Marriage and the Family, 37*, 471–478.

McCubbin, H., Hunter, E., & Dahl, B. (1975). Residual of war: Families of prisoners of war and servicemen missing in action. *Journal of Social Issues, 31*(4), 95–109.

McCubbin, H., & McCubbin, M. (1988). Typologies of resilient families: Emerging roles of social class and ethnicity. *Family Relations, 37*, 247–254.

McCubbin, M. A., & McCubbin, H. I. (1996). Resiliency in families: A conceptual model of family adjustment and adaptation in response to stress and crises. In H. McCubbin, A. Thompson, & M. McCubbin, (Eds.), *Family assessment: Resiliency, coping and adaptation-Inventories for research and practice,* (pp. 1–64). Madison: University of Wisconsin System.

McCubbin, H., & Patterson, J. (1983). *Systematic assessment of family stress, resources and coping.* St. Paul: University of Minnesota Press.

McCubbin, H., & Thompson, A. (1989). *Balancing work and family on Wall Street: Stockbrokers and families coping with economic instability.* Edina, MN: Bellwether.

McCay, B. (1988). Fish guts, hair nets and unemployment stamps: Women and work in cooperative fish plants. In P. Sinclair (Ed.), *A question of survival: The fisheries and Newfoundland Society,* (pp. 105–131) St. John's, Newfoundland: Social and Economic Papers No. 17. Memorial University of Newfoundland, Institute of Social and Economic Research.

Mederer, H. (1993, August). *Fishing space and family space: Negotiating gendered role boundaries under fishery changes.* Paper presented at the annual meeting of the Rural Sociological Society, Orlando, FL.

Metres, P., McCubbin, H., & Hunter, E. (1974). Families of returned prisoners of war: Some impressions on their initial reintegration. In H. McCubbin, B. Dahl, P. Metres, Jr., E. Hunter, & J. Plag (Eds.), *Family separation and reunion: Families of prisoners of war and servicemen missing in action,* (pp. 147–157) Washington, DC: U.S. Government Printing Office, Superintendent of Documents.

Nadel-Klein, J., & Davis, D. L. (Eds.). (1988). *To work and to weep: Women in fishing economies.* St. John's, Newfoundland: Social and Economic Papers No. 18. Memorial University of Newfoundland, Institute of Social and Economic Research.

National Marine Fishery Service. (1991). *Public hearing document for landings of groundfish species in New England ports.* Saugus, MA.

National Marine Fishery Service. (1995). *Public hearing document for Amendment #7 to the Northeast Multispecies Fisheries Management Plan.* Saugus, MA.

New England Fishery Management Council. (1992). *Public hearing document for Amendment #5 to the Fishery Management Plan for the multispecies fishery.* Narragansett: Rhode Island Sea Grant.

Newman, K. (1988). *Falling from grace.* New York: Free Press.

O'Neill, J. (1991, August 18). Fishermen's success in '80s robs the sea: Greed leaves local waters overfished. *Providence Journal Bulletin,* p. A-01.

Orbach, M. K. (1978). Social and cultural aspects of limited entry. In R. B. Rettig & J. C. Ginter (Eds.), *Limited entry as a fishery management tool* (pp. 211–229). Seattle: University of Washington Press.

Palsson, G. (1989). The political ecology of Icelandic fishing. In J. S. Thomas, L. Maril, & E. P. Durrenberger (Eds.), *Marine resource utilization: A conference on social science issues* (pp. 131–135). Mobile: University of South Alabama Publication Services.

Pearlin, L., Lieberman, M., Menaghan, E., & Mullan, J. (1981). The stress process. *Journal of Health and Social Behavior, 22,* 337–356.

Pearlin, L., & Schooler, C. (1978). The structure of coping. *Journal of Health and Social Behavior, 19*, 2–21.

Pollack, S. (1992, September). Fishermen's wives respond to hard times. *National Fisherman*, pp. 20–22.

Ransom, D. C., Fisher, L., & Terry, H. E. (1992). The California family health project II: Family world view and adult health. *Family Process, 31*, 251–267.

Reiss, D. (1981). *The family's construction of reality*. Cambridge, MA: Harvard University Press.

Reiss, D., & Oliveri, M. E. (1980). Family paradigm and family coping: A proposal for linking the family's intrinsic adaptive capacities to its responses to stress. *Family Relations, 29*, 425–433.

Repetti, R. L. (1989). Effects of daily workload on subsequent behavior during marital interaction: The roles of social withdrawal and spouse support. *Journal of Personality and Social Psychology, 57*, 651–659.

Rutter, M. (1987). Psychosocial resilience and protective mechanisms. *American Journal of Orthopsychiatry, 57*, 316–331.

Sabella, J., Dixon, R., & Hepburn, M. (1979). Aspects of family and kinship in a North Carolina coastal community: A comparative study. *Maritime Political Management, 6*(2), 93–99.

Smith, S., & Jepson, M. (1993). Big fish, little fish: Politics and power in the regulation of Florida's marine resources. *Social Problems, 40*, 39–49.

Solheim, J. & Bauer, H. (1983). *Complexity and communality on a North Sea platform*. Work Research Institutes, Oslo.

Thompson, P. (1985). Women in the fishing: The roots of power between the sexes. *Comparative Studies in Society and History, 27*, 3–32.

Voydanoff, P. (1990). Economic distress and family relations: A review of the eighties. *Journal of Marriage and the Family, 52*, 1099–1115.

Voydanoff, P., & Donnelly, B. W. (1988). Economic distress, family coping, and quality of family life. In P. Voydanoff & L. C. Majka (Eds.), *Families and economic distress: Coping strategies and social policy*. Newbury Park, CA: Sage.

Voydanoff, P., & Majka, L. C. (Eds.). (1988). *Families and economic distress: Coping strategies and social policy*. Newbury Park, CA: Sage.

West, C., & Zimmerman, D. H. (1987). Doing gender. *Gender & Society, 1*, 125–151.

Zvonkovic, A., Schmiege, C., & Hall, L. (1994). Influence strategies used when couples make work-family decisions and their importance for marital satisfaction. *Family Relations, 43*, 182–188.

8

Resilience in Postdivorce Mother-Child Relationships[1]

Barbara J. Golby and Inge Bretherton

The Challenges of Postdivorce Parent-Child Relationships

The bulk of research on postdivorce parent-child relationships is based on group comparisons of divorced and nondivorced families. Findings reveal that, on average, custodial mothers tend to have poorer communication with their children than do those who are married, and that they are inclined to be less consistent, less affectionate, and less effective in eliciting cooperation from their children (e.g., Hetherington, 1987; Hetherington, Cox, & Cox, 1982; Stanley Hagen, Hollier, O'Connor, & Eisenberg, 1992; for reviews, see Emery, 1988, 1994). Although these differences are most pronounced during the first 2 years following the divorce, continuing differences in divorced versus nondivorced parenting have been reported in studies in which families were followed for longer periods of time (e.g., Hetherington, 1989; Hetherington & Clingempeel, 1992).

Findings based on group comparisons of nondivorced and divorced families can lead to the erroneous assumption that most postdivorce families are destined for a myriad of continuing problems in the parent-child relationship. However, although meta-analyses (Amato & Keith, 1991; Grych & Fincham, 1991) document several statistically significant differences based on divorced versus nondivorced family status, the effect sizes are generally quite small.

Findings on variations *within* the group of divorced families, by contrast, illuminate many aspects of healthy growth and favorable adaptation in many postdivorce families (e.g., Hetherington, 1989; Wallerstein & Kelly, 1980), especially 2 years or more beyond the divorce decree. When parents are able to adaptively reorganize their postdivorce lives, they tend also to regain their ability to respond sensitively to their children's needs and to manage discipline issues effectively, with beneficial effects for all family members (Hetherington, 1989; Hetherington & Clingempeel, 1992). Along these lines, Hanson (1986) found that postdivorce parents' and children's ratings of good parent-child communication were significantly correlated with assessments of family members' physical and mental health. Furthermore, in some families, the challenge of divorce enhances children's maturity (Weiss, 1979). We therefore suggest that greater insight into bonadaptive postdivorce family functioning may be gained by focusing on variations in resilience *within* this family form.

Studying Postdivorce Families From a Resilience Perspective

Resilience has been conceptualized in a number of ways. Both Hill's (1949, 1958) ABCX Model and McCubbin and McCubbin's (1993, 1996) Resiliency Model examine family resilience in terms of satisfactory adaptation in the face of adversity. In the ABCX Model, a stressor event (A) interacts with the family's crisis-meeting resources (B) and the family's interpretation of the event (C) to produce a crisis (X), defined as the level of disruptiveness and disorganization in the family. To account for the fact that crises are not one-time events but evolve and are resolved over a period of time, McCubbin and Patterson (1983) expanded Hill's model into the Double ABCX Model. McCubbin and McCubbin (1993, 1996) further expanded the model, emphasizing the family's relational processes of adaptation and appraisal to form the Resiliency Model. In the aftermath of a major stressor, families are likely to experience a pile-up of additional stressors (aA). Some of these are causally related to earlier strains experienced by the family; some are precipitated by the major stressor event; and others are due to normative and nonnormative transitions, or even arise as consequences of the family's efforts to cope. To respond to these stressors, families must call upon old and new resources (bB) from family members, the family as a system, and from the community. At the same time, families must give meaning to and redefine (cC) the total situation, that is, the various stressors, the old and newly developed resources, as well as the available and emerging coping strategies. The outcome of this process is family bon- or maladaptation (xX).

The Resiliency Model is especially relevant to the study of postdivorce families. In one sense, the legal divorce presents the family with a defined event to which all members must respond, but in another sense, the divorce is better understood as an ongoing process (Hetherington, Law, & O'Connor, 1993). The legal decree not only precipitates immediate changes in family roles and structure but also has been preceded by stressors leading up to the divorce and is, in turn, likely to be followed by further normative and nonnormative transitions, such as renewed custody disputes, remarriage by one or both parents, or the birth of half-siblings, in addition to the children's normative developmental changes. What resources, meanings, and coping strategies are in evidence at any one time after the marital dissolution will, therefore, differ depending not only on the time elapsed since the legal divorce but also on the particular transitions the family is undergoing at that time. Viewed this way, adaptation by all members is never completely achieved, and resilience does not focus on whether parents and children experience difficulties but, rather, on how they renegotiate relationships, create new structures, reorganize their lives, and create new meanings in response to these events. Families who manage to adapt well often do so in the face of considerable emotional pain and economic hardship as they renegotiate the postdivorce parent-child and coparenting relationships.

An alternative approach to the study of resilience derives from Garmezy's (1991) and Rutter's (1983, 1987) research on children's reactions to negative life events, wherein resilience is defined as competent functioning in the face of emotional stressors. In their work, the primary emphasis is on identifying protective versus risk factors. A greater number of protective factors balanced by a smaller number of risk factors tends to be associated with greater resilience. The advantage of the Garmezy/Rutter approach is its emphasis on searching out various factors associated with bon- and maladaptation. The advantage of the McCubbin and McCubbin Resiliency Model is its systems approach, in which these factors are viewed interactively and in which meaning making is regarded as a potent contributor to the quality of adaptation.

The resilience approach is in contrast to the "deficit model" that underlies group comparisons of divorced and nondivorced families and whose usual goal is to discover the extent to which the strains and stresses of divorce have adverse effects on family members. A focus on resilience, by contrast, highlights family strengths, particularly the individual, familial, and community resources that allow family members to respond with what McCubbin and McCubbin (1993, 1996) call bonadaptation. At the same time, this approach also provides greater insight into the lives of those families who adapt less well.

In this chapter, we examine divorced mothers' narratives on child rearing, collected as part of a lengthy interview consisting of structured but open-ended questions about the mother-child relationship. These narratives provide a window on mothers' appraisals of how they are negotiating and experiencing the complex task of postdivorce parenting. In terms of the Resiliency Model, our study's goal is to shed light on the Cc component, that is, to document in the mothers' own words the varied ways in which they attempt to define and redefine their parenting values and experiences as well as the relationship with their child. Although most of these mothers now carry the primary responsibility for parenting their children, many describe themselves as coping very competently and as effectively engaging their children's cooperation, whereas others feel overwhelmed by their situation and experience great difficulties in guiding their children's behavior.

Method

Participants

Participants were 71 mothers who had at least one preschool child. Families from a wide range of socioeconomic backgrounds were included in the sample. However, an effort was made to exclude families receiving public assistance (except those in which the mother was a student) in order to avoid the effects of stress due to poverty.

The great majority of mothers were found through the public court divorce records. A few families were contacted through local preschools or by word of mouth. All participants were living in or near a midwestern university town. Mothers' ages ranged from 23 to 47 years, with an average of 33 years. For 19 of the mothers, high school was the highest level of education completed. An additional 32 mothers had completed some college. Eleven of the mothers had college degrees, and nine had completed advanced degrees. Sixty-five mothers were either employed full-time or were full-time students, and six mothers were employed part-time. Income for this group of mothers ranged from $6,000 to $80,000, with a mean of $25,000. All mothers were Euro-American with the exception of two, who were of Latino/Hispanic descent.

All mothers had been permanently separated or divorced for at least 2 years. None of the mothers had remarried at the time of the study, although almost two thirds were involved in relationships. Twelve mothers (17%) were living with new partners at the time of the study, five (7%) with parents, and seven (10%) were living with another adult in the home. Sixty-five mothers were assigned primary physical placement of their child or children, and six shared equal placement with the children's fathers. Seventy-five percent of the children had contact with their fathers every 2 weeks or more frequently. The father's educational and occupational levels resembled the mothers', but 28% of the fathers were reported to have severe drinking or drug problems.

The target children (i.e., those about whom the mothers were interviewed) were between 4.5 and 5 years of age, with a mean of 4.7 years. Thirty of the children were girls, 41 were boys. Twenty-four of the target children had no siblings, 35 had one sibling and 12 had more than one sibling. One child in the group was biracial, and one had been adopted as a newborn.

Procedure

Mothers were individually interviewed in a quiet, comfortable office setting at the university while their children were engaged in a task in a nearby lab. Occasionally, an interview had to be continued at the participant's home. Most of the interviews were conducted by the first author, but about one third of them were conducted by the second author. Interviews lasted from 1 to 3 hours and were audiotaped and transcribed verbatim for analysis.

The Parent Attachment Interview. The Parent Attachment Interview (PAI) was developed by Bretherton, Biringen, Ridgeway, Maslin, and Sherman (1989) to assess a mother's perception of the mother-child attachment relationship through 25 structured, open-ended questions. In answer to all questions, mothers are encouraged to illustrate general statements with detailed memories of actual events.

During the PAI, parents are asked about various aspects of their relationship with their children. For example, they are asked to discuss their thoughts and feelings during pregnancy and at the time of the child's birth; to describe the child with five adjectives or phrases, and then to illustrate these with examples; to comment on how they and their children respond to each other's positive and negative emotions; and to discuss how they and their children feel during times of separation and reunion. They are also asked to talk about aspects within the relationship that they find disappointing, frustrating, or worrisome, and to describe how they handle situations in which they and their children have different goals. Additional questions focus on similarities and differences between the mother- and father-child relationships and between the mother's relations with her own parents in childhood and her relationship with her own child.

The interview questions were not specifically designed to elicit mothers' thoughts and feelings about issues relating to discipline, cooperation, and conflict. However, mothers talked so extensively about these topics in answer to various questions that a decision was made to analyze this material separately. The interview focused on the mother-child relationship in general, and only one question touched on divorce issues directly (i.e., how the mother's relationship with the child had changed since the divorce). Nevertheless, the mothers themselves brought up issues particularly related to postdivorce coparenting.

Data Analysis

Analyses of the PAI transcripts were based on a modified grounded theory approach (Glaser & Strauss, 1967; Strauss, 1987). The first step was to extract all sections of the interview transcripts in which mothers specifically addressed issues related to guidance, cooperation, and the negotiation of control. Next, each individual vignette or idea was printed on a separate card and assigned a provisional code that described the passage. An effort was made to use the mothers' own words in creating these in vivo codes. Piles were then formed by placing cards with the same or similar codes together, but rereading the text often resulted in the creation of new categories. When two or more categories greatly overlapped or were judged to be closely related, they were combined into a single category. As the cards were organized and reorganized, four general categories started to emerge that are presented in the results section.

Results

Mothers' narratives about child rearing fell into four bipolar categories that conveyed (a) a mother's sense of effectiveness versus her sense of ineffectiveness in child rearing, (b) her flexibility versus inflexibility in dealing with parent-child conflict, (c) her sensitivity in communication versus insensitivity in communication about feelings, and (d) her firmness and demandingness versus two forms of permissiveness: less demanding by choice and nondemanding under pressure.

A picture of resilience or bonadaptation emerged from narratives in which mothers talked about their sense of effectiveness in child rearing, their flexibility in dealing with parent-child conflict, their firmness or lower demands by choice, and their sensitivity in communication about feelings. By contrast, difficulties in adaptation were conveyed by narratives in which mothers talked about their sense of ineffectiveness and their inflexibility, were nondemanding due to feeling overwhelmed and fatigued, and their insensitivity in communicating with their children about feelings.

In all narrative excerpts below, personal names have been replaced with pseudonyms to protect the identity of the families. Furthermore, placement of narratives into particular categories should not be taken as an indicator that the mother possessed this quality as a general trait or typically interacted with her child as portrayed in the vignette. A mother might speak of herself as flexible in discussing one event and then inflexible in describing another. However, on the whole, mothers painted a fairly consistent picture of themselves. Finally, it must be noted that our descriptive categories are based on mothers' own perceptions as reflected in their reports, not on our observations of their behavior.

Narratives Indicative of Resilience

Traditional assessments of parental discipline styles (e.g., Baumrind, 1967, 1971) tend to focus primarily on the parents' child-rearing behavior and then examine its correlates with the child's functioning in other contexts, such as the preschool. In contrast, when mothers in this study discussed child-rearing issues, they placed their own behavior in the context of the relationship with the child. Not only did they talk about what they themselves said, felt, and did about a particular situation, but they also described the child's behavior and emotional expressions toward themselves or others and usually noted how the situation was resolved. In short, they described aspects of the relationship rather than merely commenting on their parenting techniques or the child's characteristics.

Sense of Effectiveness. An important topic for many mothers was whether or not they felt effective in handling actual or potential conflicts with their children. In narratives that portrayed their sense of effectiveness, mothers recognized openly that problems existed, but they appeared reasonably satisfied with how these situations were resolved. When these mothers talked about the challenges they faced, they generally conveyed a sense of being in charge, often emphasizing instances where positive change had occurred. Not only did they express pleasure in seeing their children's demanding behavior improve, but they also spoke about changes in their own behavior that helped bring about more positive interactions. In short, they evaluated both themselves and their children as basically cooperative:

> Sometimes, it's kind of hard when we disagree about something. Usually, it's a real tug of war about who is going to win because he is very stubborn and so am I. . . . But we both learn from being

stubborn, too; somebody's got to give in, and he's learning that, too. And he's getting better at giving in, and I am, too.

This mother expressed her satisfaction in what she generally described as some of her child's welcome behaviors and characteristics:

She listens pretty well . . . she is usually a pretty cooperative kid.

Another mother gave an overall assessment of the relationship itself as she saw it:

We have a good relationship. It's getting better and better and better.

Mothers who conveyed a sense of effectiveness did not idealize their relationship with their children. As the following examples illustrate, these mothers spoke candidly both about positive aspects of the relationship and about problems and frustrations while maintaining an overriding sentiment of confidence:

I think [the relationship is] working. We don't have any great struggles; just normal things, the normal struggles.

I'm very happy with the way he is, although at times he drives me up the wall [laugh].

Of course, he has his good days and his bad days, but generally he is . . . I can't think of any *real* bad days.

One mother conveyed her sense of effectiveness in comparing herself with the child's father:

I always thought that [child's father] would be more of the disciplinarian because I'm always kind of free spirited and stuff. [Child's father] is a pushover. Johnny's got him [his father] wrapped around his little finger, and I, I think that's the difference. Johnny runs [child's father]. I can tell when they're together. Johnny's upset about it, [child's father] is like doing everything but standing on his head to make him smile again and then he's, when he's with me, I won't do it. It's just "no" or whatever. That surprised me. But that's a very, very obvious difference.

Another mother was pleased that she had been able to successfully teach her child that the rules in mother's and father's houses were different:

I haven't wanted her to chew gum 'cause I don't, I didn't, I didn't want her choking on it and swallowing it and chomping on it [laugh]. Her dad lets her chew gum and has since she's been 2. Well, she didn't understand that and I said: "When you're 5 [years old], um . . . then you can chew gum, but not until then." "Well, how come Daddy let me chew gum?" "Well, those are his rules." And it's to the point now where she can walk out of the [father's] house and be chewing gum, and she'll just take it out of her mouth and hand it to me to throw away, and there's . . . it's just "When I'm five, I can chew gum with Mom, and I can chew gum with my Dad now. So here, Mom, it's your rules, take the gum."

Flexibility in Parent-Child Conflict. Resilience and flexibility have similar connotations, suggesting bending without breaking. Mothers' resilience was reflected in narratives in which they discussed their ability and willingness to negotiate differences between themselves and their children. These mothers gave in when they believed that situations called for it without feeling that this undermined their authority and sense of effectiveness in the relationship. They were not afraid that making exceptions to rules would lead them to lose control as a parent.

In contrast to mothers who made blanket statements such as, "I'll always just do it for him" or "I'll just make her stay there until she does it," these mothers took into account the different factors at play in the situation and generated solutions they felt were appropriate for that particular circumstance. Hence, they used phrases like, "it depends on the situation" and "I decide if it's worth making an issue over." In addition, flexible mothers looked at situations from the child's point of view, evaluating his or her individual needs and capabilities, before making a decision on whether to stand firm or not. For example, one mother talked about how she understood that a small child cannot eat as much as an adult and therefore did not expect her child to finish everything on her plate. Other mothers said that they would allow their children to sleep with them occasionally if, in the middle of the night, the children were upset over a bad dream or thunderstorm, and provided it did not become a habit. As one of these mothers stated, "You gotta make allowances once in a while. You can't be hard-nosed all the time." One mother commented:

If we're coming back from a playground and she's tired and she could probably make it but we'll both be miserable by the time we get home, I just pick her up. It's no big deal. I guess I measure it. If she's being a wimp and she can make it and I can talk to her about it, I'll try to get her to do it. But if I just think it's going to be a war of wills, I tend to just do it.

Being flexible also meant affirming children's struggle for independence, providing support and encouraging autonomy, while at the same time maintaining limits.

> Using a knife at the table . . . he insists on doing it himself. I say, "No, knives are very sharp." We compromise, and I say, "We'll get you a special knife for little boys at the table." So, then, the next day, we will go out and buy a special one. We normally talk back and forth of what would work the best.

These mothers were understanding of their children's individual quirks and rituals, explaining that sometimes the best way to gain their children's cooperation was to have patience and respect for their views, ideas, and feelings, and to allow them the freedom to do things their own way.

Sensitivity in Communication. Mothers differed substantially on how they discussed and evaluated their children's negative emotions, such as sadness, anger, and frustration. Mothers' attitudes toward these emotions played an important role in the way disagreements with the child were resolved. Sensitivity was reflected in the way mothers said they handled communication about their children's needs and emotions, how they fostered open communication in the relationship, and whether they tried to understand the reasons behind their children's acting out.

In narratives reflecting sensitivity in communication, mothers showed awareness, understanding, and often also acceptance of their children's negative feelings. Children's anger was a feeling that mothers frequently discussed in relation to misbehavior, but the way they handled their children's anger was in large part dependent upon what they believed the source of the anger to be. For example, mothers rarely accommodated anger expressed in response to the request to perform an undesirable task. If, however, the mother believed there was a deeper reason why her child might be acting out or feeling angry, she showed more tolerance:

> The more I've been a parent, the more I've learned that her actions all depend on how her day goes. Like if she hasn't had her nap, if she's hungry, then they get tired, they get ornery. It's like, you know, you just gotta realize they're acting this way because, you know, there's a reason behind it.

A common situation during which mothers became the recipients of their children's angry feelings was upon returning from a weekend with their fathers.   Sensitive mothers appeared to have extra empathy for their children's negative feelings during this time:

> He very frequently is very angry . . . with me when he comes back [from spending time at Dad's], and it takes just like one explosive type of thing, for him, to have happened, and then he is fine . . . it's like he has to work something out and he is not able to verbalize it to me.

Another mother expressed a similar sentiment, and added that she believed it was the two parents' different standards and expectations for behavior that was contributing to her child's experienced difficulty making the transition between houses.

> I notice a . . . difference in parenting, and it's frustrating, probably more so for him [child] than it is for me, because he doesn't understand and I do. And he can only react, and sometimes I have to . . . take a step back and know that he's not deliberately trying to be bad. He just needs a day to get reacclimated to a different household and a different rule, and things like that.

Some sensitive mothers expressed concern about their children's sadness and anger, and about the effect they felt these feelings had on their children's behavior.   Several said they enlisted a therapist to help them understand and relate to their children better:

> This therapist that I've gone to, he gave me some really good skills about talking to the kids . . . they can't articulate what's wrong, so what I can do is label things. I'll have no idea what's wrong, and I'll start naming the teacher, kids at school, the baby-sitter, missing the TV show, "oh no, oh no."   But when you hit on it, you know, like dinner wasn't very good, "Yes, I'm still hungry." . . . So that's been really helpful because I'd get real frustrated. I'd go, "You don't need to cry, there's nothing wrong," that's how I used to be. "Why are you so upset?" But now it's like, if they're crying, even if it's nothing that I think is reasonable, [I know] there's something wrong.

Open communication was something that sensitive mothers said they worked hard at obtaining. For some, the accepting home they tried to create was different from the experience they had growing up. A few said that they set aside specific times to give everyone in the family a chance to express his or her feelings:

> I have always really tried to talk to the kids and given them an opening to discuss their feelings, and sometimes, if they don't take it, we'll sit down and discuss it. We just started having family meetings, where we could have a safe place to say whatever we felt . . . and I said, "This is time for criticism. If you don't like what I'm

doing, you can bring it up," you know. So I've always had this open relationship with them.

In vignettes categorized as sensitive, mothers acknowledged their children's negative emotions, but they did not condone all negative behavior. Talking and reasoning, as well as helping the children find appropriate ways of expressing their negative feelings, were some of the ways these mothers said they handled their children's undesirable behavior:

> I try to say, "It's okay to be angry, but it's not okay to hit. You have to use your words if you want him to know what . . . if you want him to stop." Because if she whines about something, he [sibling] won't stop. If she tells him, "Please stop that," sometimes he will. So I'm trying to teach her appropriate ways to be angry.

In a further vignette, a mother discussed how she acknowledged her son's negative feelings concerning her work situation, even though she did not feel she could change it:

> He disagrees with my having to work long hours. He doesn't like that at all. And so we really talk about these things. And he very much holds his own in the conversation. He still doesn't like it, and I tell him that I really understand that and that he's entitled to that, but I still have to do it.

In another narrative describing sensitive responses to negative feelings, a mother noticed her child's fearful reaction to "We're going to have to talk about this (misbehavior) with your dad." Because the mother felt that "I don't want it to be like that, I don't want to instill the fear that if Betsy, (father), and I all have to sit down and talk about something, that it's bad." She reassured the child, "Maybe just you and I can talk about it."

In a few of the sensitive vignettes, mothers remarked on how impressed they were with their children's capacity for emotional understanding. They greatly valued and took advantage of their children's increasing ability to communicate rationally, and they felt that because of these changes their interactions became smoother and more enjoyable as their children grew:

> [Returning from a stay with father] used to be a lot more frustrating when he was younger, when he couldn't talk, when he couldn't tell me what was on his mind and the only thing he could do was act out. And so now that he can talk and has a much better capacity to reason, and understand, and communicate, and talk about his feelings, that makes it tremendously easier.

Firm and Demanding Child Rearing. In narratives depicting the related qualities of firmness and demandingness, mothers portrayed themselves as consistent and unwavering in their decisions about child rearing. They did not talk about feeling guilty or uncertain about how to handle such situations; they described themselves as calm and fair in dealing with their children, but never irritated or condescending. Neither were these mothers punitive in their approaches to gaining compliance. Their narratives suggested that they were able to use persuasion to obtain cooperation, even if after some resistance.

Firm mothers explained that, for them, running a tight household was vital for maintaining control, given the added pressures of postdivorce parenthood. Some said that their hectic lifestyles and the added responsibility of having to take care of everything themselves made it necessary to be firm. Others said they were firm because there was no second adult in the house to enforce rules and demands:

> You're not really wishy-washy . . . you're very firm, you don't buckle under and let the kid win, just being real consistent and, you know, asking them to listen or behave well or forewarning them, you know. "Okay, I've already warned you once, next time . . . ," you know. . . . So just being real consistent and firm and letting them know in the end that they can't really manipulate you when you're trying to enforce something . . . the fact that you're the single parent and not having anyone else behind you to enforce what you're trying to get across. That's why I'm probably pretty firm on trying to get him to listen now, 'cause later on if he can't listen to me, then that's going to be a lot harder.

For these mothers, being firm was not just a matter of following through. It also meant having demands and expectations. One mother described how her child-rearing style changed as a result of the postdivorce situation:

> I decided that I could no longer be wishy-washy about certain things, that I really had to be very strong, as consistent as I possibly could be, and, you know, a perfect Mom, Super Mom, and really, really be tougher with them. . . . I have learned that children really do need discipline, they do need guidelines, they do need consistency, and other parents might think I'm strict, but I don't think so, because I see my children able to do things these other children aren't doing . . . and I don't see any reason why they shouldn't be.

Several mothers commented on firmness in the context of differences between themselves and the child's father:

> I think I'm a lot more strict than he is. Of course, I have to live with them a lot more than he does, so I expect them to respect me and to do what I ask them to do. Of course, that takes a lot of work, to get your kids to actually do that.

The difference in parenting for another mother had to do with the degree to which maturity demands were made and routine structure was provided.

> He [father] doesn't have rules. I do. . . . Like when I went out there this weekend, and this is just an example, it was in the afternoon. I picked them up and brought their presents for their dad, for his birthday. It was his birthday, and they bought him house-warming presents too, it was really cute. So I went out there to pick them up and, um, their beds were, like, totally not made, you know, just. . . . And I said "You guys, why aren't your beds made?" And Sally went: "Oh, we don't have to at Dad's." And I, so I went into the kitchen and I said: "You know, David, they make their beds, you can ask them to make their beds and they'll do that." And Sam [son] went "Mom, shhhh." And David [father] went: "They do? They make their beds?" But he lets them stay up, there is no bedtime. . . . And Sally's relationship with her dad, she tells him what to do and what she wants to do, and he'll comply. . . . He thinks that makes him a good father. I mean, he loves them and so to him that's love. So, there's a difference, you know. With me they have, you know, we have rules, we have structure.

A few mothers gave the postdivorce situation as one reason why they were "more strict" than their own mothers had been:

> Sometimes, I think I am more strict than my mother, but I think she [mother's mother] understands that it's because I'm a single parent and I'm doing it on my own, and that is why I am more strict.

Other mothers said that they felt that it was important that their children have the security of knowing that they, the parent, were in charge:

> . . . I'm able to be, whether I am on the inside or not, put across the appearance of, "This is the decision. I made it. This is what we're going for." I'm confident in my decision, so that she can see a strong parental unit that way: "Oh, Mom made this decision, this is what we're doing, cool, let's go for it."

In short, firm mothers were confident in their role as authority figures. They were not intimidated by their children or afraid to make reasonable demands. One way in which they displayed their authority was by emphasizing generational boundaries. Unlike mothers who were not firm, these mothers did not feel subject to the same rules and restrictions they placed on their children:

> Usually, I'll say, "Two minutes bed time," or I'll say, "Two minutes to get your pajamas on," and then he will slowly and surely get his pajamas on and I help him put on his pajama top and then he is usually pretty good. He'll say, "Well, after I get my pajamas on can I play or watch TV for a few more minutes?" And I'll say either yes or no. If I say no, I get some resistance. Then it's like, "Well, why is it bedtime, you always get to stay up later than me," and I'll just explain, "Well, I'm an adult and you're not." He's actually pretty good.

Less Demanding by Choice. In narratives identified as "less demanding by choice," mothers portrayed themselves as less concerned about behavioral standards because they embraced lower demands as part of their child-rearing philosophy. That is, they did not believe in imposing what they regarded as unnecessarily high expectations on their children. The more indulgent permissiveness described in these mothers' narratives differed greatly from other narratives in which mothers attributed their lack of follow-through on demands to feeling overwhelmed, tired, and frustrated (later described under the rubric "nondemanding under pressure"). In short, less demanding mothers—although more lenient than those who described themselves as firm/demanding—felt themselves to be in charge of the situation and the relationship.

Some of these mothers said that they sometimes enjoyed doing things for their children, even things they knew their children could do themselves:

> I think that I tend to run things in a more kind of, I hate to say loving, but it's just, it's a softer relationship I guess [as compared to the child's father]. Their dad has more expectations of, sort of, you know, the "grow up," you know. Always put on your own clothes because you can do it, you know, you can do that so you do it type of thing. Move on in life. Whereas, it's like this morning he wanted me to dress him. That's fine, you know. Or we play a game at bedtime where he wants me to say, "OHHH!" when I take his socks off, like everything smells, and it's a fun game. I know he can take all his clothes off, but I don't always have him do it, you know.

In these narratives, mothers explained that they did not always make high-maturity demands on their children because they did not see the need to require their children to do things for themselves all the time. The mother in the following example talked about how her nondemanding style was guided by her child-rearing philosophy:

> He always, after going to the bathroom he wants me to buckle his pants up for him. . . . I don't have the expectations for them to be as independent as they do in day care. . . . I guess I don't see that as too important. I think it's just a difference in philosophy, and I guess I'm not going to judge myself as right or wrong, just the thinking that makes it so.

Another mother admitted that there were times when being less demanding made life easier, and that once in a while, she would find herself thinking twice about her approach. But the underlying ideas conveyed were that her decision to relate to her child in this way was made deliberately, not reluctantly, and that she was generally satisfied with the way she handled these situations:

> It happens a lot in the morning, she will want me to dress her, and simply because it saves time, you know, I do. And some mornings I think, you really shouldn't be doing this, but, you know, I don't think it's hindering her from dressing herself, it just makes life easier. So, in that case, I just go ahead with it.

Less demanding mothers also talked about generational differences. One mother felt that the difference between her relationship with her child and her childhood relationship with her mother had to do with the more hectic schedules of today's families:

> He's got a pretty rigorous schedule. He plays hard all day . . . he's tired when he comes home, too. And there are times when I won't [ask him to pick up his toys] because he's pooped, and we'll just kind of . . . turn on a movie.

She later went on to explain:

> I'm more lenient than my mom was . . . I think the big difference is the mother being at home full time and they're, you know, just being there all the time, and the kids aren't so tired. I mean, they could sleep in a little longer, they're not rushed from, you know, you put them in the car in the morning and you drop them off here and you rush them there, you take them to the store, and you come back. We didn't have that big rush, like the working mom does nowadays. . . . I think I do discipline Marty but I'm more lenient . . . [he's] going to be more tired because he has a more rigorous schedule. . . . It's more relaxed when they're at home, and I think the parents are more relaxed . . . I would love being at home with him.

In contrast to mothers who felt that being a single parent required them to be demanding and strict in following through, nondemanding mothers explained that their family structure allowed them to be more laid-back about certain things such as meal schedules, what their children ate, or their children's table manners, because they did not have to compromise and negotiate with another parent regarding how to handle such issues. They tended to be less worried about things, such as whether their children got a bath every night, and they enjoyed both granting their children more freedom than they had growing up and having the freedom to run their homes the way they wanted:

> My friend was just laughing so hard because Timothy was bouncing on the bed and I wasn't even saying anything to him, and I said, "Well, if he wants to bounce on the bed he can bounce on the bed" . . . I don't believe in all of this, you have to do this because you have to . . . I don't like that kind of stuff. . . . All these, like, parent rules that I don't really believe in or understand where they ever came from. So, as long as you're not having ice cream every night, I mean, I don't believe in that, but I mean if we want to have fun and we end up having french fries and ice cream for supper, sometimes that's what we do.

Another mother, recollecting her own childhood, explained:

> I don't remember ever being as sassy as he can be . . . I know I wasn't. But I still always have to tell myself, too, that when I was his age, I was normally scared to death all the time, and that makes a big difference . . . it was kind of like, you didn't speak unless spoken to kind of place. So, I have to always remind myself that he's not in that. He has the freedom to act silly and goof off at the dinner table and not feel like you're going to choke on your food because you're scared to swallow. . . . I was probably a lot better behaved, but I think it's more healthy that he can be bratty [laugh]. So, I always have to pull back and think, no, just kind of let it go, it's not that big of a deal.

Less demandingness as a deliberate approach was less commonly mentioned by mothers in this study than was taking a firm/demanding or flexible stance. It was also much less common than the approach that is discussed under lack of resilience.

Lack of Resilience

In contrast to mothers who were able to negotiate the postdivorce situation with a sense of effectiveness, accompanied by flexibility, sensitivity, and feeling in charge, some mothers described a preponderant sense of frustration and dissatisfaction.

Sense of Ineffectiveness. In vignettes reflecting a sense of ineffectiveness, sometimes even helplessness, mothers commented that they had no control over their children. They described how their children showed disregard for their authority by ignoring them, mimicking them, and even belittling them with derogatory remarks that they might have learned from their older siblings or fathers:

> If I try to discipline him sometime and he doesn't, like . . . he'll come back with a snide comment, all the time. I think he gets it from his brother, too . . . sometimes I catch him swearing. . . . There was one time, his dad used to threaten me all the time, one time I told Jimmy that he needed to do something, he called me a bitch.

In these narratives, mothers expressed self-doubts about their judgments or decisions. Their reports suggested that this lack of self-confidence was hindering their ability to parent with authority. Some were afraid that they gave in too easily or were inconsistent. Others felt guilty about the divorce, some were afraid they were not good mothers, and some feared their behavior was negatively affecting their children's emotional development:

> I have mixed feelings as to how I should discipline him when he is naughty, you know, when he's out of my control. I mean, I don't want him to be my robot, but I just want him to be good, you know, don't be so rotten.

A few mothers expressed fear in anticipation of not being able to control their children (especially sons) as they grew older and bigger and stronger:

> It's kind of scary to think, if he's like what he is now, I'm going to have a handful because sometimes, not that a parent should control a child . . . but sometimes I feel like he's going to try to run me over, you know? Like, there's many times when he won't even listen to me now. What's going to happen 10 years down the road when he's developed all these other tools of manipulation [laugh] and, you know, be really rotten?

Some mothers felt they were ineffective because their children exhibited no internal motivation to behave in a desirable fashion. Neither the mothers' praise for good behavior nor their anger over poor behavior seemed to move the children to comply:

> He's harder to motivate to do what you want him to do . . . it's real hard to get him to want to keep his room clean. He just doesn't care, he just doesn't care . . . he doesn't seem to need pleasing a lot, you know, he does things because he wants to do them because it makes him feel good, rather than, I'm going to clean my room and please

Mom. That's not what motivates him, and that frustrates me. I don't quite know how to get him to do certain things like that.

Another mother, describing a similar experience, added:

They will pretty much ignore me. I mean, I have not found a way to get mad yet, whether it's quietly or loudly or whatever that makes either one of them respond. They just do what they are going to do, and they don't care if I'm mad or not, or they don't seem to.

Many mothers in the study were frustrated by the behavior their children exhibited upon returning from their father's house, and they did not feel able to resolve the situation:

She's different . . . she doesn't seem to respect me as much when she first comes home from there, and I guess that brings on a fear that as she gets older, there is just going to be longer episodes of disrespect and more, um, harshness and aggressiveness.

Although the situation had fortunately changed somewhat for the better in the past 6 months, another mother described her feelings of helplessness in response to her son's behavior after returning from the father's house, behavior that even the neighbors noticed:

People, um, that wouldn't . . . that wouldn't know our schedule, which weekend they were gone, they could tell. . . . They'd say, "Oh, they were gone again this weekend, weren't they?" I can tell the way they acted, too, or the way they both of them would act the next day. The sassing, the swearing, which they don't do around here. Um, the attitudes towards women. This is mainly Eric, um, just a little, I mean, you just have to do everything you can just not to strangle him. It would be like an obscene drunk or something. Just, you can't even stand to be around him, and then that would be like that and he'd be violent, more violent, more prone to be aggressive, more bossy, more pushy, more selfish, more "I don't want to play with anybody today," that type of thing.

Another mother ascribed her ineffectiveness in eliciting cooperation to the fact that the child's father was undermining her authority:

He [son] may not say it in so many words, but it's basically, like, "You don't have to listen to your mom." I mean, the kids have gotten in the car after being with their dad, they go: "We don't have to listen to you." "Oh, is that right?" "Dad says we don't."

Some mothers wondered why their own parents had been so much more effective in gaining compliance to demands than they were with their children. As the following two examples illustrate, mothers remembered being fearful and respectful of their own parents, both mothers and fathers, and seemed puzzled as to why they could not elicit the same obedient response:

> She [mother's mother] had this look, I mean, that can wilt a line-backer. . . . Oh, if I could generate one tenth of that look to keep my children in control, I would [laugh].

> You just did whatever my dad said. It was, like, how did that ever come about? You just did. I can't explain why. You just did. Sometimes, it was out of respect, sometimes, it was just because my dad said it, you just did it. And I'd like her [daughter] to do that once in a while [laugh]. But that just wouldn't be her [laugh] . . . I try to do that [and] it just doesn't work [laugh].

Inflexibility in Child Rearing. In a number of narratives, mothers described their parenting behavior as power-assertive and inflexible. In the child socialization literature, this style would be characterized as authoritarian or autocratic (Baumrind, 1967, 1971; Maccoby & Martin, 1983). However, despite the fact that obedience appeared to be these mothers' main objective, most described their children as not willing to comply, if not defiant. Hence, conflicts became an issue of who controlled whom in the relationship. Mothers felt they could not let their children win and possibly gain control, even if it meant becoming tired and frustrated in the process. Because most of their descriptions were of power struggles that were resolved by force or coercion, and because of the dissatisfactions and frustrations these mothers expressed, inflexibility was not regarded as a helpful adaptation:

> He will continue to argue and argue and finally he will break down, if I stand my ground, and by that time I'm frustrated, and I'm ready to just root my hair out, but if I can, you know, and I've been really managing to stand my ground, but he'll change, he'll back down.

What was most striking about these mothers as a group was the feeling of exasperation they described in response to power struggles that often escalated after their refusal to seek a compromise. Yet they did not appear willing to break the pattern and find alternative ways of handling conflictual situations. In vignettes describing inflexibility, mothers did not talk about negotiating and working through problems to arrive at win-win situations. Instead, they focused on obtaining compliance by issuing threats, explaining how they "won't tolerate" misbehavior. They described giving ultimatums rather than choices:

Sometimes, like zipping up her coat, and I know she can do it because she has done it before, and all of a sudden she says, "I can't do it, I can't do it." And I just tell her, "Well, it's like this: You're doing it or you can just suffer," you know [laugh]? She will start whining and stuff, and if we're not in a hurry she will go to her room, otherwise, I let her go out the door without it zipped, and if you freeze it's your problem.

Some of the mothers felt that they had to use physical force in order to get their children to comply:

Yesterday, he wanted to watch a movie and I told him, "No," because he wasn't behaving very well. And he started putting the movie into the VCR: "I want to watch this movie!" And I said, "No, you can't." "But I want to watch it, Mom!" And it kept going back and forth: "I want to watch it!" "No you can't!", you know. And I said, "If you say it one more time you're going to your room." And I didn't even get that whole sentence out and he was saying it again. And I tried to send him to his room, and he wouldn't go, so I had to drag him to his room, and when he got in there, he screamed and kicked his feet, "But I want to see the movie!"

In the context of describing power struggles, several of these mothers also spoke about their children in somewhat derogatory, condescending terms that seemed to reflect feelings of anger and irritation toward them:

If he finishes drinking his Kool-Aid and he sets it on the table, I says, "Now go put that in the kitchen." "No, you do it, Mom. I don't want to do it. I'm too tired." He'll say, "I'm too tired." He'll justify that way. [Interviewer: What do you do?] I don't do it. I just keep on him and tell him to go do it . . . It's almost like I have a power struggle with him. . . . That little turd, he can go put it in the sink himself [laugh]. He's supposed to be my slave [laugh]. You know what I mean? It's almost comical sometimes the way he, you know, is like, "No, Mom, you do it, I'm too tired." Like I'm not tired. He just played all day, that's his job, you know?

Nondemanding Under Pressure. This category contrasts importantly with the permissiveness of mothers who purposefully chose a somewhat less demanding child-rearing strategy (described as "less demanding by choice" in the section on resilience). When mothers portrayed themselves as "nondemanding under pressure," they ascribed their behavior to feeling burdened and overwhelmed, both physically and emotionally. They talked about their difficulties in taking charge, commenting that they often felt as if their efforts at controlling their children's behavior were futile, in part because the children "did not care." They mentioned their tendency not to follow through on demands and to give in to their children's whining, manipulation, and noncompliance to obtain respite. Insisting that their children cooperate with requests had simply become too emotionally taxing. Many said they did not know what to do to get their children to "listen":

> Like today, when he was running ahead of me and . . . I told him, "Don't run." He still runs. So what am I supposed to do there?

Mothers gave different reasons why they might have had a difficult time in gaining compliance or cooperation. Whereas some talked about the fear of losing their children to the children's fathers, others felt sorry for their children because of the divorce situation. Two mothers were afraid that their children would charge them with child abuse if they were too harsh. One of these mothers said that her older son had actually threatened to report her. "It makes you afraid to spank him," she admitted. And several mothers feared that if they were too strict, their children would not love them or would choose to live with their father:

> I don't want to be real strict with her, real, you know, a lot of hard discipline or anything because her brother just left [to live with father] a couple months ago . . . and I guess in the back of my mind I'm thinking, God, you know . . . if I don't give her the attention in what she needs or I'm yelling at her a lot or something or she's just not listening and I just get frustrated and just have had enough, you know, she's going to want to say, "I want to go to Daddy's," and she'll mean it, you know. And I don't want that to happen, so it's kind of hard.

These mothers indicated that they gave in, not because they felt it was the right thing to do but because they did not know how to handle the situation any other way. They gave in, they said, because it was easier than fighting, or because they could not tolerate their children's behavior, and then they described feeling worried that they were not firm or consistent enough. Those in this category who were aware of their tendency to give in believed that it probably made things worse. As one mother stated, "The more I give in, the more he knows he can play the game with me." A few talked about the desire to be firmer and described some of their desperate attempts to engage their children's cooperation (one mother said she tried unsuccessfully to get her child to sleep in her own room by buying her a brand new bedroom set, including her own VCR). But most agreed that, when faced with time constraints, fatigue, and high levels of frustration, giving in was the easiest way to get things done. As this mother set forth:

They usually pretty much get what they want, unfortunately. I gotta try to get them used to, you know, not always getting their way and to be happy with when I say, "No." But it doesn't always work that way. When I'm tired at night, "Okay, you can have it. Get whatever you want. Let's just go home and get ready for bed."

Lack of Sensitivity in Communication About Feelings. A number of mothers found it difficult to understand their children and feel empathy toward them when they were angry or distressed. Some said they had such difficulty handling their children's anger that they would simply ignore it:

I guess I somewhat kind of close it out. I'll just, like, go into another room. Like I said, I'll go into another room and just keep going on with my normal things. I don't drop everything and get into a screaming match with him.

In contrast to vignettes categorized as sensitive, in which mothers talked of accepting their children's negative emotions because they trusted that those feelings had a cause, insensitive vignettes revealed mothers' difficulties in acknowledging and accepting situations when their children expressed anger, sadness, and frustration. One mother, when asked how she felt when her child got angry, said she would think to herself (addressing the child), "Why do you have to have an attitude like that? Where do you get that from?" This inability to understand and reflect on things from the children's point of view seemed to contribute to the difficulty these mothers experienced in responding to their children's needs in an effective manner, and hence enhanced rather than counteracted their high levels of frustration.

Many mothers who portrayed themselves as insensitive explained that they had no patience for expressions of sadness and anger if they did not judge them to be warranted, and they talked about punishing their children if they showed anger toward the mothers that the mothers considered to be unjustified. Such a scenario is illustrated in the following description of what typically happens in one mother's home:

If I feel he's being rebellious or his anger is because of his own feelings, and I feel that, you know, he shouldn't be feeling that way, I'll scold him and put him in the corner.

However, what these mothers often discovered was that the harder they tried to get their children to stop crying or expressing anger, the more frustrated the children became:

> If she wants to do something and I tell her, "No," she will pout. I'm not real big on spanking . . . I'll send her to her room or say, "Stop crying or you'll . . ." and I always want to say, "Or I'll give you something to cry about," because that's what I heard every day when I was growing up from my father . . . I'll say, "Go to your room and cry," or, "I don't want to hear it," you know. "I don't like to hear little girls crying. There's no reason for you to be crying. Why are you crying?" And she gets stubborn and frustrated at that point, and she will go in her room and lay down once in a while, or she'll go and she'll find a corner and she'll like kind of hide.

Many of these mothers did not attempt to reason with their children. Some said they gave orders without explaining their demands, and others talked about punishing and threatening their children for their feelings rather than trying to help them resolve their problems. Insight into why mothers responded this way might be found in the following two excerpts. In the first, the mother said she did not think her child had the capability of being rational. According to her descriptions, she and her daughter communicated mostly via arguments and power struggles.

> We just kind of argue about it. I mean, we are almost like sisters when it comes to arguing. You don't try to reason with a 4-year old.

The second mother explained that she had neither the time nor the patience to communicate rationally with her child:

> I think sometimes just her age is frustrating too . . . she's still at an age where some things just don't quite sink in and, you know, when you're running around all day and you've got two kids, it's just . . . and when you take that extra 5 minutes to explain something or, you know what I mean? Sometimes that just is like, I'm just sick of dealing with this and I won't do it anymore [laugh].

In another case, a mother ascribed her daughter's negative feelings to the father's influence, but without trying to gain a deeper understanding:

> I think some of her dark, her dark side, I think, is really coming from her dad. I think he's really putting it on her 'cause it's the same kind of stuff he does. It's a manipulation and using, pulling, playing people off against each other and, uh, that kind of stuff.

In short, inflexible discipline and lack of follow-through, as well as insensitivity toward the child's negative feelings, appeared to exacerbate difficulties in the parent-child relationship. In child socialization studies, autocratic or lax styles of parental behavior have been studied with a view of predicting the children's successful adaptation to peer relations and even school achievement. In many such studies, only the parental side of a particular style is examined (for a review, see Maccoby & Martin, 1983). Narratives by mothers who parent in postdivorce families show that when mothers describe their own behavior as inflexible, lax, and insensitive to children's negative feelings, children tend to reciprocate with disregard for parental requests, disrespect, and often defiance. That is, both partners' adaptations in the relationship are maladaptive, setting in train a vicious circle of negativity similar to the coercive cycles described by Patterson (1980).

Discussion

The mothers in this study were faced with challenges few bargained for when their children were born. All struggled with the realities of raising children as divorced parents, often without the help of another adult in the household. In most of these families, children had relationships with both parents, although mothers did the brunt of the child rearing. However, there were enormous variations in how mothers reported managing the task of postdivorce parenting. In contrast to many studies that dwell on the negative consequences of divorce for families, and especially for children, our qualitative analysis of divorced mothers' narratives reveals a great deal of resiliency in the mother-child relationship, but also makes the difficulties some families experience stand out more poignantly.

Resilient mothers did not paint an idealized picture of miraculously cooperative children who always "listen" to maternal requests. Nevertheless, 2 or more years after their permanent separation and divorce, many felt quite confident in their roles as parents and about the parent-child relationship because they were able to elicit their children's cooperation, even if after some resistance.

It is particularly noteworthy that the narratives of more and less resilient mothers often describe very similar issues or situations. What varied were the mothers' interpretations and responses. Although resiliency was not the original focus of the study, the topic of adjustment and adaptation was one that was addressed by many of the mothers, whether resilient or not. Some were aware of their own processes of adaptation and spoke openly about them. Others felt that little had changed since the separation. Some discussed these processes in response to the question of how they felt their relationship with their children had changed since the divorce. Others brought up the topic of adaptation on their own in the context of other questions.

Talking about change, some firm and demanding mothers felt that it had become more important that they be "strict" and "enforce" their demands. They had made these changes in response to the hectic lifestyles and the added responsibilities brought on by having to do everything on their own. Some nondemanding mothers, on the other hand, explained that they felt it necessary to take a more laid-back approach to child rearing. They explained that with mothers so busy all the time and having to leave for work early, children felt more tired, and it was therefore important to be more relaxed and lenient about the demands they placed on them. Both of these strategies were effective for the mothers. Some mothers reported that the changes precipitated by divorce actually enabled them to have more positive interactions with their children. Release from an unhappy or abusive relationship had a beneficial effect on their mental health, which, in turn, allowed them to be more responsive and sensitive to their children's needs than before the divorce. In contrast, other mothers felt that parenting largely alone was so physically and emotionally draining that they could not respond as they would have liked to. For others, feelings of guilt, fear of losing the children's love, or losing them to the child's father led to a conflicted leniency that was not adaptive for the mother-child relationship or the mother's sense of effectiveness.

Another commonly discussed situation was children's negativism after returning from a weekend at their fathers' houses, but again, maternal interpretations and responses varied greatly. Resilient mothers understood the behavior as a temporary reaction to a stressful transition and reflected on how they could help calm their children, whereas less resilient mothers focused on how the defiant or aggressive behavior affected them and the relationship without feeling able to respond effectively, and fearing what this behavior portended for the future.

Likewise, differences between the mother's and the father's parenting philosophies were mentioned by resilient and less resilient mothers. However, resilient mothers felt able to accept the father's practices, even though they disagreed with them, but they were also able to explain to the child that their own expectations were different, and gain the child's cooperation. Less resilient mothers dwelt on the problems that the different disciplinary styles presented for them but could not find a satisfactory solution.

Incipient power struggles were common in all families, but resilient mothers described strategies or compromises that led the child to go along with maternal requests. Children of firm mothers might offer resistance but ultimately "listened" and cooperated. Flexible mothers negotiated or chose alternatives that were mutually satisfactory. In contrast, inflexible mothers described power struggles that escalated until they felt compelled to use physical force to overcome their children's oppositional behavior. Alternatively, the nascent conflict might be short-circuited because the mother could not muster sufficient energy to insist or come up with an alternative strategy. Ultimately, however, this strategy left her feeling manipulated and powerless.

One of the factors that distinguished the narratives of more resilient mothers was their ability and willingness to look at a situation from their children's, not just their own, point of view. If a mother expressed an understanding of her child's personality, abilities, and feelings, she tended to tailor her demands to the child's capacity for self-regulation and mastery, and, in some cases, was willing to tolerate emotional outbursts she regarded as temporary. Even when she could not accommodate the child's needs and desires, such as shorten her work hours, she accepted the child's negative feelings about the situation.

The distinction between mothers' thinking about firmness, here taken as an indicator of resilience, and inflexibility, here regarded as maladaptive, is also instructive. Firm and inflexible mothers appeared to have different goals. We had the impression that mothers who believed in inflexibility regarded their parenting task as inculcating *obedience*. Yet inflexible maternal behavior was rarely associated with voluntary compliance and, hence, not usually accompanied by a sense of effectiveness despite the fact that some inflexible mothers remembered being in awe of the "withering looks" they received from their own parents. Rather, the resulting interactions resembled the "coercive cycles" that Patterson (1980) observed in studies of children with behavioral problems. In contrast, firm mothers most often mentioned *rules* that they hoped their children would learn.

The contrast between mothers' descriptions of flexible child-rearing strategies and those assigned to the category "nondemanding under pressure" is similarly telling. Viewed by outside observers, both types of behavior might be labeled inconsistent. However, in the flexible case, mothers felt in charge and provided reasons why they were willing to bend the rules at times. In very similar situations, mothers portraying themselves as "nondemanding under pressure" felt powerless vis-a-vis their children and controlled or manipulated by them. Where flexible mothers saw special circumstances, the seemingly lax, nondemanding-under-pressure mothers tended to see misbehavior that they could not influence. It also appeared that these less resilient mothers had not been able to adjust their goals for child behavior to their own coping resources and hence reported themselves to be deeply frustrated.

In summary, what emerges from the narratives we have classified as resilient and nonresilient are bonadaptive and maladaptive circles. The bonadaptive circle is characterized by mothers seeing themselves as in charge yet able to view situations from the child's perspective and able to tailor their demands for prosocial, cooperative, and self-regulatory behavior to the particular child's competencies. This approach is likely to generate what some have called committed or receptive compliance in the child (Kochanska, 1995; Maccoby & Martin, 1983), making disciplinary interventions less necessary and hence fostering a more positive relationship in which stresses are lessened. In such a relationship, a child is more likely to respond positively to circumspect firmness, but it is also easier for a parent to behave flexibly and sensitively with the child in the expectation that the relationship will remain cooperative (see Bretherton, Golby, & Cho, in press).

When caught in a maladaptive circle, mothers make inflexible demands to which their children respond only under duress. Or, they cave in quickly in the hope of avoiding confrontations. Their children, in turn, respond with defiant, demanding, and manipulative behavior. As a result, the relationship takes on a negative tone in which each party expects negative and coercive behavior of the other. At this point, the relationship itself becomes a stressor.

Of course, in describing postdivorce mother-child relationships in terms of bon- and maladaptive circles, one could start by describing difficulties in the relationship caused by the child rather than the mother. Apart from the possible influences of child temperament, the child's cooperativeness with the mother may be affected by whether the father undermines or supports the child's respect and love for the mother and vice versa. Parental conflict, whether pre- or postdivorce, has consistently been identified as a risk factor in child development (Amato & Keith, 1991).

In addition, bonadaptation or maladaptation in the postdivorce mother-child relationship may be influenced by whether or not the mother receives social support or is able to call on friends, relatives, and coworkers; the flexibility of her work and child care situations; her financial situation; and her physical and mental health, as well as the child's health and functioning in preschool (Bretherton, Walsh, & Lependorf, 1996). In other words, resilience should not be treated as a static trait inherent in the mother, the child, or even the relationship, but open to a host of risk and protective factors outside the family (Cicchetti & Garmezy, 1993).

On the other hand, the maternal narratives we have presented in this chapter show that meaning making, too, plays an important role in resilience. McCubbin, McCubbin, and Thompson (1993) talk about how families legitimize and make sense of the changes in patterns of functioning by changing their values and expectations. Our examples illustrate how, in response to becoming divorced parents, some mothers changed both their child-rearing styles and their standards of what was and was not acceptable behavior from their children or retained prior effective parenting despite the strains of the divorce situation. Mothers whose narratives we characterized as resilient did, nonetheless, encounter difficulties in parenting. The difference lay in how mothers interpreted initially quite similar situations, such as power struggles or disagreements with the child's father. Mothers' own narratives, we suggest, can provide useful insight into their own views of how bonadaptive circles in the parent-child relationship foster, and maladaptive circles hamper, a sense of effective and resilient parenting. This insight, in turn, can help us search for more flexible familial, community, and societal supports and policies that enhance, rather than undermine, adaptive postdivorce parenting.

Note

1. This study was supported by grant R01 HD267766-01 from NIH and funds awarded by the University of Wisconsin Graduate School Research Committee to the second author. We especially thank the mothers and children who participated in our study and shared their experiences with us. We also acknowledge Reghan O. Walsh for her assistance in coordinating the study, and Margaret Peterson and Julia North for typing the interview transcripts.

References

Amato, P. R., & Keith, B. (1991). Parental divorce and the well-being of children: A meta-analysis. *Psychological Bulletin, 110,* 26–46.

Baumrind, D. (1967). Child care practices anteceding three patterns of preschool behavior. *Genetic Psychology Monographs, 75,* 43–88.

Baumrind, D. (1971). Current patterns of parental authority. *Developmental Psychology Monographs, 4,* 1–103.

Bretherton, I., Biringen, Z., Ridgeway, D., Maslin, C., & Sherman, M. (1989). Attachment: The parental perspective. *Infant Mental Health Journal, 10,* 203–221.

Bretherton, I., Golby, B., & Cho, E. (in press). Attachment and the acquisition of values. In J. Grusec & L. Kucszynski (Eds.). *Handbook of parenting and the socialization of values.* New York: Plenum.

Bretherton, I., Walsh, R., & Lependorf, M. (1996). Social support in postdivorce families: An attachment perspective. In G. R. Pierce, B. R. Sarason, & I. G. Sarason (Eds.), *Handbook of social support and families* (pp. 345–373). New York: Plenum.

Cicchetti, D., & Garmezy, N. (1993). Prospects and promises in the study of resilience. *Development and Psychopathology, 5,* 497–502.

Emery, R. E. (1988). *Marriage, divorce and children's adjustment.* Newbury Park, CA: Sage.

Garmezy, N. (1991). Resilience in children's adaptation to negative life events and stressed environments. *Pediatric Annals, 20,* 459–466.

Glaser, B., & Strauss, A. (1967). *The discovery of grounded theory.* New York: Aldine.

Grych, J. H., & Fincham, F. C. (1991). Marital conflict and children's adjustment: Cognitive-developmental framework. *Psychological Bulletin, 108,* 267–290.

Hanson, S. M. H. (1986). Healthy single parent families. *Family Relations, 35,* 125–132.

Hetherington, E. M. (1987). Family relations six years after divorce. In K. Pasley & M. Ihinger-Tollman (Eds.), *Remarriage and stepparenting: Current research and theory* (pp. 185–205). New York: Guilford.

Hetherington, E. M. (1989). Coping with family transitions: Winners, losers and survivors. *Child Development, 60,* 1–14.

Hetherington, E. M., & Clingempeel, W. G. (1992). Coping with marital transitions. *Monographs of the Society for Research in Child Development, 57* (Serial. No. 227).

Hetherington, E. M., Cox, M. J., & Cox, R. (1982). Effects of divorce on parents and children. In M. E. Lamb (Ed.), *Nontraditional families* (pp. 233–288). Hillsdale, NJ: Erlbaum.

Hetherington, E. M., Law, T. C., & O'Connor, T. G. (1993). Divorce: Challenges, changes, and new chances. In F. Walsh (Ed.), *Normal family processes* (pp. 208–234). New York: Guilford.

Hill, R. (1949). *Families under stress.* New York: Harper & Row.

Hill, R. (1958). Generic features of families under stress. *Social Casework, 49,* 139–150.

Kochanska, G. (1995). Children's temperament, mother's discipline, and security of attachment: Multiple pathways to emerging internalization. *Child Development, 66,* 597–615.

Maccoby, E. E., & Martin, J. A. (1983). Socialization in the context of the family: Parent-child interaction. In E. M. Hetherington (Ed.), *Handbook of child psychology: Socialization, personality and social development* (Vol. 4, pp. 1–111). New York: Wiley.

McCubbin, H. I., McCubbin, M. A., & Thompson, A. I. (1993). Resiliency in families: The role of family schema and appraisal in family adaptation to crises. In T. H. Brubaker (Ed.), *Family relations: Challenges for the future* (pp. 153–177). Newbury Park, CA: Sage.

McCubbin, H. I. & Patterson, J. M. (1983). The family stress process: The Double ABCX model of adjustment and adaptation. In H. I. McCubbin, M. Sussman, & J. M. Patterson (Eds.), *Social stress and the family: Advances and developments in family stress theory and research* (pp. 7–37). New York: Haworth.

McCubbin, M. A. & McCubbin, H. I. (1993). Family coping with health crises: The resiliency model of family stress, adjustment and adaptation. In C. Danielson, B. Hamel-Bissell, & P. Winstead-Fry (Eds.), *Families, health and illness* (pp. 21–63). New York: Mosby.

McCubbin, M. A., & McCubbin, H. I. (1996). Resiliency in families: A conceptual model of family adjustment and adaptation in response to stress and crises. In H. I. McCubbin, A. I. Thompson, & M. A. McCubbin (Eds.), *Family assessment: Resiliency, coping and adaptation—Inventories for research and practice* (pp. 1–64). Madison: University of Wisconsin System.

Patterson, G. R. (1980). Mothers: The unacknowledged victims. *Monographs of the Society for Research in Child Development, 45* (5, Serial No. 186).

Rutter, M. (1983). Stress, coping and development: Some issues and some questions. In M. Garmezy & M. Rutter (Eds.), *Stress, coping and development in children* (pp. 1–41). New York: McGraw-Hill.

Rutter, M. (1987). Psychosocial resilience and protective mechanisms. *American Journal of Orthopsychiatry, 57*, 316–331.

Stanley Hagan, M., Hollier, E. A., O'Connor, T. G., & Eisenberg, M. (1992). Parent-child relationships in nondivorced, divorced single-mother, and remarried families. In E. M. Hetherington & W. G. Clingempeel (Eds.), *Coping with marital transitions. Monographs of the Society for Research in Child Development, 57* (2–3, Serial No. 227), 94–148.

Strauss, A. (1987). *Qualitative analysis.* New York: Cambridge University Press.

Wallerstein, J. S., & Kelly, J. B. (1980). *Surviving the breakup: How children and parents cope with divorce.* New York: Basic Books.

Weiss, R. S. (1979). Growing up a little faster: The experience of growing up in a single parent household. *Journal of Social Issues, 35*, 97–111.

Index

About the Authors and Editors

Katherine R. Allen, Ph.D., is Professor of Family Studies in the Department of Human Development at Virginia Polytechnic Institute and State University. Her research interests include family diversity, older families, qualitative research methods, and feminist family studies.

Robert Wm. Blum, M.D., M.P.H., Ph.D., is a Professor in the Department of Pediatrics at the University of Minnesota. His research interests include adolescent sexuality, chronic illness, and international adolescent health care issues.

Inge Bretherton, Ph.D., is a Professor in the Department of Child and Family Studies at the University of Wisconsin-Madison. Her research interests include attachment relationships across the lifespan and young children's play and social cognition.

Catherine A. Chesla, Ph.D., is an Associate Professor in the Department of Family Health Care Nursing at the University of California-San Francisco. Her research interests pertain to family responses to a wide variety of chronic illnesses.

Kerry J. Daly, Ph.D., is a Professor in the Department of Family Relations and Applied Nutrition at the University of Guelph, located in Guelph, Ontario. His current research interests focus on the way that men and women, parents and children negotiate and organize their time for work, family and leisure.

Jo A. Futrell, MA., MAW., is an Editor for the Center for Excellence in Family Studies. She holds master's degrees in Journalism and English from the University of Iowa and a bachelor's degree in Anthropology from Iowa State University. She currently serves as an Editor for University Relations, University of Wisconsin-Madison System Administration.

Ann W. Garwick, Ph.D., R.N., L.P., is an Associate Professor in the School of Nursing at the University of Minnesota. Her research focuses on the impact of chronic illness and disability on children and families from diverse cultural backgrounds.

Jane F. Gilgun, Ph.D., is a Professor in the School of Social Work at the University of Minnesota. Her research interests include how persons overcome adversities, the development of violent behaviors, and the meanings of violence to perpetrators.

Barbara J. Golby, C.S.W., is clinical coordinator for the pediatric AIDS program at Elmhurst Hospital in New York, NY. Her research interests focus on the experiences of mothers and children with AIDS.

Claire H. Kohrman, Ph.D., is a Professor in the Department of Pediatrics at the University of Chicago. Her research interests include families and children facing illness.

Hamilton I. McCubbin, Ph.D., is Dean of the School of Human Ecology and Professor of Child and Family Studies and Social Work at the University of Wisconsin-Madison. His research interests include families over the life cycle and families under stress, with emphasis on family postcrisis responses and resiliency.

Helen J. Mederer, Ph.D., is Associate Professor in the Department of Sociology at the University of Rhode Island. Her research interests include work-family connections, and the effects of economic changes on family life.

Anne I. Thompson, Ph.D., is Assistant Dean of the School of Human Ecology at the University of Wisconsin-Madison. Her research interests include families and the workplace, and families and health.

Elizabeth A. Thompson, Ph.D., is Research Scientist and Postdoctoral Scholar at the Center for Excellence in Family Studies and the Institute for the Study of Resiliency in Families at the University of Wisconsin-Madison. Her research interests include the advancement of qualitative methods with families faced with stigmatized hardships and adversities.

Janet C. Titus, Ph.D., is Project Coordinator for the "Cannabis Youth Treatment Project", affiliated with Chestnut Health Systems in Bloomington, Illinois. Her current research interests include educational, vocational, and motivational aspects related to treatment effectiveness, and measuring the quality of the parent-child relationship when a child has a chronic illness or disability.

Clara Wolman, Ph.D., is Assistant Professor in the School of Education at Barry University in Miami Shores, Florida. Her research interests include children with learning disabilities.